Communications
in Computer and Information Science   **458**

T0215838

More information about this series at http://www.springer.com/series/7899

Sebastiano Battiato · Sabine Coquillart
Robert S. Laramee · Andreas Kerren
José Braz (Eds.)

Computer Vision, Imaging and Computer Graphics – Theory and Applications

International Joint Conference, VISIGRAPP 2013
Barcelona, Spain, February 21–24, 2013
Revised Selected Papers

 Springer

Editors
Sebastiano Battiato
Università di Catania
Catania, Catania
Italy

Andreas Kerren
Linnaeus University
Växjö
Sweden

Sabine Coquillart
Inria/ZIRST
Saint Ismier
France

José Braz
Escola Superior de Tecnologia do IPS
Setúbal
Portugal

Robert S. Laramee
Swansea University
Swansea
UK

ISSN 1865-0929   ISSN 1865-0937   (electronic)
ISBN 978-3-662-44910-3   ISBN 978-3-662-44911-0   (eBook)
DOI 10.1007/978-3-662-44911-0

Library of Congress Control Number: 2014950073

Springer Heidelberg New York Dordrecht London

Printed on acid-free paper

Springer is part of Springer Science+Business Media (www.springer.com)

Preface

This book includes the extended versions of the selected papers from VISIGRAPP 2013, the International Joint Conference on Computer Vision, Imaging and Computer Graphics Theory and Applications, which was held in Barcelona, Spain, during 21 to 24 February 2013 and organized by the Institute for Systems and Technologies of Information, Control and Communication (INSTICC).

VISIGRAPP comprises three conferences, namely, the International Conference on Computer Vision Theory and Applications (VISAPP), the International Conference on Computer Graphics Theory and Applications (GRAPP), and the International Conference on Information Visualization Theory and Applications (IVAPP).

VISIGRAPP received a total of 445 paper submissions from more than 50 countries. After a rigorous double-blind evaluation, only 13 % of the papers were accepted and published as full papers. These numbers clearly show that this conference is aiming at high quality standards and is now an established venue for researchers of the broad fields of computer vision, image analysis, computer graphics, and information visualization. From the set of full papers, 15 were selected for inclusion in this book. The selection process was based on quantitative and qualitative evaluation results provided by the Program Committee reviewers as well as the feedback on paper presentations provided by the session chairs during the conference. After selection, the accepted papers were further revised and extended by the authors. Our gratitude goes to all contributors and reviewers, without whom this book would not have been possible. Apart from the full papers, 23 % of the papers were accepted for short presentations and 23 % accepted for poster presentations. These works were not considered for the present book selection process.

As VISAPP 2013 constituted the largest part of VISIGRAPP with 319 submissions, we decided to select and integrate 9 full papers aiming to cover different aspects and areas related to computer vision such as image formation and pre-processing, image and video analysis and understanding, motion tracking, stereo vision as well as diverse computer vision applications and services.

We would also like to mention that when we selected the papers from VISAPP for this book our intention was to cover and highlight research from different areas and sub-areas related to computer vision. Therefore, papers were mainly competing with other papers having similar content and therefore we want to acknowledge that other high quality papers accepted at the conference could have been integrated in this book if we had space for them.

Concerning GRAPP 2013, 84 papers were submitted and it was decided to include 4 full papers. The papers selection was based on both the reviewers' feedback and the quality of the oral presentation appreciated by the GRAPP program co-chairs. We tried to cover the main areas of computer graphics to make the content of the book similar to the research addressed in the conference.

The 2 selected IVAPP 2013 papers are not only excellent representatives of the field of information visualization but also form a quite balanced representation of the field itself. Above all, they are almost as diverse and exciting as the field of information visualization itself.

It is not to be expected that any single reader is equally interested in all 15 of the selected VISIGRAPP papers; however, the diversity of these papers makes it very likely that all readers can find something of interest in this selection.

VISIGRAPP 2013 included four invited keynote lectures, presented by internationally renowned researchers, whom we would like to thank for their contribution to reinforce the overall quality of the conference, namely, in alphabetical order: Frank van Ham (IBM Software Group, United Kingdom), Alfred Inselberg (Tel Aviv University, Israel), Roberto Scopigno (Visual Computing Lab, CNR-ISTI, Italy) and Jeffrey Ventrella (Visual Music Systems, United States).

We wish to thank all those who supported VISIGRAPP and helped to organize the conference. On behalf of the Conference Organizing Committee, we would like to especially thank the authors, whose work was the essential part of the conference and contributed to a very successful event. We would also like to thank the members of the Program Committee, whose expertise and diligence were instrumental to ensure the quality of the final contributions. We also wish to thank all the members of the Organizing Committee whose work and commitment was invaluable. Last but not least, we would like to thank Springer for their collaboration in getting this book to print.

December 2013

Sebastiano Battiato
Sabine Coquillart
Robert S. Laramee
Andreas Kerren
José Braz

Organization

Conference Chair

José Braz — Polytechnic Institute of Setúbal, Portugal

Program Co-chairs

GRAPP

Sabine Coquillart — Inria, France
Carlos Andujar — Universitat Politècnica de Catalunya, Spain

IVAPP

Robert S. Laramee — Swansea University, UK
Andreas Kerren — Linnaeus University, Sweden

VISAPP

Sebastiano Battiato — University of Catania, Italy

Organizing Committee

Marina Carvalho — INSTICC, Portugal
Helder Coelhas — INSTICC, Portugal
Andreia Costa — INSTICC, Portugal
Bruno Encarnação — INSTICC, Portugal
Ana Guerreiro — INSTICC, Portugal
André Lista — INSTICC, Portugal
Carla Mota — INSTICC, Portugal
Raquel Pedrosa — INSTICC, Portugal
Vitor Pedrosa — INSTICC, Portugal
Cláudia Pinto — INSTICC, Portugal
Cátia Pires — INSTICC, Portugal
Susana Ribeiro — INSTICC, Portugal
Sara Santiago — INSTICC, Portugal
Margarida Sorribas — INSTICC, Portugal
José Varela — INSTICC, Portugal
Pedro Varela — INSTICC, Portugal

GRAPP Program Committee

Francisco Abad, Spain
Marco Agus, Italy
Tremeau Alain, France
Marco Attene, Italy
Dolors Ayala, Spain
Jacob Barhak, USA
Marco Di Benedetto, Italy
Bernd Bickel, Switzerland
Jiri Bittner, Czech Republic
Manfred Bogen, Germany
Martin Bokeloh, USA
Kadi Bouatouch, France
Stephen Brooks, Canada
Stefan Bruckner, Austria
Carlos Buchart, Spain
Matthias Bues, Germany
Patrick Callet, France
Pedro Cano, Spain
Maria Beatriz Carmo, Portugal
L.G. Casado, Spain
Teresa Chambel, Portugal
Antoni Chica, Spain
Hwan-gue Cho, Republic of Korea
Miguel Chover, Spain
Ana Paula Cláudio, Portugal
Sabine Coquillart, France
Nuno Correia, Portugal
António Cardoso Costa, Portugal
Victor Debelov, Russia
John Dingliana, Ireland
Thierry Duval, France
Ramsay Dyer, France
Francisco R. Feito, Spain
Petr Felkel, Czech Republic
Jie-Qing Feng, China
Luiz Henrique de Figueiredo, Brazil
Ioannis Fudos, Greece
Alejandro García-Alonso, Spain
Enrico Gobbetti, Italy
Stephane Gobron, Switzerland
Peter Hall, UK
Vlastimil Havran, Czech Republic
Nancy Hitschfeld, Chile

Toby Howard, UK
Ludovic Hoyet, Ireland
Andres Iglesias, Spain
Jiri Janacek, Czech Republic
Frederik Jansen, The Netherlands
Juan J. Jimenez, Spain
Robert Joan-Arinyo, Spain
Chris Joslin, Canada
Josef Kohout, Czech Republic
Marc Erich Latoschik, Germany
Miguel Leitão, Portugal
Heinz U. Lemke, Germany
Suresh Lodha, USA
Adriano Lopes, Portugal
Steve Maddock, UK
Joaquim Madeira, Portugal
Nadia Magnenat-Thalmann, Switzerland
Stephen Mann, Canada
Michael Manzke, Ireland
Maud Marchal, France
Francho Melendez, UK
Ramon Molla, Spain
Guillaume Moreau, France
David Mould, Canada
Gennadiy Nikishkov, Japan
Marc Olano, USA
Manuel M. Oliveira, Brazil
Renato Pajarola, Switzerland
Georgios Papaioannou, Greece
Alexander Pasko, UK
Giuseppe Patané, Italy
Daniel Patel, Norway
João Madeiras Pereira, Portugal
João Pereira, Portugal
Steve Pettifer, UK
Ruggero Pintus, Italy
Nicolas Pronost, The Netherlands
Anna Puig, Spain
Paul Richard, France
María Cecilia Rivara, Chile
Inmaculada Rodríguez, Spain
Przemyslaw Rokita, Poland
Timo Ropinski, Sweden

Manuel Próspero dos Santos, Portugal
Rafael J. Segura, Spain
Roberto Seixas, Brazil
Ari Shapiro, USA
A. Augusto Sousa, Portugal
Milos Sramek, Austria
Frank Steinicke, Germany
Ching-Liang Su, India
Veronica Sundstedt, Sweden
Antonio Susín, Spain
Matthias Teschner, Germany
Daniel Thalmann, Singapore

Juan Carlos Torres, Spain
Torsten Ullrich, Austria
Anna Ursyn, USA
Pere-Pau Vázquez, Spain
Luiz Velho, Brazil
Àlvar Vinacua, Spain
Andreas Weber, Germany
Daniel Weiskopf, Germany
Burkhard Wuensche, New Zealand
Lihua You, UK
Jian J. Zhang, UK
Jianmin Zheng, Singapore

GRAPP Auxiliary Reviewers

Nico van der Aa, The Netherlands
Artem Amirkhanov, Austria
Aiert Amundarain, Spain
Fernando Birra, Portugal
Annelies Braffort, France
Pere Brunet, Spain
Leonardo Carvalho, Brazil
Marta Fairen, Spain
Ángel Luis García Fernández, Spain
Fernando de Goes, USA
Carlos González, Spain
Jesus Gumbau, Spain
Min Jiang, UK

Wenxi Li, UK
Francisco Lopez Luro, Argentina
Peter Mindek, Slovak Republic
Gabriel Mistelbauer, Austria
Adolfo Muñoz, Spain
Alexis Paljic, France
Sofia Reis, Portugal
Inmaculada Remolar, Spain
Isaac Rudomin, Spain
Richard Southern, UK
Andreas Vasilakis, Greece
Dennis Wiebusch, Germany

IVAPP Program Committee

Wolfgang Aigner, Austria
Daniel Archambault, Ireland
Lisa Sobierajski Avila, USA
Rita Borgo, UK
Maria Beatriz Carmo, Portugal
Hamish Carr, UK
Remco Chang, USA
Guoning Chen, USA
Carlos Correa, USA
Chi-Wing Fu, Singapore

Zhao Geng, UK
David Gotz, USA
Georges Grinstein, USA
Dongfeng Han, USA
Seokhee Hong, Australia
Weidong Huang, Australia
Alfred Inselberg, Israel
Johannes Kehrer, Austria
Jessie Kennedy, UK
Andreas Kerren, Sweden

Martin Kraus, Denmark
Simone Kriglstein, Austria
Denis Lalanne, Switzerland
Robert S. Laramee, UK
Chun-Cheng Lin, Taiwan
Lars Linsen, Germany
Giuseppe Liotta, Italy
Ross Maciejewski, USA
Krešimir Matkovic, Austria
Silvia Miksch, Austria
Benoît Otjacques, Luxembourg
Margit Pohl, Austria
Edmond Prakash, UK
Philip J. Rhodes, USA

Adrian Rusu, USA
Filip Sadlo, Germany
Shigeo Takahashi, Japan
Laura Tateosian, USA
Sidharth Thakur, USA
Martin Turner, UK
Huy T. Vo, USA
Chaoli Wang, USA
Yunai Wang, China
Matt Ward, USA
Huub van de Wetering, The Netherlands
Hsu-Chun Yen, Taiwan
Ji Soo Yi, USA
Xiaoru Yuan, China

IVAPP Auxiliary Reviewers

Bilal Alsallakh, Austria
Pierrick Bruneau, Luxembourg
Paolo Federico, Austria
Yi Gu, USA
Jiaxin Han, USA
Yifan Hu, USA
Radu Jianu, USA
Karsten Klein, Australia

Tim Lammarsch, Austria
Jun Ma, USA
Paulo Pombinho, Portugal
Amalia Rusu, USA
Jun Tao, USA
Ming Zhang, USA
Björn Zimmer, Sweden

VISAPP Program Committee

Amr Abdel-Dayem, Canada
Tremeau Alain, France
Sileye Ba, France
Reneta Barneva, USA
Arrate Muñoz Barrutia, Spain
Sebastiano Battiato, Italy
Fabio Bellavia, Italy
Diego Borro, Spain
Adrian Bors, UK
Alain Boucher, Vietnam
Djamal Boukerroui, France
Valentin Brimkov, USA
Alfred Bruckstein, Israel
Pascual Campoy, Spain
Xianbin Cao, China

Barbara Caputo, Switzerland
Pedro Latorre Carmona, Spain
Gustavo Carneiro, Portugal
Vicent Caselles, Spain
M. Emre Celebi, USA
Vinod Chandran, Australia
Chin-Chen Chang, Taiwan
Jocelyn Chanussot, France
Chung Hao Chen, USA
Samuel Cheng, USA
Hocine Cherifi, France
Albert C.S. Chung, Hong Kong
Laurent Cohen, France
Carlo Colombo, Italy
David Connah, UK

Andreja Samcovic, Serbia
Raimondo Schettini, Italy
Mário Forjaz Secca, Portugal
Chan Chee Seng, Malaysia
Fiorella Sgallari, Italy
Xiaowei Shao, Japan
Lik-Kwan Shark, UK
Gaurav Sharma, USA
Li Shen, USA
Maryam Shokri, Canada
Chang Shu, Canada
Luciano Silva, Brazil
Bogdan Smolka, Poland
Ferdous Sohel, Australia
Lauge Sørensen, Denmark
José Martínez Sotoca, Spain
Ömer Muhammet Soysal, USA
Jon Sporring, Denmark
Filippo Stanco, Italy
Liana Stanescu, Romania
Changming Sun, Australia
Yajie Sun, USA
Shamik Sural, India
David Svoboda, Czech Republic
Tamás Szirányi, Hungary

Ryszard Tadeusiewicz, Poland
Johji Tajima, Japan
João Manuel R.S. Tavares, Portugal
YingLi Tian, USA
Hamid Tizhoosh, Canada
Shoji Tominaga, Japan
Georgios Triantafyllidis, Greece
Yulia Trusova, Russia
Muriel Visani, France
Frank Wallhoff, Germany
Joost van de Weijer, Spain
Christian Wöhler, Germany
StefanWörz, Germany
Qingxiang Wu, UK
Pingkun Yan, China
Vera Yashina, Russia
Shan Yu, USA
Jun Zhang, Japan
Lei Zhang, Hong Kong
Huiyu Zhou, UK
Yun Zhu, USA
Li Zhuo, China
Peter Zolliker, Switzerland
Ju Jia (Jeffrey) Zou, Australia

VISAPP Auxiliary Reviewers

Luis Almeida, Portugal
Carlos Buchart, Spain
Neal Checka, USA
Marco Fanfani, Italy
João Filipe Ferreira, Portugal
Guangwei Gao, China
Wenjuan Gong, Spain
Rene Grzeszick, Germany
Jiaxin Han, USA
Michael Hödlmoser, Austria
Britta Hummel, USA
Zhang Kaihua, Hong Kong
Ibai Leizea, Spain
Marco Moltisanti, Italy
Fabio Pazzaglia, Italy
Giovanni Puglisi, Italy

Daniele Ravì, Italy
Hugang Ren, USA
Kamrad Khoshhal Roudposhti, Portugal
Michael Sapienza, UK
Chao Wang, USA
Jin Wang, USA
Qixin Wang, USA
Shenlong Wang, Hong Kong
Shuang Wang, USA
Yong Xia, Australia
Sebastian Zambanini, Austria
Kaihua Zhang, Hong Kong
Ming Zhang, USA
Pengfei Zhu, China
Andreas Zweng, Austria

Invited Speakers

Jeffrey Ventrella	Visual Music Systems, USA
Roberto Scopigno	Visual Computing Lab, CNR-ISTI, Italy
Frank van Ham	IBM Software Group, UK
Alfred Inselberg	Tel Aviv University, Israel

Contents

Computer Graphics Theory and Applications

Real-Time Lattice Boltzmann Shallow Waters Method for Breaking Wave Simulations

Jesus Ojeda[1]([✉]) and Antonio Susín[2]

[1] Dept. LSI, Universitat Politècnica de Catalunya, Barcelona, Spain
jojeda@lsi.upc.edu
[2] Dept. MA1, Universitat Politècnica de Catalunya, Barcelona, Spain

Abstract. We present a new approach for the simulation of surface-based fluids based in a hybrid formulation of Lattice Boltzmann Method for Shallow Waters and particle systems. The modified LBM can handle arbitrary underlying terrain conditions and arbitrary fluid depth. It also introduces a novel method for tracking dry-wet regions and moving boundaries. Dynamic rigid bodies are also included in our simulations using a two-way coupling. Certain features of the simulation that the LBM can not handle because of its heightfield nature, as breaking waves, are detected and automatically turned into splash particles. Here we use a ballistic particle system, but our hybrid method can handle more complex systems as SPH. Both the LBM and particle systems are implemented in CUDA, although dynamic rigid bodies are simulated in CPU. We show the effectiveness of our method with various examples which achieve real-time on consumer-level hardware.

Keywords: Fluid simulation · Natural phenomena · Physically-based animation

1 Introduction

In the last years, professionals from real-time rendering and interactive fields have become more aware of physically-based effects as new graphics hardware can be used for such purposes. Among the most common features in actual computer games we find particle systems, rigid bodies and fluid simulations, being the last one the most complex and difficult to achieve in real-time. Moreover, the possibility of coupling all these simulations opens a wide range for building rich scenes with more interactivity.

Regarding fluid simulations, the restrictions of the equations and the extension of the simulations make them difficult to solve. Eulerian fluid simulations compute the fluid properties at fixed points in space, distributed over a grid. On the other hand, Lagrangian approximations evaluate the fluid properties at points that are advected with the fluid itself. Whatever the chosen method, the visualization of the fluid is usually based on its surface, which, for great volumes of water, can be simplified to this boundary, so the 3D simulation could potentially be reduced to a 2D simulation of an evolving height field.

© Springer-Verlag Berlin Heidelberg 2014
S. Battiato et al. (Eds.): VISIGRAPP 2013, CCIS 458, pp. 3–18, 2014.
DOI: 10.1007/978-3-662-44911-0_1

Solving the 2D wave equation is a common technique to simulate fluid surfaces as height fields, but it can not resolve effects based on horizontal velocity fields as whirlpools. To account for this, a shallow water framework is preferred. Derived from the more common Navier-Stokes equations, it is implemented based on a discretization on time and space over a grid. A less commonplace alternative derivation of these equations is based on the Lattice Boltzmann Method, which simplifies the implementation, restricting the maximal wave speed.

A 2D heightfield representation of a fluid can not account for many interesting phenomena that could happen in a full 3D simulation, like breaking waves. To improve this situation, we propose an implementation of an hybrid system that couples a Shallow Water Lattice Boltzmann with particle systems in CUDA for real-time fluid simulation with the following key features:

– Use of arbitrary underlying terrain.
– A method to maintain stability and to track dry-wet regions in the simulation.
– Two-way simplified coupling with rigid body simulations using a proxy system.
– Breaking wave detection conditions.
– Full particle generation, simulation and reintegration with the heightfield system.

Although we have used a ballistic particle system for the present work, it is easily interchangeable with other, more sophisticated methods, like SPH.

1.1   Related Work

A simple way to simulate water surfaces is based in procedural methods, as those based in the Fast Fourier Transform like [1] or [2]. These methods are well suited for the generation of high resolution and large scale animations, and have been used extensively in commercial products as movies or videogames; however, they are not easily coupled with solid objects and are unable to simulate eddies.

In computer graphics, among the first to use a shallow waters framework, [3] implemented a pipe model, which was later extended by [4], by using particles for the splashes generated from falling objects. More recently, [5] ported this model to GPUs for the simulation of hydraulic erosion. As an alternative, [6] presented a novel approach using wave trains on 2D particles to solve the wave equation. These methods, however, can not simulate the effects of horizontal flow.

On the other hand, the Shallow Water Equations (SWE) can simulate these phenomena. In addition to the heightfield description of the fluid surface, it also simulates a 2D horizontal velocity field. Reference [7] were the first to introduce them to the graphics field. Among other works, [8] used them to simulate breaking waves and later were ported to CUDA by [9], coupling it with a particle system.

A Smooth Particle Hydrodynamics (SPH) system can also be used to solve these equations. Reference [10] coupled an SPHSW with the wave equation to obtain higher detail fluid surfaces. Reference [11] ported the SPHSW simulation to CUDA and has already been extended by [12].

Yet another formulation can be stated with the Lattice Boltzmann Method (LBM). The LBMSW derivation can be found in [13] and has been used in various scenarios. Among others, [14] coupled it with a full 3D LBM simulation and [15] used it to simulate the currents in the strait of Gibraltar. More recently, [16] simplified the force terms of the formulation.

As the LBM is quite similar to a cellular automaton, it can be implemented in a parallel setting without much effort with regard to other methods. There are already GPU implementations as [17], where it was adapted using textures; but more recently, with the advent of general programmability of GPUs we find CUDA implementations like [18,19]. Reference [20] proposed an alternative kernel implementation to reduce memory usage and [21] targeted multiple different parallel architectures using higher-level libraries for solving the LBMSW model.

2 Methodology

The main steps our hybrid particle-LBM coupling executes for one time step can be summarized as:

1. LBMSW fluid simulation.
2. Rigid body simulation.
3. Two-way coupling of rigid bodies and LBMSW.
4. Particle generation and simulation.
5. Render.

The first step is to advance the LBMSW simulation explained in Sect. 2.1. This takes into account external forces and the dry-wet region tracking from Sect. 2.2. Using any external package, as the Bullet Physics library in our case, rigid bodies are simulated. These are then coupled with the fluid as presented in Sect. 2.3. This two-way coupling affects the movement of the dynamic objects but also modifies the behaviour of the fluid. Next, particles are generated and simulated for all the fluid regions the LBMSW can not handle, as breaking waves. These particles subtract some volume from the LBMSW in their generation and restore it back when they fall to the surface again. Details about this process will be discussed in Sect. 2.4. Finally, the render of the scene should be done.

Further details about the CUDA implementation are given in Sect. 3.

2.1 Lattice Boltzmann Shallow Waters

In contrast to other methods where a set of partial differential equations is discretized and solved directly, the Lattice Boltzmann Method already provides a discrete model suitable for parallel computations using only arithmetic operations. The fluid is simulated by particle distributions over a regular grid (distribution functions dfs). The particle's movement is restricted to certain directions $\mathbf{e}_i$ defined by the Boltzmann discretization used.

We use the D2Q9 model, pictured in Fig. 1, and assuming an adimensional parametrization as in [14], the velocity vectors $\mathbf{e}_{0..8}$ take the values: $\mathbf{e}_0 = (0,0)^T$, $\mathbf{e}_{1,2} = (\pm 1, 0)^T$, $\mathbf{e}_{3,4} = (0, \pm 1)^T$ and $\mathbf{e}_{5..8} = (\pm 1, \pm 1)^T$.

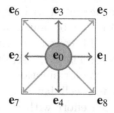

Fig. 1. D2Q9 model: nine velocity square lattice.

The Lattice Boltzmann Equation, then, defines the behaviour of the fluid by the chosen collision operator. We employ here the common BGK operator [22]

$$f_i(\mathbf{x} + \mathbf{e}_i \Delta t, t + \Delta t) = f_i(\mathbf{x}, t) - \omega(f_i - f_i^{eq}) + \mathcal{F}_i, \tag{1}$$

where f_i^{eq} is the df for the $\mathbf{e}_i$ direction, ω is the relaxation parameter, in close relation with the viscosity of the fluid, and f_i^{eq} is the local equilibrium distribution function, which defines the actual equations that are being solved. The original SWE can be recovered by applying Chapman-Enskog expansion if f^{eq} is defined like in, e.g., [13]

$$f_i^{eq}(h, \mathbf{u}) = \begin{cases} h\left(1 - \frac{5}{6}gh - \frac{2}{3}\mathbf{u}^2\right), & i = 0, \\ \lambda_i h\left(\frac{gh}{6} + \frac{\mathbf{e}_i \cdot \mathbf{u}}{3} + \frac{(\mathbf{e}_i \cdot \mathbf{u})^2}{2} - \frac{\mathbf{u}^2}{6}\right), & i \neq 0, \end{cases} \tag{2}$$

where $\lambda_i = 1$ for $i = 1..4$ and $\lambda_i = 1/4$ for $i = 5..8$. g is the gravity and h and $\mathbf{u}$ are the macroscopic fluid properties; height level from the underlying terrain and velocity, respectively, calculated as

$$h(\mathbf{x}, t) = \sum_i f_i, \tag{3}$$

$$\mathbf{u}(\mathbf{x}, t) = \frac{1}{h} \sum_i \mathbf{e}_i f_i. \tag{4}$$

From Eq. 1, $\mathcal{F}_i$ are the external forces applied to the LBMSW. In contrast to how these forces are applied in, e.g., [15] or [21]; [16] stated them with simpler arithmetic operations as

$$\mathcal{F}_i = \mathcal{X}_i + \mathcal{Z}_i. \tag{5}$$

From a constant underlying terrain $z_b(\mathbf{x})$ defined as a heightfield, $\mathcal{X}_i$ is the force caused by its slope as

$$\mathcal{X}_i = \begin{cases} \frac{g[h(\mathbf{x} + \mathbf{e}_i \Delta t, t) + h(\mathbf{x}, t)]}{2}[z_b(\mathbf{x} + \mathbf{e}_i \Delta t) - z_b(\mathbf{x})], & i = 1..4, \\ 0, & \text{otherwise.} \end{cases} \tag{6}$$

$\mathcal{Z}_i$ internalises other forces F, as friction or the Coriolis effect, defined as

$$\mathcal{Z}_i = \begin{cases} 0, & i = 0, \\ \frac{F_\alpha}{6e_{i_\alpha}}, & i \neq 0, \end{cases} \tag{7}$$

where α is a Cartesian index and Einstein summation convention is used. The same can be applied to e_{i_α}. We only consider the friction with the underlying terrain, so F_α is defined as

$$F_\alpha = C_t u_\alpha \sqrt{u_\beta u_\beta}, \tag{8}$$

where β is the other Cartesian index and C_t is the terrain friction coefficient, defined as a constant. u_α and u_β are the components of the fluid velocity in the α and β directions, respectively.

As boundary conditions, we use a no-slip boundary which is implemented as a bounce-back rule: the *df*s that should be streamed from boundary cells are just inverted as

$$f_i(\mathbf{x}, t + \Delta t) = f_{\bar{i}}(\mathbf{x}, t), \tag{9}$$

where $f_{\bar{i}}$ is the *df* in the opposite direction of f_i, i.e., $\mathbf{e}_i = -\mathbf{e}_{\bar{i}}$.

Additionally, we use for the rest of the paper the value η defined as

$$\eta(\mathbf{x}, t) = h(\mathbf{x}, t) + z_b(\mathbf{x}). \tag{10}$$

2.2 Dry-Wet Region Tracking

In order to be able to track dry regions, i.e., cells that do not contain fluid, we modify the original algorithm. We define a threshold ϵ as the minimal height a cell must satisfy to be considered a Fluid cell. After an iteration of the LBM has been executed, we must look for cells whose level has dropped below the threshold. For all the found cells, we must tag them as Empty. In order to not lose fluid mass, we also distribute the remainder of the fluid between the Fluid neighbours favoring the direction of the underlying terrain gradient as follows:

$$f_i(\mathbf{x} + \mathbf{e}_i \Delta t) = f_i(\mathbf{x} + \mathbf{e}_i \Delta t) + h(\mathbf{x}) \cdot (\zeta_i / \zeta_{total}), \tag{11}$$

where ζ_{total} is the sum of all weights ζ_i, which are computed as

$$\zeta_i = \begin{cases} -(\nabla z_b \cdot \mathbf{e}_i) & \text{if } -(\nabla z_b \cdot \mathbf{e}_i) > 0 \text{ and cell at} \\ & (\mathbf{x} + \mathbf{e}_i) \text{ is a Fluid one,} \\ 0 & \text{otherwise.} \end{cases} \tag{12}$$

Seamlessly, we search also for Fluid cells whose fluid level is above the threshold and whose neighbours are Empty cells. We tag these Empty cells as Fluid, in order to allow the advance of the fluid from the Fluid tagged cell.

This addition enables for the tracking of dry-wet regions, but Eq. 4 still poses a limitation: as the fluid level goes down, the velocities can grow very large and lead to inevitable instabilities. In contrast to [21], where they used a modified minmod flux limiter to solve this, we use the Froude number, which relates the characteristic velocity of the fluid to a gravitational wave velocity

$$Fr = \frac{\sqrt{\mathbf{u} \cdot \mathbf{u}}}{\sqrt{gh}}, \tag{13}$$

Fig. 2. Image stills from the breaking dam over noisy ground example. Using values of $\epsilon = 0.1$ and $\varphi = 0.95$.

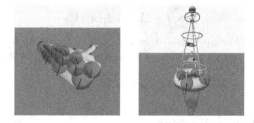

Fig. 3. Sphere discretization example for the boat and buoy models. The spheres are positioned and sized within the models, their normal vectors represented by the black short lines.

and is defined as $Fr < 1$ for subcritical flows, just the case of the LBMSW simulations [23]. We define an upper limit parameter φ for that ratio. When, due to low fluid height, the ratio does not hold, we compute a new suitable velocity $\mathbf{u}$ for the fluid and replace the dfs of the cell with new ones computed from Eq. 2. Also, we can further use this condition to dampen high velocities through the full body of fluid and ensure a stable simulation.

Although not physically correct, this method ensures stability in a similar fashion to the Smagorinsky method [24]: it changes the local viscosity of the fluid and dampens high velocities, as can be seen in Fig. 2.

2.3 Two-Way Coupling of Dynamic Rigid Bodies

For the introduction of rigid bodies to the LBMSW simulation we propose the use of a proxy model to decouple the complexity of the interaction of the fluid with the object mesh, in contrast to [9], where they use a tessellated mesh to the level of using triangles of areas similar to Δx^2, from the fluid simulation.

Our proxy model is composed of a set spheres and can be understood as a rough discretization of the object mesh. The properties defined for the spheres are the radius r, the position $\mathbf{p} = (p_x, p_y, p_z)^T$ and a normal $\mathbf{n} = (n_x, n_y, n_z)^T$. During the simulation, the spheres will also hold a velocity $\mathbf{v} = (v_x, v_y, v_z)^T$.

For our examples, we have used manually discretized models, as the boat in Fig. 3. Depending on the discretization of the model in spheres, the simulation becomes more accurate but also more expensive. For a regular discretization with spheres of radius $r < \Delta x/2$ our results are visually similar to [9].

Fluid to Rigid Body. For the implementation of the fluid to solid coupling we follow the path of [6,9]. There are three main forces a fluid induces to a solid body: buoyancy, drag and lift. We will compute them at the sphere positions of the proxy object. Assuming the simulation plane is xz, then $\hat{y} = (0,1,0)^T$.

The buoyancy force points upward and is proportional to the weight of the displaced fluid, we can define it for sphere i as

$$\mathbf{f}_i^{buoy} = \begin{cases} 0 & \text{if } S_i^p - S_i^r > \eta_p, \\ g\rho V_{sub}\hat{y} & \text{otherwise,} \end{cases} \tag{14}$$

where, η_p is the water level at the sphere position, S_i^r is the sphere radius, S_i^p is the y coordinate of the location of the sphere, ρ is the density of the fluid and V_{sub} is the volume of the submerged part of the sphere calculated as

$$V_{sub} = \int_{-S_i^r}^{top} \pi(S_i^{r2} - x^2)dx, \tag{15}$$

with $top = (\eta_p - (S_i^p - S_i^r))$.

Drag force is a resistive force and is dependent on the actual velocity of the obstacle with regard to the fluid. Lift is a force perpendicular to the oncoming flow direction, but is also dependent on the actual fluid velocity. For sphere i, they are defined as

$$\mathbf{f}_i^{drag} = -\frac{1}{2}C_D A_{2D}\|\mathbf{u}_{rel}\|\mathbf{u}_{rel}, \tag{16}$$

$$\mathbf{f}_i^{lift} = -\frac{1}{2}C_L A_{2D}\|\mathbf{u}_{rel}\| \left(\mathbf{u}_{rel} \times \frac{S_i^n \times \mathbf{u}_{rel}}{\|S_i^n \times \mathbf{u}_{rel}\|} \right), \tag{17}$$

where C_D and C_L are the drag and lift coefficients, $\mathbf{u}_{rel}$ is the relative velocity of the sphere with respect to the fluid, S_i^n is the normal defined for the sphere and A_{2D} is the area of the circle that cuts the sphere at water level η_p.

The forces are finally added to the ith sphere. The rigid body simulator will take care of the evolution of the proxy model and will provide the corresponding transform which will be applied in the render phase.

Rigid Body to Fluid. In this case, the rigid body will modify the behaviour of the fluid. As before, the computations are done per sphere. To change the fluid correctly, we get the velocity of the obstacle for the ith sphere as $\mathbf{v}$ and the difference between the submerged height of the sphere and the fluid level as *depth*. We compute the following values

$$decay = \exp(-depth), \tag{18}$$

$$h_o = decay \cdot C_{dis} \cdot depth, \tag{19}$$

$$\mathbf{u}_o = decay \cdot C_{adp} \cdot \mathbf{v}, \tag{20}$$

Fig. 4. A buoy is being dragged by the fluid (left). The boat introduces some new fluid waves at its tail as a result of the coupling (right).

and input these h_o and $\mathbf{u}_o$ into the LBM equilibrium distribution, Eq. 2, updating the previous dfs as

$$f_0 = f_0 - h_o,$$

$$f_i = f_i + f_i^{eq}(h_o, \mathbf{u}_o) + \frac{f_0^{eq}(h_o, \mathbf{u}_o)}{\mathsf{w}_o}, \text{ where } \mathsf{w}_o = \begin{cases} 5 & i = 1..4, \\ 20 & i = 5..8. \end{cases} \quad (21)$$

The values of w_o are calculated from the contribution each $\mathbf{e}_i$ gives on the D2Q9 model [25]. With this computation we push the fluid the obstacle is displacing to the neighbour cells, taking into account in this process the obstacle velocity. Additionally, to avoid high differences between lattice neighbours, we distribute the h_o and $\mathbf{u}_o$ among the nearest cells using linear interpolation.

decay takes into account the depth the sphere is at and limits accordingly the effect it has over the fluid surface. C_{dis} and C_{adp} are parameters in the range $[0, 1]$ that allow to dampen the effect of the coupling as desired. We have used the values $C_{dis} = 0.8$ and $C_{adp} = 0.5$ for the examples of Fig. 4.

2.4   Coupling of Particle Systems

The LBMSW model described so far is only capable of representing fluids as heightfields and certain phenomena is limited, e.g., breaking waves can not be resolved. In order to deal with this restriction, we have coupled it with a ballistic particle system and adapted the detection of breaking waves and generation of the respective particles from [9]. They also proposed other detection conditions for when to generate particles for the interaction with obstacles and terrain discontinuities like waterfalls, which could also be adapted to our system. In this case, however, we restrict ourselves to the breaking wave example. In contrast, we will present an implementation that allows alternative particle systems like SPH with minor changes in Sect. 3.

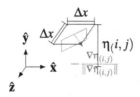

Fig. 5. For breaking wave detected particles, they are placed within the red rectangle in their generation step. (Color figure online)

Breaking Wave Detection. Waves that would break in a full 3D simulation just produce singular waves due to numerical instability in a Shallow Waters simulation. The detection of this situation for a given cell (i, j) is done via three parametrized conditions:

$$\|\nabla \eta_{i,j}\| > \Phi g, \tag{22}$$

$$\eta_{i,j} - \eta_{i,j}^{prev} > \Psi, \tag{23}$$

$$\nabla^2 \eta_{i,j} < \Upsilon, \tag{24}$$

where $\eta_{i,j}^{prev}$ is the fluid height in the previous time step and Φ, Ψ and Υ are parameters, which should be tailored per scene, and more specifically by its scale. Equation 22 ensures the wave is steep enough to break. Equation 23 requires that the cell is part of the front of the wave and it is raising fast, introducing a comparison with the previous value of fluid height. Finally, Eq. 24 makes sure particles are only generated near the top of the wave.

The computation of $\nabla \eta_{i,j}$ is done using the maximum among the one-sided derivatives and $\nabla^2 \eta_{i,j}$ is computed using central differences

$$\nabla \eta_{i,j} = \begin{bmatrix} \frac{max(|\eta_{i+1,j}-\eta_{i,j}|,|\eta_{i,j}-\eta_{i-1,j}|)}{\Delta x} \\ \frac{max(|\eta_{i,j+1}-\eta_{i,j}|,|\eta_{i,j}-\eta_{i,j-1}|)}{\Delta x} \end{bmatrix}, \tag{25}$$

$$\nabla^2 \eta_{i,j} = \frac{\eta_{i+1,j} + \eta_{i-1,j} + \eta_{i,j+1} + \eta_{i,j-1} - 4\eta_{i,j}}{\Delta x^2}. \tag{26}$$

If all three conditions are met, the next step will generate and initialize particles for the given cell. The total volume V_{total} the added particles will subtract from the LBMSW is proportional to $\|\nabla \eta_{i,j}\| - \Phi g$ and can be controlled introducing a new parameter θ, as

$$V_{total} = \theta(\|\nabla \eta_{i,j}\| - \Phi g). \tag{27}$$

Particle Generation. For each cell detected in the previous step, a number of particles will be generated for the volume of Eq. 27.

The particles are positioned within a cell-centered rectangle of width equal to the LBMSW cell width and height V_{total} as shown in Fig. 5. This rectangle is oriented with the opposite direction of the gradient computed in Eq. 25.

The particle velocities in the xz plane are defined by the wave speed as in [8] and the y component can be defined as a fraction of the height differences from Eq. 23 as

$$\mathbf{v}_{xz} = \frac{-\nabla\eta_{i,j}\sqrt{gh}}{\|\nabla\eta_{i,j}\|}, \tag{28}$$

$$v_y = \lambda_y(\eta_{i,j} - \eta_{i,j}^{prev}), \tag{29}$$

where λ_y controls the fraction. We have used here a value of $\lambda_y = 0.1$.

Additionally, we lightly perturb the velocity of each particle and jitter their initial positions between $[\frac{-\Delta x}{2}, \frac{\Delta x}{2}]$ in the gradient direction, which helps to add variation and result in less uniform, more chaotic, particle movement.

The total volume the particles supply must be subtracted from the LBMSW, as well as the momentum they get. We do this by computing the equilibrium distribution function from Eq. 2; using as input values V_{total} and the xz velocity components from the particle velocities, prior to the perturbations we apply. These newly computed equilibrium dfs will be subtracted from the cell's original df set as

$$f_i = f_i - f_i^{eq}\left(\frac{V_{total}}{\Delta x^2}, \mathbf{v}_{xz}\right). \tag{30}$$

As said previously, particles are not restricted to be generated only from the detected breaking waves of the previous step. We can generate and initialize particles with other requirements in mind, like a faucet pouring fluid into a basin as demonstrated by Fig. 6.

Particle Reintegration. Finally, the particles must be reintegrated to the LBMSW when they hit the surface of the fluid, i.e., $p_y \leq \eta_{i,j}$. The volume the particles carry, as well as their momentum, must be absorbed by the cell they fall on.

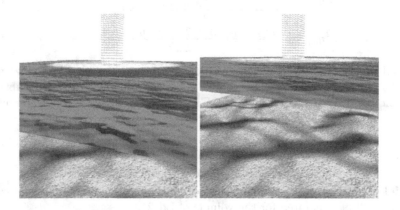

Fig. 6. Particles generated in middle air (like a heavy rain or some pipe open tab), integrated afterwards to the bulk of the fluid. After a few seconds, the level of the LBMSW is effectively raised.

As the LBMSW has no explicit method to input vertical velocities, we introduce an interpolation for the absorption of the volume of the particle among the cell's dfs. This interpolation is based on the terminal speed the particle could achieve, defined as

$$v_T = \sqrt{\frac{8rg}{3C_D}}, \tag{31}$$

where C_D is the drag coefficient. We normalize the particle's vertical speed with v_T and clamp the result to the range $[0, 1]$, as $\chi = clamp(v_y/v_T, 0, 1)$.

Taking into account the previous consideration, we can update the dfs of the cell using the following computations

$$f_0^{eq\chi} = f_0^{eq}\left(\frac{V_p}{\Delta x^2}, \mathbf{v}_{xz}\right), \tag{32}$$

$$f_0 = f_0 + (1 - \chi) \cdot f_0^{eq\chi}, \tag{33}$$

$$f_i = f_i + f_i^{eq}\left(\frac{V_p}{\Delta x^2} + \chi f_0^{eq\chi}, \mathbf{v}_{xz}\right). \tag{34}$$

Similarly to the obstacle to fluid coupling from Sect. 2.3, using the interpolation with the terminal speed, the added volume is pushed from the cell's center to its neighbours with more energy, the faster the particle drops. Figure 2 shows how particles generated from a breaking dam wave are reintegrated even in dry sections and Fig. 6 shows how the water level of a basin is effectively raised from the mid-air dropped particles.

3 Implementation Details

In this section we give some implementation details of the Particle-LBMSW coupling. As there is no simple way to maintain a dynamic data structure for the particles on the GPU, we have resorted to a fixed number of particles from the beginning of the simulation. In addition to the usual particle properties as position and velocity, we add two more: a TTL (time-to-live) value and an active (ACTIVE/INACTIVE) flag. We will explain their use in the particle-related functions.

In Algorithm 1 we show high-level pseudo-code for the full simulation. All CUDA functions are kernels, except the sort, remove and prefix_sum parallel operations, which are provided by the Thrust library. The kernels that are only targeted to a limited group of cells or particles provide an early exit condition for the elements that are not to be changed. Below, we will explain the different kernels, starting from the LBM simulation to the Particle coupling at last.

The LBM core, executed in the LBM_stream_collision kernel is the same as previous LBM implementations in CUDA like, e.g., [18,21] or [19]; using the BGK collision operator instead of the MRT one. This is done in an inner loop, as the $\Delta t'$ for the LBM can be smaller than the Δt of the frame and depends on the parametrization used. In contrast to [20], where they proposed an A-A memory access pattern to reduce memory requirements, we have used an A-B memory access pattern; there are two arrays for the *dfs* in memory and they are interchanged after each iteration. The reason for this choice is the additional operations we are doing, they would have required to double the kernels, as the A-A memory access pattern needs two kernels just for the core simulation.

The LBM_applyForce kernel adds the force terms from Eq. 5 for the underlying slope and friction.

The three kernels upd_CellTags_* are the ones responsible for the actual Dry-Wet region tracking. Fluid cells that have a height above the threshold ϵ must convert their Empty neighborhood to Fluid in order to allow the fluid to advance. Seamlessly, Fluid cells with a height below the threshold must be changed back to Empty. In CUDA, we could fall into race conditions in this change of type for the cells, so we have to serialize the reflaging operations, thus the three kernels. upd_CellTags_pre checks the height of the cells against the threshold and preflags

---

Algorithm 1. Full per frame Particle-LBMSW high-level algorithm.

dt = (Δt) frame time step (16ms)
dt' = ($\Delta t'$) LBM dimensional time step

```
foreach(frame) {
  //CPU
  ObstacleSimulation();
  ObstacleFluidCoupling();
  //CUDA
  ReintegrateParts_S1();
  sort_tuples();
  remove_nonValidTuples();
  prefix_sum_tuples();
  ReintegrateParts_S2();

  for(i=0; i<dt; i+=dt') {
    LBM_stream_collision();
    LBM_applyForce();
    upd_CellTags_pre();
    upd_CellTags_Fluid();
    upd_CellTags_Empty();
  }
  computeLBM_GradLaplacian();

  sort_particlesByTTL();
  stepParticles();
  detectBreakingWaveCells();
  prefix_sum_NeededPartsPerCell();
  initParticles();

  //Render
}
```

---

them with an additional type if necessary: tobeFluid or tobeEmpty. Next, we change the type of the cells conservatively, first the Fluid-to-be ones and then the Empty ones, ensuring that no cells are changed prematurely if they should be needed in the next iteration.

Then, the computation of the gradient and laplacian of the fluid height is done for further use in the breaking wave detection kernel.

The particles are then sorted by their TTL in ascending order and the simulation is advanced in stepParticles, which depends on the chosen particle system. For a ballistic particle system, the interaction between particles is ignored. The particles' TTL are also updated, subtracting the current Δt and their status is set to ACTIVE. If a particle has died (TTL ≤ 0) before being reintegrated, we let them be ACTIVE but out of view. This ensures we don't lose mass because of dead particles in the particle generation step.

From the previously computed gradient and laplacian and Eqs. 22 to 24 we detect the cells that have a breaking wave. Each cell will output the needed particle count that it needs. Then, with a prefix sum operation we can obtain an accumulated sum of the needed particles and use this result as the index at the particle array from which each cell will take their needed particle count. As particles have been sorted by TTL, we ensure the particles first taken in this step are those who had a lower TTL. With a bad parametrization this can lead to artifacts, as disappearing particles from frame to frame as they are needed. initParticles will, then, initialize the particles needed for each cell as explained in Sect. 2.4, marking them as ACTIVE2 which ensures they are alive at least for a frame. Their TTL is also set up as the maximum allowed time to live for a particle, which is a user-defined parameter. For particles that were previously marked as ACTIVE, no fluid will be subtracted from the LBMSW, ensuring no mass loss; thus, only INACTIVE particles will take fluid from the LBMSW.

Finally, the particles are reintroduced. Only ACTIVE particles will be looked for. For these particles, the reintegration should be as easy as the explanation from Sect. 2.4 but we can fall in race conditions if multiple particles fall in the same cell. As our hardware, a GTX280, does not support atomic float operations, we had to solve it from another perspective: ReintegrateParts_S1 relates which particles have fallen in which cells and how many there are for each cell; from the cell point of view, ReintegrateParts_S2 will gather the fallen particles and update the local dfs. In order to do so, for each particle, S1 will write a tuple associating the cell id with the particle id, as well as the particle count for each cell. Particles not to be reintegrated are associated to a fake cell, in this case we use the cell 0 that we ensure is a Boundary cell for all examples. Sorting the tuples by the cell id, removing those with the fake cell id and doing a prefix sum on the particle-in-cell count will lead us to the cells having the index where their particle count starts in the tuple array. S2 will, for each cell, take their counted fallen particles and reintegrate them, marking them as INACTIVE with TTL $= 0$.

While the rigid body simulation is done in CPU, we update the values as in Sect. 2.3 using the CUDA memory arrays mapped to CPU memory space.

4   Results and Discussion

We have tested our implementation both on CPU with OpenMP and GPU with CUDA, timings shown in Table 1 for various examples. Our test system was an Intel Core2Duo E8400 with 4 GB of RAM memory and a Nvidia GTX280. The size of the grid used throughout the examples is set to 128×128 and we fix the time step for each frame to $\Delta t = 16$ ms. For the boat and buoy scenes, the particle coupling was deactivated to allow us a better timing and similarly, for the wave examples, the object coupling was deactivated. The wavegr example is basically the same as the others, a breaking wave generated from a breaking dam, but in this case the rest of the domain is totally empty as shown in Fig. 2.

Table 1. Timings per frame for various examples in milliseconds; the number in the name indicates the number of particles used, where $k = 2^{10}$. LBM includes the LBM simulation and the dry-wet region tracking. Solids accounts for the coupling of rigid bodies. PGen, PSim and PReint are the timings for the generation, simulation and reintegration of the particles, respectively. The timings for the sort operation from the Thrust library are noted in Psort and PReint_sort; they do not depend directly on the other steps but have a significant impact on the results. Psort is for the sorting of particles by their TTL. PReint_sort is the sort of the (cell_id, particle_id) tuples.

		Total	LBM	Solids	Psort	PGen	PSim	PReint	PReint_sort
CPU	boat	10.78	10.69	0.09	0.00	0.00	0.00	0.00	0.00
	buoy	10.91	10.85	0.06	0.00	0.00	0.00	0.00	0.00
	drop 32k	372.96	9.97	0.00	214.56	1.16	1.46	31.50	114.31
	drop 128k	1635.36	9.75	0.00	1001.35	2.09	2.79	114.92	504.46
	wave 32k	410.88	9.62	0.00	224.04	3.68	4.85	32.58	136.11
	wave 128k	1694.87	9.62	0.00	1007.30	3.37	10.71	117.51	546.36
GPU	boat	0.82	0.35	0.47	0.00	0.00	0.00	0.00	0.00
	buoy	0.87	0.35	0.52	0.00	0.00	0.00	0.00	0.00
	drop 32k	14.30	0.35	0.00	7.03	0.45	0.10	1.24	5.13
	drop 128k	23.50	0.34	0.00	10.71	0.41	0.14	1.75	10.15
	wave 32k	15.28	0.36	0.00	7.26	0.99	0.12	1.32	5.23
	wave 128k	25.71	0.36	0.00	11.21	1.42	0.32	2.01	10.39
	wavegr 64k	18.79	0.39	0.00	9.48	1.18	0.18	1.64	5.92

Although a direct comparison with [9] would not be totally fair because of the difference in the hardware and their lack of implementation details, at least for the particle simulation in CUDA, we think that our LBM-based hybrid system is a great alternative up to the challenge for real-time fluid simulations.

To ensure all the particles were reintroduced correctly without loss mass and because the GTX280 had no support for float atomic operations, we had to separate the reintroduction step in two kernels plus some other Thrust powered operations; the particles are not directly reintroduced but gathered by the cells. These additional operations add more time to the processing of the particles than what it should be needed with more modern hardware.

Nevertheless, we have shown that a coupling of LBMSW with a particle system is feasible for higher-detail fluid simulations. The particle system, however, is not limited to the ballistic version used in here. While the coupling should be the same, i.e., generation and reintegration, TTL of particles and active flag; the simulation and behaviour of the particles can be defined alternatively. A CUDA implementation of SPH like [26] could be easily adapted to our hybrid system.

One limitation our system has, however, is the sudden disappearance of particles due to high demanding simulations, i.e., more particles are needed per frame than what is available. It will be interesting to look at LOD techniques that relax this situation: if more particles than available are needed, the ones actually being active could be represented with simpler primitives, grouping nearby particles, etc. Alternatively, it also would be worth to try and prioritize the preservation of visible particles, i.e., those that fall in the actual view frustum.

Although we have not explained how the visualization is done, the render of the fluid is based in triangle meshes in OpenGL. This can provoke some visual artifacts in the dry-wet region boundaries, which should also be considered.

Other future work also includes the use of a rigid body simulation totally in the GPU, improve the detection conditions for breaking waves and add other particle generation conditions to further broaden the use of this method.

Acknowledgements. With the support of the Research Project TIN2010-20590-C02-01 of the Spanish Government.

References

1. Tessendorf, J.: Simulating ocean water. In: SIGGRAPH Course Notes (1999)
2. Hinsinger, D., Neyret, F., Cani, M.P.: Interactive animation of ocean waves. In: SCA, pp. 161–166 (2002)
3. Kass, M., Miller, G.: Rapid, stable fluid dynamics for computer graphics. In: SIGGRAPH, pp. 49–57 (1990)
4. O'Brien, J.F., Hodgins, J.K.: Dynamic simulation of splashing fluids. In: Proceedings of the Computer Animation, CA '95, pp. 198–205 (1995)
5. Šťava, O., Beneš, B., Brisbin, M., Křivánek, J.: Interactive terrain modeling using hydraulic erosion. In: SCA, pp. 201–210 (2008)
6. Yuksel, C., House, D.H., Keyser, J.: Wave particles. ACM Trans. Graph. **26**, 99 (2007)
7. Layton, A.T., van de Panne, M.: A numerically efficient and stable algorithm for animating water waves. Vis. Comput. **18**, 41–53 (2002)
8. Thürey, N., Müller-Fischer, M., Schirm, S., Gross, M.: Real-time breaking waves for shallow water simulations. In: 15th Pacific Conference on Computer Graphics and Applications, pp. 39–46 (2007)
9. Chentanez, N., Müller, M.: Real-time simulation of large bodies of water with small scale details. In: SCA, pp. 197–206 (2010)

10. Cords, H.: Mode-splitting for highly detailed, interactive liquid simulation. In: GRAPHITE, pp. 265–272 (2007)
11. Lee, H., Han, S.: Solving the shallow water equations using 2d sph particles for interactive applications. Vis. Comput. **26**, 865–872 (2010)
12. Solenthaler, B., Bucher, P., Chentanez, N., Müller, M., Gross, M.: SPH based shallow water simulation. In: VRIPHYS, pp. 39–46 (2011)
13. Salmon, R.: The lattice boltzmann method as a basis for ocean circulation modeling. J. Mar. Res. **57**, 503–535 (1999)
14. Thürey, N.: Physically based animation of free surface flows with the lattice boltzmann method. Ph.D. thesis, Dept. of Computer Science 10, University of Erlangen-Nuremberg (2007)
15. Thömmes, G., Seaïd, M., Banda, M.K.: Lattice boltzmann methods for shallow water flow applications. Int. J. Numer. Meth. Fluids **55**, 673–692 (2007)
16. Zhou, J.G.: Enhancement of the labswe for shallow water flows. J. Comput. Phys. **230**, 394–401 (2011)
17. Wei, X., Li, W., Mueller, K., Kaufman, A.: The lattice-boltzmann method for simulating gaseous phenomena. IEEE Trans. Vis. Comput. Graph. **10**, 164–176 (2004)
18. Tölke, J.: Implementation of a lattice boltzmann kernel using the compute unified device architecture developed by nvidia. Comput. Vis. Sci. **13**, 29–39 (2010)
19. Obrecht, C., Kuznik, F., Tourancheau, B., Roux, J.J.: A new approach to the lattice boltzmann method for graphics processing units. Comput. Math. Appl. **61**, 3628–3638 (2011)
20. Bailey, P., Myre, J., Walsh, S., Lilja, D., Saar, M.: Accelerating lattice boltzmann fluid flow simulations using graphics processors. In: International Conference on Parallel Processing, pp. 550–557 (2009)
21. Geveler, M., Ribbrock, D., Göddeke, D., Turek, S.: Lattice-Boltzmann simulation of the Shallow-Water equations with fluid-structure interaction on multi- and manycore processors. In: Keller, R., Kramer, D., Weiss, J.-P. (eds.) Facing the Multicore-Challenge. LNCS, vol. 6310, pp. 92–104. Springer, Heidelberg (2010)
22. Qian, Y.H., D'Humières, D., Lallemand, P.: Lattice BGK models for Navier-Stokes equation. EPL (Europhysics Letters) **17**, 479 (1992)
23. Zhou, J.G.: Lattice Boltzmann Methods for Shallow Water Flows. Springer, New York (2004)
24. Hou, S., Sterling, J., Chen, S., Doolen, G.D.: A lattice boltzmann subgrid model for high reynolds number flows. Fields Inst. Commun. **6**, 151–166 (1996)
25. He, X., Luo, L.S.: Theory of the lattice Boltzmann method: from the Boltzmann equation to the lattice Boltzmann equation. Phys. Rev. E **56**, 6811–6817 (1997)
26. Goswami, P., Schlegel, P., Solenthaler, B., Pajarola, R.: Interactive SPH simulation and rendering on the GPU. In: SCA, pp. 55–64 (2010)

Asymmetry Patterns Shape Contexts to Describe the 3D Geometry of Craniofacial Landmarks

Federico M. Sukno[1,2](✉), John L. Waddington[2], and Paul F. Whelan[1]

[1] Centre for Image Processing and Analysis,
Dublin City University, Dublin 9, Ireland
federico.sukno@gmail.com
[2] Molecular and Cellular Therapeutics,
Royal College of Surgeons in Ireland, Dublin 2, Ireland

Abstract. We present a new family of 3D geometry descriptors based on asymmetry patterns from the popular 3D Shape Contexts (3DSC). Our approach resolves the azimuth ambiguity of 3DSC, thus providing rotational invariance, at the expense of a marginal increase in computational load, outperforming previous algorithms dealing with azimuth ambiguity. We build on a recently presented measure of approximate rotational symmetry in 2D, defined as the overlapping area between a shape and rotated versions of itself, to extract asymmetry patterns from a 3DSC in a variety of ways, depending on the spatial relationships that need to be highlighted or disabled. Thus, we define Asymmetry Patterns Shape Contexts (APSC) from a subset of the possible spatial relations present in the spherical grid of 3DSC; hence they can be thought of as a family of descriptors that depend on the subset that is selected. The possibility to define APSC descriptors by selecting diverse spatial patterns from a 3DSC has two important advantages: (1) choosing the appropriate spatial patterns can considerably reduce the errors obtained with 3DSC when targeting specific types of points; (2) Once one APSC descriptor is built, additional ones can be built with only incremental cost. Therefore, it is possible to use a pool of APSC descriptors to maximize accuracy without a large increase in computational cost.

Keywords: 3D geometric descriptors · Rotational symmetry · Craniofacial landmarks

1 Introduction

Geometric descriptors for three dimensional (3D) data are important for a wide range of applications, as they constitute a core element for the identification of corresponding points in relation to object retrieval [26], recognition [9], surface registration [2] and landmark identification [5,16].

The increased availability of 3D data in the last decade has generated much research in this area and several 3D descriptors have been proposed. Depending

© Springer-Verlag Berlin Heidelberg 2014
S. Battiato et al. (Eds.): VISIGRAPP 2013, CCIS 458, pp. 19–35, 2014.
DOI: 10.1007/978-3-662-44911-0_2

on the data that is targeted, the descriptors can be purely geometric [4,13,17, 28] or include additional functions that are attached to the geometry, such as radiometric information [20,27].

Among purely geometric descriptors, which are the most general type, 3D shape contexts (and extensions derived from them) have attracted considerable interest due to their good performance in diverse applications. A recent comparison of geometric descriptors in the context of craniofacial landmark localization highlighted 3D shape contexts as one of the most accurate algorithms [21].

Shape contexts in 3D are based on the distribution of distances with respect to the point of interest, estimated by means of a histogram over a spherical grid (elevation, azimuth and radius). The spherical grid is centered at the point of interest and its North Pole is oriented in the direction of the normal to the surface. This is enough to uniquely determine the elevation and radial bins but leaves unresolved the origin of azimuth bins. Different approaches have been taken to resolve this ambiguity:

- In one of the earliest works [9], the 3D Shape Contexts descriptor (3DSC) was introduced, without actually resolving the azimuth ambiguity. The authors compute multiple descriptors to account for all possible rotations (as many as the number of azimuth bins). During matching, when comparing descriptors of different points, all possible rotations are tested and the one that produces the highest similarity score is retained.
- As an alternative that achieves invariance to the azimuth angle, Frome et al. explored the use of Spherical Harmonics. Similarly to other descriptors based on symmetry [14], they proposed to keep only the magnitude of the Spherical Harmonic coefficients, which are rotationally invariant. We will refer to this approach as Harmonic Shape Contexts (HSC) [9].
- A third option [15,26] consists of performing Singular Value Decomposition (SVD) on the support region (i.e. all points within the considered sphere) to identify the principal axes and disambiguate the sign by considering the heaviest tail of each axis as the positive direction. Thus, a unique axis can be identified to set the azimuth origin, obtaining the Unique Shape Contexts (USC) descriptor.

It would be desirable to avoid the evaluation of multiple descriptors as done by [9]. Such a strategy increases the computational load during matching, can suffer from false matches (due to an unfortunate rotation of the descriptor of a non-corresponding point) and adds considerable complexity to the application of machine learning techniques that can be useful upon the availability of a training set. Despite the above efforts to obtain shape context descriptors without azimuth ambiguity, the best performance is still obtained by using 3DSC (i.e. computing multiple descriptors).

The performance of HSC was found comparable to 3DSC in some cases [9] but at the expense of a huge increase in computational load. On the other hand, USC was reported to perform slightly better than 3DSC in terms of precision-recall curves for a task of feature matching on synthetically transformed shapes [26]. However, USC was found considerably less accurate than 3DSC when targeting specific points on a craniofacial landmark localization task [21]. This can be explained by the instability of the sign disambiguation on objects that present a high variability, such as the human face. That is, it cannot be assured that the directions determined by the proposed disambiguation step are consistent across a population of facial scans. Since USC rely on the unique definition of azimuth bins, the lack of consistency has an important effect on accuracy [23].

In this paper we present a different approach to resolve the azimuth ambiguity, based on asymmetry patterns, and show that it is possible to attain rotationally invariant shape contexts that obtain comparable accuracy to 3DSC for the localization of craniofacial landmarks and remarkably outperform 3DSC for specific points like the outer eye corners and nose corners.

We build on a recently presented measure of approximate rotational symmetry in 2D [10], defined as the overlapping area between a shape and rotated versions of itself. We show that such a measure can be extended to 3DSC and derive asymmetry based on the absolute differences between overlapping bins of the descriptor and rotated versions of itself. Both measures depend on the rotation angle but not on the selection of the origin of azimuth bins, which allows us to obtain patterns that capture the rotational asymmetry of the descriptor over the azimuth but are invariant to the rotation of its bins.

The asymmetry patterns can be defined in a variety of ways, depending on the spatial relationships that need to be highlighted. Thus, we define Asymmetry Patterns Shape Contexts (APSC) [23] from a subset of the possible spatial relations present in the spherical support region; hence they can be thought of as a family of descriptors that depend on the subset that is selected.

Concrete examples of APSC are evaluated by defining some of the simplest possible spatial patterns. We show that the performance of APSC depends heavily on the selection of these spatial patterns, which can be useful to target different types of points. The computation of an APSC descriptor is slightly more expensive than a single 3DSC but produces considerable savings in matching time and memory (APSC requires half the memory of 3DSC). This computational efficiency contrasts with prior work exploring the use of symmetry in geometric descriptors using Spherical Harmonics [14].

In the next section we provide the definition of APSC, as well as a brief review of 3DSC. Experimental evaluation is presented in Sect. 3, followed by a discussion of results (Sect. 4) and concluding remarks (Sect. 5).

2 Asymmetry Patterns Shape Contexts

Computation of the APSC descriptor starts by computing a 3DSC descriptor [9], from which the asymmetry patterns are later extracted.

2.1 3D Shape Contexts

This descriptor is based on a 3D-histogram computed on a spherical support region centered at the interest point, $\mathbf{v}$, considering a neighborhood $\mathcal{N}_v = \{\mathbf{w} \mid \|\mathbf{w} - \mathbf{v}\| \leq r_N\}$, namely all points within a radius r_N. The North pole of the sphere is oriented with the normal vector at the interest point $\mathbf{n}_v$. The default structure has $N_E = 11$ elevation bins and $N_A = 12$ azimuth bins, both uniformly spaced, and $N_R = 15$ radial bins logarithmically spaced as follows:

$$r_k = \exp\left(\ln(r_{min}) + \frac{k}{N_R}\ln\left(\frac{r_N}{r_{min}}\right)\right) \tag{1}$$

where r_k is the k-*th* radial division from a total of N_R, r_N is the radius of the spherical neighborhood and r_{min} is the radius of the smallest bin.

The logarithmic sampling is aimed at assigning more importance to shape changes that are closer to the interest point. The contribution to the histogram of each point is normalization by bin volume and sampling density.

As the spherical support region is defined based on $\mathbf{v}$ and $\mathbf{n}_v$, there is an ambiguity in the origin of the azimuth bins. This is dealt with by calculating N_A descriptors per point, covering all possible shifts. The computation of multiple descriptors is done for the model (i.e. during training), so that during matching only one descriptor is computed and matched to the multiple descriptors by choosing the one that yields the smallest Euclidean distance:

$$d(\mathbf{x}, \mathbf{y}) = \min_{0 \le a < N_A} \sqrt{\sum_{i=0}^{N_E-1} \sum_{j=0}^{N_A-1} \sum_{k=0}^{N_R-1} (x_{i,j+a,k} - y_{i,j,k})^2} \tag{2}$$

where $\mathbf{x}$ and $\mathbf{y}$ are the descriptors to compare and the addition $j + a$ is modulo N_A (i.e. circular) so that $\mathbf{x}_{i,j+a,k}$ is an azimuth rotation of $\mathbf{x}_{i,j,k}$ (i.e. about the North-South axis of the sphere) by a bins.

2.2   Rotational Symmetry

In a recent work, Guo et al. [10] presented continuous measures of approximate bilateral and rotational symmetry. Given a shape $\mathbf{m}$ in 2D and a rotation angle ϕ about the z-axis (i.e. perpendicular to the plane containing the shape), they defined the rotational central symmetry degree $\mathcal{S}_c(\mathbf{m}, \phi)$ to be the area of intersection of shape $\mathbf{m}$ with a rotated version of itself by an angle ϕ, $R(\mathbf{m}, \phi)$, normalized by the area of shape $\mathbf{m}$:

$$\mathcal{S}_c(\mathbf{m}, \phi) = \frac{\text{Area}(\mathbf{m} \cap R(\mathbf{m}, \phi))}{\text{Area}(\mathbf{m})} \tag{3}$$

Defined in this way, $\mathcal{S}_c(\mathbf{m}, \phi)$ measures the degree of rotational symmetry of shape $\mathbf{m}$ from 0 (no symmetry) to 1 (perfect symmetry at the considered angle).

We can adapt this symmetry measure to the 3DSC descriptor by converting the area overlap into the minimum value of overlapping bins. That is, as the support region of the descriptor is spherical, the overlap of rotated shapes (in terms of area or volume) is always perfect, but not the values assigned to the coinciding bins. For example, assume we extract from a 3DSC descriptor $\mathbf{x}$ the ring composed by all the bins at a given elevation i and radius k; this will generate a shape $\mathbf{m}$ represented as a sequence of N_A non-negative values from the corresponding bins:

$$m_j = x_{i,j,k}, \quad m_j \geq 0 \, \forall j \in [1; N_A] \tag{4}$$

We can define the symmetry degree of the sequence $\mathbf{m}$ as follows:

$$\mathcal{S}(\mathbf{m}, a) = \frac{\sum_j \min(m_j, m_{j+a})}{\sum_j m_j} \tag{5}$$

where, as before, $j + a$ is the addition modulo the cardinality of $\mathbf{m}$ (N_A in this example). Notice that the angular parameter ϕ used in the area-based definition is replaced by the shift parameter a, which represents a discrete azimuth rotation of $2\pi/N_A$. Thus, $\mathcal{S}$ behaves analogously to $\mathcal{S}_c$.

By considering asymmetry as the complement of symmetry, we obtain a particularly simple formulation:

$$\mathcal{A}(\mathbf{m}, a) = 1 - \mathcal{S}(\mathbf{m}, a) = \frac{\sum_j m_j - \sum_j \min(m_j, m_{j+a})}{\sum_j m_j}$$
$$= \frac{\frac{1}{2} \sum_j (\max(m_j, m_{j+a}) - \min(m_j, m_{j+a}))}{\sum_j m_j} = \frac{\sum_j |m_j - m_{j+a}|}{2 \sum_j m_j} \tag{6}$$

which holds because for every pair (m_j, m_{j+a}) one element is the maximum and the other one the minimum, hence adding both guarantees to include each element of $\mathbf{m}$ exactly twice in the summation [23].

The asymmetry degree $\mathcal{A}(\mathbf{m}, a)$ defined in (6) is the mean of absolute differences between $\mathbf{m}$ and $R(\mathbf{m}, a)$ with an appropriate normalization factor. While such normalization is important to facilitate a meaningful interpretation of the asymmetry value in $[0; 1]$, it is not desirable in our case as it removes potentially useful information. Thus we define:

$$\mathcal{A}_1(\mathbf{m}, a) = \sum_j |m_j - m_{j+a}| \tag{7}$$

2.3 Asymmetry Patterns

We obtain asymmetry patterns by considering all possible azimuth rotations of the sequence that generate distinct values:

$$\mathcal{P}_A(\mathbf{m}) = \mathcal{A}_1(\mathbf{m}, 1), \mathcal{A}_1(\mathbf{m}, 2), \ldots, \mathcal{A}_1(\mathbf{m}, \lfloor \frac{N_A}{2} \rfloor) \tag{8}$$

where $\lfloor x \rfloor$ is the integer part of x. Defined in this way the asymmetry pattern accounts for approximately half the possible rotations, because those remaining would generate only repeated values. This happens because $\mathcal{A}_1(\mathbf{m}, a)$ is an even function with respect to a:

$$\forall a \in [1; N_A] : \mathcal{A}_1(\mathbf{m}, a) = \mathcal{A}_1(\mathbf{m}, -a) = \mathcal{A}_1(\mathbf{m}, N_A - a) \tag{9}$$

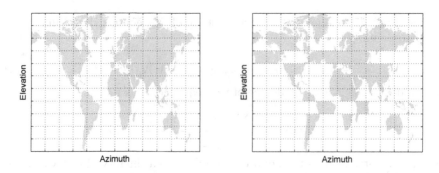

Fig. 1. Left: the World map as an example of a shell with (ideally) constant radius. The azimuth (longitude) and elevation (latitude) bins are also indicated. Right: the same spherical shell after arbitrary and independent azimuth rotations of two rings with constant elevation (4-th and 8-th bins).

where both addition and substraction are modulo N_A operations. Intuitively, this can be understood from the definition as an overlap between $\mathbf{m}$ and a rotated version of itself by an angle $\phi = 2\pi a/N_A$ that we can call $\mathbf{m}' = R(\mathbf{m}, \phi)$. The overlap between the two would be the same if we rotate both $\mathbf{m}$ and $\mathbf{m}'$ by any angle, for example $-\phi$, which would transform shape $\mathbf{m}$ into $R(\mathbf{m}, 2\pi - \phi)$ and shape $\mathbf{m}'$ into $\mathbf{m}$. Hence, the overlap between $\mathbf{m}$ and $R(\mathbf{m}, \phi)$ is equivalent to the overlap between $\mathbf{m}$ and $R(\mathbf{m}, 2\pi - \phi)$.

Thus, the sequence $\mathcal{P}_A(\mathbf{m})$ is the asymmetry pattern of the sequence $\mathbf{m}$, indicating how asymmetric is the ring that originated $\mathbf{m}$ for different angles of azimuth rotation. However, from the definition of $\mathcal{A}(\mathbf{m}, a)$, it is clear that the generated pattern is invariant to the origin chosen for the azimuth bins, i.e.

$$\mathcal{P}_A(\mathbf{m}) = \mathcal{P}_A(R(\mathbf{m}, a)), \forall a \in \mathbb{Z} \tag{10}$$

2.4   Spatial Relationships

So far, we have worked with a sequence $\mathbf{m}$ defined as in (4), namely the bins of a ring at fixed elevation and radius from the spherical support of a 3DSC. This choice seems natural, as it allows to transform each $(i-k)$ ring of a 3DSC descriptor $\mathbf{x}$ into an asymmetry pattern that is invariant to the choice of azimuth.

However, such a choice takes into account only the spatial relationships within each $(i-k)$ ring. To illustrate this, suppose that we consider all bins of $\mathbf{x}$ at a fixed radius. This is a spherical shell and we could represent it on a Cartesian plane similarly to a World map, as shown in Fig. 1, where latitude is the elevation and longitude is the azimuth. If we consider the representation of each ring independently, then any azimuth shift of a ring has no effect in our representation and both the *correct* World map of Fig. 1(left) and the example with shifted rings in Fig. 1(right) will generate the same set of patterns. A similar reasoning can be applied to the relation between shells of different radii. While this is not

Table 1. Description of some specific spatial patterns for APSC descriptors. In all cases the sequences are generated by varying the azimuth index j.

Abbreviation	Sequence(s) equation		Description
A	$m_j = x_{i,j,k}$		Azimuth ring
D_{AE}	$m_j = x_{i+j,j,k}$		Azimuth-Elevation diagonal
D_{AR}	$m_j = x_{i,j,k+j}$		Azimuth-Radius diagonal
D_{AER}	$m_j = x_{i+j,j,k+j}$		Azimuth-Elevation-Radius diagonal
$A+E$	$m_{1,j} = x_{i,j,k},$	$m_{2,j} = x_{i+1,j,k}$	Azimuth ring + Elevation neighbors
$A+R$	$m_{1,j} = x_{i,j,k},$	$m_{2,j} = x_{i,j,k+1}$	Azimuth ring + Radial neighbors
$A+D_{AE}$	$m_{1,j} = x_{i,j,k},$	$m_{2,j} = x_{i+j,j,k}$	Azimuth ring + Az-Elev diagonal
$A+D_{AR}$	$m_{1,j} = x_{i,j,k},$	$m_{2,j} = x_{i,j,k+j}$	Azimuth ring + Az-Rad diagonal
$A+D_{AER}$	$m_{1,j} = x_{i,j,k},$	$m_{2,j} = x_{i+j,j,k+j}$	Azimuth ring + Az-Elev-Rad diag

necessarily negative (e.g. it might be useful to *disable* certain spatial relations), in the general case it can lead to a loss of discriminant information.

The choice of what spatial relations are considered is related to the definition of **m**. Straight-forward alternatives include considering adjacent rings (either in elevation or radius) or, if relaxing the rotational invariance requirement, *diagonal rings*, i.e. jointly changing the bin indexes of azimuth with radius and/or elevation. In Table 1 we indicate the sequences to generate eight other simple patterns resulting from combinations of diagonals, adjacent rings and azimuth rings. When jointly considering two rings, e.g. $A+E$, $A+D_{AR}$, the overlap is computed only between rings with the same definition:

$$\mathcal{A}_2(\mathbf{m}, a) = \sum_j |m_{1,j} - m_{1,j+a}| + |m_{2,j} - m_{2,j+a}| \tag{11}$$

All additions are circular, modulo the corresponding number of bins (N_E, N_A and N_R respectively for i, j and k). In principle, the definition of the sequences can be arbitrary and the above are just a few intuitive choices. Thus, APSC can be though of as a family of descriptors with a flexible definition that allows their adaptation so as to highlight or disable specific spatial relationships.

3 Experimental Evaluation

In this section we compare the performance of APSC to the following three algorithms, which constitute competing alternatives:

- 3DSC [9], which generate descriptors that are not invariant to azimuth rotations.
- HSC [9], which achieve invariance to azimuth rotations by decomposing each spherical shell at fixed radius r_k of a 3DSC descriptor into Spherical Harmonics keeping only the modulus of the resulting coefficients.

- USC [26], which compute a 3DSC with a unique orientation of the spherical support region based on the principal axes in a neighborhood of the interest point and a sign disambiguation step.

In all cases we used the default configuration as indicated in the original papers: $N_E = 11$ elevation bins, $N_A = 12$ azimuth bins and $N_R = 15$ radial bins. The radius of the spherical support region was set to $r_N = 30$ mm and the minimum radius to $r_{min} = 1$ mm (see (1)). Spherical Harmonics were computed up to order $N_{SH} = 16$. Thus, 3DSC and USC had a total of $N_E \times N_A \times N_R = 1980$ bins while HSC had a total of $N_R \times N_{SH} \times (N_{SH} + 1)/2 = 2040$ bins.

For APSC, we test the 9 descriptors indicated in Table 1, computed starting from a $3DSC$ descriptor $\mathbf{x}$, whose elements are indexed by $(i, j, k) =$ (elevation, azimuth, radius). We always generate sequences for all possible combinations of i and k (while varying j), which results in full coverage of the bins of $\mathbf{x}$. For each sequence of length $N_A = 12$ bins, an asymmetry pattern of length $\lfloor N_A/2 \rfloor = 6$ is generated. Thus, each $APSC$ descriptor has only $N_E \times N_A \times 6 = 990$ bins.

3.1   Craniofacial Landmarks

We frame our evaluation in the task of craniofacial landmark localization. This landmark-based evaluation has two important advantages with respect to evaluations based on *keypoints* (i.e. points that are considered highly discriminant or *salient* from the point of view of a descriptor): (*i*) all descriptors are evaluated in the same set of points which are not necessarily salient and, as in the case of facial landmarks, can include diverse (local) geometries that pose different degrees of challenge to the descriptor; (*ii*) the evaluation is done on *real world* examples (e.g. a population of faces where anatomical correspondences have been manually annotated), instead of using synthesized instances obtained by modifying a given example by some set of transformations [3,20,26].

Our test dataset consisted of 144 facial scans acquired by means of a hand-held laser scanner[1]. Special care was taken to avoid occlusions due to facial hair. The extracted surfaces were subsampled by a factor of 4 : 1, resulting in an average of approximately 21.3 thousand vertices per mesh. The dataset contains exclusively healthy volunteers who acted as controls in the context of craniofacial dysmorphology research. Each scan was annotated with a set of anatomical landmarks, in accordance with definitions in [12] (based on [8]), from which we target the 22 points indicated in Fig. 2(a).

The fact that the test dataset was acquired in the context of clinical research makes it especially suited for tests of localization accuracy. As can be observed in Fig. 2(a), these are high quality scans that have been carefully annotated by experts based on anthropometric definitions. Recent studies indicate that the intra- and inter-observer uncertainty of this type of annotation are typically between 1 mm and 2 mm [1,25].

---

[1] Polhemus FastSCAN^{TM}, Colchester, VT, USA. An example is available at http:// www.cipa.dcu.ie/videos/face3d/Scanning_DCU_RCSI.avi [Accessed on 20.05.2013].

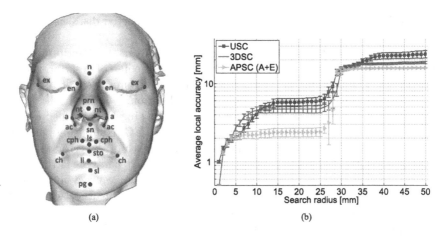

(a)   (b)

Fig. 2. (a) A scan from the clinical dataset with the 22 landmarks used in this study: en = endocanthion; ex = exocanthion; n = nasion; a = alare; ac = alar crest; nt = nostril top; prn = pronasale; sn = subnasale; ch = cheilion; cph = crista philtrum; li = labiale inferius; ls = labiale superius; sto = stomion; sl = sublabiale; pg = pogonion; [12]; (b) average accuracy curves of USC, 3DSC and APSC (using $A + E$ rings) targeting the nose corners (ac). Error bars indicate a 95 % confidence interval.

3.2 Accuracy

In this section we evaluate the performance of each descriptor for the different landmarks on an individual basis. This is done using the expected local accuracy $\bar{e}_L(r_S)$, as defined in [21]. For each descriptor and landmark that is targeted, $\bar{e}_L(r_S)$ is computed as follows:

1. Start from an annotated set of facial surfaces represented by meshes $\mathcal{M}_i$.
2. For every vertex $\mathbf{v} \in \mathcal{M}_i$ compute a descriptor *score*, $s(\mathbf{v})$, which measures how similar is the descriptor of vertex $\mathbf{v}$ to that of the targeted landmark.
3. For every vertex $\mathbf{v} \in \mathcal{M}_i$ compute also the Euclidean distance to the *correct* position of the targeted landmark, say $d(\mathbf{v})$.
4. For each $\mathcal{M}_i$ consider a neighborhood of radius r_S around the ground truth position of the targeted landmark and select $\mathbf{v}_i^{max}$ as the vertex with highest score in this neighborhood. Its distance to the ground truth is $d(\mathbf{v}_i^{max})$.
5. There is one value of $d(\mathbf{v}_i^{max})$ for each mesh; $\bar{e}_L(r_S)$ is their expected value over the test set:

$$\bar{e}_L(r_S) = E[d(\mathbf{v}_{i,r_S}^{max})] \qquad \mathbf{v}_{i,r_S}^{max} = \underset{\mathbf{v}\in\mathcal{N}_{i,r_S}}{\arg\max}\left(s(\mathbf{v})\right) \qquad (12)$$

$$\mathcal{N}_{i,r_S} = \{\mathbf{v} \in \mathcal{M}_i \,|\, d(\mathbf{v}) \leq r_S\} \qquad (13)$$

where $E[x]$ is the expected value of x. That is, given a target landmark, for each mesh $\mathcal{M}_i$ we consider a neighborhood of radius r_S around the ground truth position of the landmark and select $\mathbf{v}_i^{max}$ as the vertex with the maximum score in this neighborhood. We are interested in the expected distance of these maximum-score vertices to the targeted landmark.

We used the negative Euclidean distance to a template as the descriptor score. The template for each landmark was computed as the median of descriptors over a training set. The training and test sets were obtained from the set of 144 facial scans described above by means of 6-fold cross validation.

An indicative example is provided in Fig. 2(b), showing the obtained curves of $\bar{e}_L(r_S)$ for the nose corner using USC, 3DSC and APSC (computing patterns over A + E rings). The three curves show an initial growth of the error with the search radius until they reach a nearly flat region or *plateau*. This is the most important part of the curve, because it provides both the accuracy and usable local range of the descriptor for the analyzed landmark. In other words, for search radii at which $\bar{e}_L(r_S)$ is flat the descriptor shows stable behavior. Hence, the first plateau is identified as the main feature of the local accuracy curves, allowing their characterization with just three numbers: the value of $\bar{e}_L(r_S)$ at the plateau and the plateau limits in terms of r_S [21]. Table 2 summarizes the results for HSC, USC, 3DSC and 5 selected APSC patterns[2].

Continuing with the example from Fig. 2(b), it is interesting to analyze the behavior of $\bar{e}_L(r_S)$ for radii beyond the plateau: for the three descriptors in the plot there is a sudden increase in the error at radii between 25 and 30 mm. Typically this is caused by the presence of a strong source of false positives (i.e. points with a very high score but not close to the targeted landmark) at the distance where the error increase is observed. In this case, the source of false positives is the bilaterally symmetric point (i.e. *the other* nose corner), typically located at 25 to 30 mm. This explains the strong coincidence in the upper plateau limits shown in Table 2 for nose corners (*ac*) or the inner eye-corners (*en*), as the bilaterally symmetric points are relatively close to each other.

The sources of false positives are not necessarily the symmetric point to the one targeted and depend on the descriptor that is used. There are also two special types of points: (*i*) the ones without false positives in the analyzed range (which we set to 200 mm); (*ii*) points that do not show stable behavior in terms of $\bar{e}_L(r_S)$, which are indicated in Table 2 by *n.p* (no plateau).

From the results in Table 2 we can conclude that:

- For the majority of landmarks, at least one of the specific patterns of APSC that we tested showed comparable performance to the best descriptor.
- For eight landmarks (*ex*(2), *ac*(2), *nt*(2) and *cph*(2)) there were one or more APSC descriptors that significantly outperformed 3DSC. Interestingly, HSC also outperformed 3DSC for *ac*, *nt* and *cph*, but not for *ex*.
- There were four landmarks (*a*(2), *li* and *sl*) for which none of the tested APSC achieved sufficient performance when compared to 3DSC.
- The performance of APSC descriptors strongly depends on the spatial patterns that are considered. Jointly considering two rings produced lower errors than APSC derived from single rings.

---

[2] The complete results for all patterns listed in Table 1 are available at http://www.cipa.dcu.ie/pubs_full.html [Accessed on 15.07.2013].

Table 2. Expected local accuracy [mm]. If a plateau is found, its value and limits are indicated, otherwise n.p (no plateau) is indicated. For each landmark (rows), the best descriptor is highlighted in boldface as well as those with no statistically significant difference from it. The latter are further highlighted with an asterisk.

Lmk	HSC	USC	3DSC	APSC				
				D_{AR}	D_{AER}	A+E	A+R	A+D_{AER}
en	**1.3***	1.9	1.4	1.5	1.5	**1.4***	**1.3**	**1.3***
(2)	**(2–24)**	(3–25)	(3–25)	(3–25)	(3–25)	**(3–24)**	**(3–25)**	**(3–25)**
ex	4.5	n.p	4.3	**2.9**	3.9	5.4	4.7	**3.1***
(2)	(16–90)		(13–88)	**(6–67)**	(19–48)	(13–88)	(14–89)	**(8–88)**
n	1.8	4.6	**1.5**	**1.6***	**1.6***	2.3	2.0	**1.7***
	(3–200)	(5–12)	**(3–200)**	**(4–200)**	**(4–64)**	(4–200)	(3–200)	**(4 - 200)**
a	**1.4***	n.p	**1.4**	2.9	n.p	2.1	1.8	2.0
(2)	**(3–26)**		**(4–27)**	(6–12)		(4–25)	(4–26)	(6–26)
ac	**2.1***	5.8	4.7	9.0	n.p	2.3	**2.1**	5.1
(2)	**(5–25)**	(14–25)	(9–25)	(16–24)		(7–25)	**(4–11)**	(14–25)
nt	**2.0**	12.2	8.0	6.9	7.5	2.3	2.2	6.6
(2)	**(4–8)**	(14–200)	(14–200)	(12–200)	(11–200)	(5–8)	(5–9)	(11–200)
prn	1.4	1.4	**1.2**	1.3	**1.3***	**1.3***	**1.3***	1.3
	(3–200)	(2–200)	**(2–200)**	(3–200)	**(2–200)**	**(2–200)**	**(2–200)**	(3–200)
sn	1.8	n.p	**1.6**	**1.8***	2.0	1.9	1.9	1.9
	(4–200)		**(4–55)**	**(4–22)**	(5–16)	(3–200)	(3–200)	(4–200)
ch	3.8	2.4	**2.1**	2.5	2.9	2.8	2.9	**2.3***
(2)	(11–22)	(4–42)	**(5–19)**	(9–29)	(10–39)	(6–18)	(5–20)	**(5–28)**
cph	**2.1**	13.3	8.4	7.1	7.0	n.p	7.7	2.7
(2)	**(4–9)**	(20–34)	(18–200)	(17–86)	(16–59)		(16–200)	(5–8)
li	5.0	2.7	**2.3**	4.4	3.4	4.9	4.8	3.8
	(16–51)	(7–48)	**(5–10)**	(16–37)	(11–45)	(10–15)	(9–15)	(15–95)
ls	4.1	n.p	**2.3***	2.7	**2.2**	5.2	5.7	3.8
	(6–14)		**(8–46)**	(8–13)	**(6–11)**	(14–200)	(10–54)	(7–200)
sto	**2.7***	2.9	**2.2**	**2.5***	6.1	4.0	4.5	3.1
	(6–14)	(8–46)	**(8–78)**	**(7–17)**	(14–40)	(9–14)	(11–89)	(12–54)
sl	5.4	**3.0**	**3.2***	5.5	7.4	4.7	6.0	6.2
	(10–54)	**(10–18)**	**(11–27)**	(13–79)	(16–29)	(11–77)	(12–84)	(17–62)
pg	7.0	11.6	**5.4**	7.9	7.1	7.6	**5.6***	**5.7***
	(10–200)	(19–120)	**(10–200)**	(19–200)	(13–200)	(13–26)	**(13–23)**	**(10–200)**

In global terms, averaging $\bar{e}_L(r_S)$ over all 22 landmarks for each descriptor, 3DSC, HSC and the APSC descriptors using patterns of two rings showed very similar overall accuracy. On the other hand, USC and the two APSC based on a single ring showed poorer performance [23]. This confirms that, in general, considering individual rings implies a loss of important information, as all spatial relationships between different rings are not taken into account (Sect. 2.4). Nevertheless, Table 2 shows that for some particular cases this might not have an impact in local accuracy (e.g. n, prn, ls) or might even be beneficial (ex).

3.3 Implementation and Complexity

Our implementations of 3DSC and USC are based on the Point Cloud Library [18] with some modifications to improve the computation speed by removing redundant operations and including multi-threading with OpenMP [7]. A trilinear interpolation was included in the construction of the histograms as it was experimentally found to improve the performance of all tested descriptors.

It is interesting to analyze the sign disambiguation step when deriving the axes for USC: the orientations of the generated normals were not consistently pointing inwards or outwards for 30 %–35 % of points. This is easy to verify and correct in our case as the input data are facial surfaces. The results reported in this paper include the correction of the reference frame orientation to ensure that all normals were pointing outwards from the object, which reduced the overall error of USC by approximately 10 %. The latter suggests that similar inconsistencies might also exist in the sign of the other axes (and hence in the origin of the azimuth bins), which explains the lower accuracy of USC with respect to the other methods that were tested.

Regarding computational complexity, there are two aspects to consider: (i) computation of the descriptor and (ii) point-wise comparisons or matching.

The fastest descriptor to compute is 3DSC, as all the others are built from it plus some additional step. In the case of USC the additional step is dominated by an SVD on a neighborhood of the point of interest. For APSC and HSC the additional step is carried out based on the 3DSC bins and is therefore decoupled from the sampling density of the mesh. However, the computation of the histogram to build the 3DSC descriptor depends on the number of neighbors considered and, therefore, on the density of the mesh.

The above hampers our ability to produce an exact analysis of complexity. Thus, in Table 3 we provide numerical results for the computation time of the descriptors, relative to the computation time of 3DSC, which in our experiments averaged 3.45 s on an Intel Xeon E5320 @1.86 GHz. Note that HSC was approximately an order of magnitude slower than all other descriptors, as it required the decomposition of each fixed-radius shell into Spherical Harmonics. Assuming that the $N_{SH} \times (N_{SH} + 1)/2$ basis functions are pre-computed, we still need to project each shell into each basis function, which roughly implies $N_A \times N_E$ complex multiplications and additions. Thus, the whole decomposition takes at least

$$O\left(N_A\, N_E\, N_R \frac{N_{SH}\,(N_{SH}+1)}{2} \right) \qquad (14)$$

The above cost is considerably higher than the cost of computing APSC, which for each ring $\mathbf{m}$ takes only $O(N_A^2/2)$ additions. Thus, if considering only

Table 3. Computational complexity of the descriptors relative to 3DSC = 1.

Descriptor	Computation	Matching
HSC	11.1	$\frac{N_{SH}(N_{SH}+1)}{2\,N_E\,N_A^2}$
USC	1.23	$\frac{1}{N_A}$
1-ring APSC	1.05	$\frac{1}{2\,N_A}$
2-ring APSC	1.09	$\frac{1}{2\,N_A}$

single rings, the complexity added by APSC to the computation of 3DSC is $O(N_E\,N_R N_A^2/2)$. This cost grows linearly with the number of rings jointly considered, so it approximately doubles for the last row of Table 3. Note that the complexity in (14) in not directly comparable to that of APSC, as the first one is a lower bound based on complex additions and multiplications while the latter involves only real additions.

The matching time depends exclusively on the bins for all descriptors. Hence, the relative complexity to that of 3DSC can be easily derived and is shown in Table 3. Being the fastest to compute, 3DSC are also the slowest to match as they require computation of the N_A distances that correspond to all possible azimuth rotations, as in Eq. (2). All other descriptors compute a single distance. In the case of HSC, as the number of bins is different to 3DSC, the relative computation time depends on the choice of N_{SH}, but approaches $(1/N_A)$ with the default parameters. Finally, all APSC have just half as many bins as 3DSC and USC, which makes them the fastest to match.

4 Discussion

From the results presented in the previous section we can conclude that APSC allows construction of descriptors that perform comparably to 3DSC in terms of overall accuracy, with little extra load in computation of the descriptor (<10 % in our experiments), and run several times faster during matching.

With respect to the previous alternatives to achieve azimuth-invariance in shape contexts, APSC showed similar accuracy to HSC at a much lower computational load (an order of magnitude) and outperformed USC both in terms of accuracy and speed. However, the greatest potential of APSC is their flexibility to derive different descriptors depending on the spatial patterns that are selected to construct the sequences **m**, from which asymmetry is extracted. As shown in Table 2, specific choices of spatial patterns might produce considerably lower errors than those obtained with 3DSC for certain landmarks.

It might be argued that none of the tested APSC was optimal for all landmarks; a potential reduction in the error generalized through the majority of points would require different APSC to target different landmarks. Nonetheless such a strategy is possible and prior work in landmark localization has indeed adopted different features to localize each of the targeted landmarks [6, 11, 19].

Table 4. Best-performing APSC descriptors for each landmark (i.e. the one with the lowest error and all those with no statistically significant difference from it) for three different annotated dataset, as indicated by the makers: clinical ($\star$), FRGC with GTA-1 ($\blacktriangledown$) and FRGC with GTA-2 ($\blacktriangle$).

APSC '	en	ex	n	prn	ac	ch	ls	li	pg
A	$\star$ $\blacktriangle$			$\star$ $\blacktriangle$	$\blacktriangledown\blacktriangle$	$\blacktriangle$			$\star$
D_{AE}							$\star$		
D_{AR}	$\blacktriangledown$	$\star\blacktriangledown$	$\star\blacktriangledown\blacktriangle$	$\star\blacktriangledown\blacktriangle$	$\blacktriangle$	$\star$			$\blacktriangledown$
D_{AER}	$\blacktriangledown\blacktriangle$		$\star$	$\star\blacktriangledown\blacktriangle$			$\star\blacktriangledown\blacktriangle$	$\star\blacktriangledown\blacktriangle$	$\blacktriangledown\blacktriangle$
A+E	$\star$ $\blacktriangle$			$\star$ $\blacktriangle$	$\star\blacktriangledown\blacktriangle$	$\blacktriangle$			
A+R	$\star$ $\blacktriangle$			$\star$ $\blacktriangle$	$\star\blacktriangledown\blacktriangle$	$\blacktriangle$			$\star\blacktriangledown$
A+D_{AE}	$\blacktriangledown$	$\blacktriangledown$		$\blacktriangle$					
A+D_{AR}	$\star\blacktriangledown$	$\star\blacktriangledown\blacktriangle$		$\star\blacktriangledown\blacktriangle$	$\blacktriangledown\blacktriangle$	$\star\blacktriangledown$	$\blacktriangledown$		
A+D_{AER}	$\star$	$\star$	$\star\blacktriangledown$	$\star\blacktriangledown\blacktriangle$	$\blacktriangle$	$\star\blacktriangledown$		$\star$	$\star\blacktriangledown\blacktriangle$

Moreover, combining two or more APSC can be far more efficient than combining other different descriptors, as the extra computation required would be rather marginal due to all spatial patterns being extracted from the same 3DSC, which would be computed only once. For example, all five APSC descriptors listed in Table 2 can be computed together with less than 1.4 times the computational load of a single 3DSC descriptor.

The spatial patterns that were tested correspond to some straightforward definitions from a large set of possibilities. While the wrong choice of spatial patterns might negatively affect performance, it would be expected that more elaborate strategies to choose these patterns, such as feature selection, would bring further improvement. While feature selection strategies would also be possible in 3DSC, the issue of azimuth ambiguity can considerably complicate the search for an optimal solution.

Another important aspect is how stable would the selected patterns be for different databases. To investigate this, we selected a subset of 100 scans from the Face Recognition Grand Challenge (FRGC) database, with two independent sets of manual Ground Truth Annotations (GTA):

- GTA-1: Made available by Szeptycki et al. [24], with some additions and corrections introduced by Creusot et al. [6], which are available on line[3].
- GTA-2: Our own manual annotations [22], also available on line[4].

The difference between these two sets is that the annotations in GTA-1 were marked up based on 2D images, while those in GTA-2 were annotated directly in 3D and were shown to be considerably more precise [22]. Hence, these sets allow us to test the influence of *noisy* ground truth in the selection of descriptors.

---

[3] http://clementcreusot.com/phd/ [Accessed on 08.07.2013].
[4] http://www.cipa.dcu.ie/pubs_full.html [Accessed on 15.07.2013].

Table 4 summarizes the results obtained by testing all APSC descriptors defined in Table 1. We targeted the 11 landmarks that are common to three annotated datasets: clinical (Sect. 3), FRGC with GTA-1 and FRGC with GTA-2 (the latter two correspond to the first 100 scans of FRGCv1; see [22] for details). For each landmark in Table 4, we indicate with a marker all best-performing descriptors, i.e. the one with the lowest error and all those with no statistically significant difference from it.

It is observed that, for a majority of the landmarks tested, the selection of best performing descriptors correlates reasonably well across the three datasets, highlighting the following set as the most stable choices: $ex \rightarrow A + D_{AR}$; $n \rightarrow D_{AR}$; $prn \rightarrow \{D_{AR}$ or D_{AER} or $A + D_{AR}$ or $A + D_{AER}\}$; $ac \rightarrow \{A + E$ or $A + R\}$; $ls \rightarrow D_{AER}$; $li \rightarrow D_{AER}$; $pg \rightarrow A + D_{AER}$. On the other hand, the selection of descriptors for en and ch showed a strong dependency on the dataset that is employed. This was true both for changes in the 3D data (from clinical data to FRGC) and for changes in the annotations (GTA-1 vs GTA-2).

5   Conclusions

In this paper we present a new family of 3D geometric descriptors based on a simple measure of rotational symmetry that has recently been proposed based on the overlap of a shape with a rotated version of itself [10]. We compute asymmetry patterns on sequences of bins extracted from a 3DSC descriptor by varying the azimuth index and, optionally, the radial and/or elevation bins. This allows: (*i*) definition of APSC descriptors with azimuth invariance, (*ii*) highlighting or disabling some of the spatial patterns present in the spherical grid of a 3DSC that can be used to specialize the descriptor for different types of points.

We evaluated nine examples of APSC in terms of local accuracy by targeting 22 craniofacial landmarks on a set of 144 facial scans. The accuracy was measured in terms of distance to ground truth consisting of expert annotations. Our results showed that APSC can provide invariance to azimuth rotations at the expense of a small overhead in computation of the descriptor, relative to 3DSC, which did not exceed 10 %. On the other hand the rotation invariance reduces the time required for matching two descriptors by a factor of twice the number of azimuth bins. APSC were also shown to perform better than previous approaches that provided azimuth invariance to shape contexts.

The greatest potential of APSC is their flexibility to derive different descriptors at an incremental computational cost. By appropriately selecting the patterns to extract, we can build descriptors especially tuned to produce highly accurate detections of one or several landmarks. While in general, the selection of these patterns depends on the dataset, our tests suggest that such variability is limited; for a majority of the landmarks that we tested, it was possible to identify APSC descriptors with stable performance across different datasets.

Acknowledgements. The authors would like to thank their colleagues in the Face3D Consortium (www.face3d.ac.uk) and financial support from the Wellcome Trust (WT-086901 MA) and the Marie Curie IEF programme (grant 299605, SP-MORPH).

References

1. Aynechi, N., Larson, B.E., Leon-Salazar, V., Beiraghi, S.: Accuracy and precision of a 3D anthropometric facial analysis with and without landmark labeling before image acquisition. Angle Orthod. **81**(2), 245–252 (2011)
2. Bariya, P., Novatnack, J., Schwartz, G., Nishino, K.: 3D geometric scale variability in range images: features and descriptors. Int. J. Comput. Vis. **99**(2), 232–255 (2012)
3. Bronstein, A.M., Bronstein, M.M., Castellani, U., Dubrovina, A., Guibas, L.J., Horaud, R.P., Kimmel, R., Knossow, D., von Lavante, E., Mateus, D., Ovsjanikov, M., Sharma, A.: SHREC 2010: robust correspondence benchmark. In: Proceedings of the Eurographics Workshop on 3D Object Retrieval (2010)
4. Chen, H., Bhanu, B.: 3D free-form object recognition in range images using local surface patches. Pattern Recogn. Lett. **28**(10), 1252–1262 (2007)
5. Creusot, C., Pears, N., Austin, J.: Automatic keypoint detection on 3D faces using a dictionary of local shapes. In: Proceedings of the 1st Joint Conference on 3D Imaging, Modeling, Processing, Visualization, and Transmission, pp. 204–211 (2011)
6. Creusot, C., Pears, N., Austin, J.: A machine-learning approach to keypoint detection and landmarking on 3D meshes. Int. J. Comput. Vis. **102**, 146–179 (2013)
7. Dagum, L., Menon, R.: OpenMP: an industry standard API for shared-memory programming. IEEE Comput. Sci. Eng. **5**(1), 46–55 (1998)
8. Farkas, L.G.: Anthropometry of the Head and Face. Raven Press, New York (1994)
9. Frome, A., Huber, D., Kolluri, R., Bülow, T., Malik, J.: Recognizing objects in range data using regional point descriptors. In: Pajdla, T., Matas, J.G. (eds.) ECCV 2004. LNCS, vol. 3023, pp. 224–237. Springer, Heidelberg (2004)
10. Guo, Q., Guo, F., Shao, J.: Irregular shape symmetry analysis: theory and application to quantitative galaxy classification. IEEE Trans. Pattern Anal. Mach. Intell. **32**(10), 1730–1743 (2010)
11. Gupta, S., Markey, M.K., Bovik, A.C.: Anthropometric 3D face recognition. Int. J. Comput. Vis. **90**(3), 331–349 (2010)
12. Hennessy, R.H., Kinsella, A., Waddington, J.L.: 3D laser surface scanning and geometric morphometric analysis of craniofacial shape as an index of cerebro-craniofacial morphogenesis. Biol. Psychiatry **51**(6), 507–514 (2002)
13. Johnson, A.E., Hebert, M.: Using spin images for efficient object recognition in cluttered 3D scenes. IEEE Trans. Pattern Anal. Mach. Intell. **21**(5), 433–449 (1999)
14. Kazhdan, M., Funkhouser, T., Rusinkiewicz, S.: Symmetry descriptors and 3D shape matching. In: Proceedings of the Eurographics/ACM SIGGRAPH Symposium on Geometry Processing, pp. 156–164 (2003)
15. Kortgen, M., Park, G.J., Novotni, M., Klein, R.: 3D shape matching with 3D shape contexts. In: 7th Central European Seminar on Computer Graphics (2003)
16. Passalis, G., Perakis, N., Theoharis, T., Kakadiaris, I.A.: Using facial symmetry to handle pose variations in real-world 3D face recognition. IEEE Trans. Pattern Anal. Mach. Intell. **33**(10), 1938–1951 (2011)
17. Rusu, R.B., Blodow, N., Beetz, M.: Fast point feature histograms (FPFH) for 3D registration. In: Proceedings of the IEEE International Conference on Robotics and Automation, pp. 3212–3217 (2009)
18. Rusu, R.B., Cousins, S.: 3D is here: point cloud library (PCL). In: Proceedings of the IEEE International Conference on Robotics and Automation, pp. 1–4 (2011)
19. Segundo, M.P., Silva, L., Bellon, O.R.P., Queirolo, C.C.: Automatic face segmentation and facial landmark detection in range images. IEEE Trans. Syst. Man Cybern. B Cybern. **40**(5), 1319–1330 (2010)

20. Steder, B., Rusu, R.B., Konolige, K., Burgard, W.: Point feature extraction on 3D range scans taking into account object boundaries. In: Proceedings of the IEEE International Conference on Robotics and Automation, pp. 2601–2608 (2011)
21. Sukno, F.M., Waddington, J.L., Whelan, P.F.: Comparing 3D descriptors for local search of craniofacial landmarks. In: Bebis, G., Boyle, R., Parvin, B., Koracin, D., Fowlkes, C., Wang, S., Choi, M.-H., Mantler, S., Schulze, J., Acevedo, D., Mueller, K., Papka, M. (eds.) ISVC 2012, Part II. LNCS, vol. 7432, pp. 92–103. Springer, Heidelberg (2012)
22. Sukno, F.M., Waddington, J.L., Whelan, P.F.: Compensating inaccurate annotations to train 3D facial landmark localization models. In: FG Workshop on 3D Face Biometrics (2013)
23. Sukno, F.M., Waddington, J.L., Whelan, P.F.. Rotationally invariant 3D shape contexts using asymmetry patterns. In: Proceedings of the International Conference on Computer Graphics Theory and Applications, pp. 7–17 (2013)
24. Szeptycki, P., Ardabilian, M., Chen, L.: A coarse-to-fine curvature analysis-based rotation invariant 3D face landmarking. In: Proceedings of the 3rd IEEE International Conference on Biometrics: Theory, Applications and Systems, pp. 1–6 (2009)
25. Toma, A.M., Zhurov, A., Playle, R., Ong, E., Richmond, S.: Reproducibility of facial soft tissue landmarks on 3D laser-scanned facial images. Orthod. Craniofac. Res. **12**(1), 33–42 (2009)
26. Tombari, F., Salti, S., Di Stefano, L.: Unique shape context for 3D data description. In: Proceedings of ACM Workshop on 3D Object Retrieval, pp. 57–62 (2010)
27. Zaharescu, A., Boyer, E., Horaud, R.: Keypoints and local descriptors of scalar functions on 2D manifolds. Int. J. Comput. Vis. **99**(2), 232–255 (2012)
28. Zhang, Y.: Intrinsic shape signatures: a shape descriptor for 3D object recognition. In: Proceedings of the 12th IEEE International Conference on Computer Vision Workshops, pp. 689–696 (2009)

Quasi-Delaunay Triangulations Using GPU-Based Edge-Flips

Cristóbal Navarro[1], Nancy Hitschfeld[1](✉), and Eliana Scheihing[2]

[1] Computer Science Department (DCC), Universidad de Chile, Santiago, Chile
{crinavar,nancy}@dcc.uchile.cl
[2] Instituto de Informática, Universidad Austral de Chile, Valdivia, Chile
escheihi@inf.uach.cl

Abstract. The edge-flip technique has been widely used for transforming any existing triangular mesh into a Delaunay mesh. Although several tools for generating Delaunay triangulations are known, there is no one that offers a realtime solution capable of maintaining the Delaunay condition on dynamically changing triangulations and, in particular, one integrable with the OpenGL rendering pipeline. In this paper we present an iterative GPGPU-based method capable of improving triangulations under the Delaunay criterion. Since the algorithm uses an ϵ value to handle co-circular or close to co-circular point configurations, a low percentage of triangles do not fulfill the Delaunay condition. We have compared the triangulations generated by our method with the ones generated by the Triangle software and by the CGAL library and we obtained less than 0.05 % different triangles for full random meshes and less than 1 % for noise based ones. Based on our experimental results, we report speedups from 14× to 50× against Lawson's sequential algorithm and of approximately 3× against the CGAL's and Triangle's constructive algorithms when processing full random triangulations. In our noise based tests we report up to 36× and 27× of speedup against CGAL and *Triangle*, respectively.

Keywords: Delaunay triangulations · Edge-flip technique · Parallel realtime applications · CUDA · OpenGL · GPGPU

1 Introduction

Delaunay triangulations are popular in several applications such as scientific simulations, terrain rendering, video-games and medical 3D reconstruction, among others. The Delaunay triangulation of a point set P is the one that maximizes the size of the smallest angle over all the possible triangulations that P can hold, making numeric computations on this kind of triangulation more precise than in the other ones [4].

Delaunay triangulations can be achieved in two ways: (a) by creating them from a PSLG (Planar straight linear graph), or (b) by transforming an already

© Springer-Verlag Berlin Heidelberg 2014
S. Battiato et al. (Eds.): VISIGRAPP 2013, CCIS 458, pp. 36–49, 2014.
DOI: 10.1007/978-3-662-44911-0_3

existing triangulation into one that satisfies the Delaunay condition. In general, in the case (a), a Delaunay triangulation is generated for the set of points of the PSLG. The segments (boundary edges) are then inserted to generate either a constrained Delaunay triangulation or a conforming Delaunay triangulation [14]. Case (b) assumes that a triangulation is given as input and the mesh needs to be transformed into a Delaunay mesh. A known technique for making this transformation is to flip the edges that do not satisfy the Delaunay condition. The edge-flip technique was first introduced by Lawson [10] and the proposed sequential algorithm has a worst-case complexity $O(n^2)$, where n is the number of points of the triangulation [5,6].

Real-time applications cannot make use of sequential algorithms when handling meshes close to a million triangles. To achieve faster computations, parallel solutions are needed. In recent years, GPU computing has become an important research area for parallel computing due to its high performance and low cost. Several applications that require geometric modeling and visualization benefits strongly from the use of a GPU. In particular, the generation of Delaunay triangulations with a fast GPU-based method is today a topic of interest.

The main contribution of this paper is the design and implementation of an iterative GPGPU-based algorithm that generates quasi-Delaunay triangulations starting from any existing triangulation. The algorithm maps threads to edges. Each thread is responsible for checking one edge Delaunay condition, doing one edge-flip and updating one edge data inconsistency if necessary. The performance and the quality of the generated meshes is compared with two well known and efficient sequential constrained Delaunay algorithms: the algorithm inside the software Triangle [14] and the algorithm available in the CGAL library [15]. As test examples we used full random triangulations (with minimum angles close to 0) and noise based triangulations, with mesh sizes ranging from 100 thousand up to 5 millions points. We are not using exact predicates nor floating point filters because these techniques can not be efficiently implemented on GPU architectures without sacrificing performance. These techniques would require adding if-else conditionals and handle irregular-data access patterns. That is why, in favor of speed, some results are quasi-Delaunay triangulations and not fully Delaunay triangulations.

In principle, the comparison of a transformation algorithm that generates quasi-Delaunay triangulations as the proposed in this paper with respect to constructive ones that generate exact Delaunay triangulations such as CGAL and Triangle can seem unfair because they solve different problems. However, since the complexity of a constructive algorithm is $O(nlog\ n)$ and the Lawson algorithm is $O(n^2)$, many times it is preferred to build the Delaunay mesh from scratch instead of improving an existing one. In some way, this research is intended to show that a parallel method based on edge-flips can become fast and useful in practice for applications that not require exact Delaunay meshes.

The paper is organized as follows: Sect. 2 describes some related work and the similarities and differences of our approach with other GPU-based approaches.

Section 3 presents our data structures and how they are compatible with OpenGL. Sections 4 and 5 cover the algorithm and implementation details. Section 6 shows experimental results with 2D random and noise inputs and 3D surface triangulations. Finally, Sect. 7 concludes our work.

A preliminary and short version of this paper was presented at the EuroCG11 workshop [11].

2 Related Work

Several parallel approaches have been already published for the generation of Delaunay meshes from set of points or from a PSLG [1, 8, 9, 13], but no one to transform an existing triangulation into a Delaunay mesh. To the best of our knowledge, only recently has the edge-flip technique been used in the design of parallel GPU-based algorithms for the generation of triangulations. Cao Thang [2] developed an algorithm for the generation of a Delaunay triangulation and its Voronoi diagram from a set of points. One step of his method performs GPU-based edge-flips; the algorithm maps threads to triangles. Cervenanský et al. [3] propose a GPU-based triangulation algorithm for image processing. Edges are flipped in parallel, as we also do, but by using a different approach for deciding which subset of them can be flipped in parallel (i.e., they do not use Delaunay conditions). Harada [7] proposed a constraint solver for rigid body simulation. In his work, threads are assigned to pairs of adjacent triangles by using atomic operations in the same way as we do for deciding which non-Delaunay edges can be flipped in parallel.

3 Data Structures

Proper data structures have been defined to efficiently represent a triangulation on the GPU. This representation is inspired by the Dynamic Render Mesh [16]. Figure 1 illustrates the three main components: Vertices, Triangles and Edges.

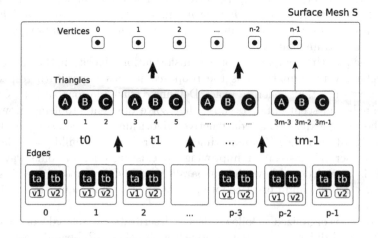

Fig. 1. Data structures for mesh rendering/processing.

Vertices are represented with a one-dimensional array in the same way as the OpenGL VBO (Vertex buffer object). Each position is of the type (x, y) or (x, y, z) depending on the used spatial dimension. The *Triangles* array is a set of indices to the *Vertices* array. For each three consecutive indices, a triangle is defined. Each edge of the *Edges* array contains a pair of indices v_1, v_2 to the *Vertices* array and two pairs of indices $t_a = \{t_{a_1}, t_{a_2}\}$ and $t_b = \{t_{b_1}, t_{b_2}\}$ to the *Triangles* array (for boundary edges, t_b remains unused). This way, an edge can know its endpoint indices directly through v_1, v_2 or indirectly via the pairs $\{Triangles[t_{a_1}], Triangles[t_{a_2}]\}$ and $\{Triangles[t_{b_1}], Triangles[t_{b_2}]\}$. This redundant information becomes useful for checking neighborhood consistency after each flip. In addition, indices to the opposite vertices per edge are stored in the *Opposites* array in order to speed up angle computations (boundary edges have only one opposite vertex). This data model can be naturally implemented and integrated with the OpenGL API and CUDA [12] or OpenCL. It is important to mention that for rendering, only the *Vertices* and *Triangles* arrays are accessed by the graphics API; the *Edges* and the *Opposites* arrays are for efficiently accessing neighbor information. All mentioned arrays use $\Theta(n)$ of memory space, where n is the number of points.

4   Algorithm Overview

We propose an iterative algorithm where each iteration consists of two consecutive phases of parallel computing:

- Phase 1: Detection, exclusion & processing.
- Phase 2: Repair.

On each iteration the algorithm transforms the mesh a step closer to the Delaunay mesh. The algorithm finishes when the Delaunay triangulation is reached. The following sub-sections explain the phases in more detail.

4.1   Detection, Exclusion and Processing

This phase is in charge of three steps: (1) detection of edges that do not fulfill the Delaunay condition, (2) exclusion of edges that can not be flipped in parallel and (3) processing the edges that can be flipped in parallel. Our algorithm maps threads to edges by using the PRAM model in such a way that thread t_i handles edge e_i with $i \in [0, ne - 1]$ (*ne* is the number of edges). The threads first detect the edges that need to be flipped (bad edges), then they go through a filter where only the independent threads survive and finally, the survivors flip their edge.

For the detection step, threads test their corresponding edge e against the Delaunay condition by computing the opposite angles λ and γ of e using the information from t_a, t_b. The test must satisfy the following condition:

$$\lambda + \gamma \leq \pi \tag{1}$$

If the test of Eq. (1) fails, the edge is a bad edge and needs to be flipped. On the other hand, if the test passes, the thread ends. Most of the time it is not possible to flip the complete set of bad edges in one iteration because the flip of a given edge e compromises the consistency of the neighbor edges that belong to t_a and t_b. However, it is possible to process a subset A of the edges that satisfy the following condition:

$$\forall e_1, e_2 \in A \quad T_{e_1} \cap T_{e_2} = \emptyset; \quad T_e = \{t \in T : e \in t\} \tag{2}$$

For implementing the exclusion step, the algorithm internally uses a *Flags* array where $Flags[i] == Taken$ if the i-th triangle was flagged by a thread, and $Flags[i] == Free$ if it was not. Each thread that needs to flip an edge requires two flags to be set, the ones associated with the triangles that share its edge. This operation is done atomically (atomic operations are sequential only when two or more threads access the same memory location). When a thread flags the first triangle, some neighbor threads will be excluded (i.e. the ones that failed to catch this flag). When a thread flags the second one, the rest of the neighbors will get excluded. Figure 2 shows an example, where edges a, b and c need to be flipped but only $\{a, c\}$ or $\{b, c\}$ can be processed at the same time. By using condition (2), the thread associated with edge a is excluded.

For the processing step, the per thread edge-flip method is designed as a swap of indices between the associated triangles t_a, t_b making a rotating effect of the triangles (see Fig. 3 (left)). For a given edge e_i, our parallel edge-flip proceeds in the following way:

1. Variables: $O[] = Opposites$, $T[] = Triangles$, $E[] = Edges$;
2. Get the opposite vertex indices o_1, o_2:
   $o_1 = O[i][0]; \qquad o_2 = O[i][1];$
3. Get $c_1 \in t_a, c_2 \in t_b$ such that $v_1 = T[c_1], v_2 = T[c_2]$:
   $c_1 = E[i].t_{a_1}; \qquad c_2 = E[i].t_{b_2};$
4. do the edge-flip:
   $T[c_2] = T[o_1]; \qquad T[c_1] = T[o_2];$

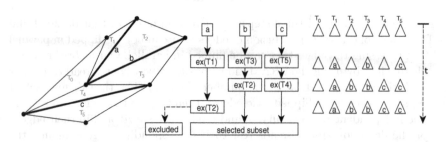

Fig. 2. Exclusion mechanism. Each thread performs an atomic operation ex(T_i) to select its triangles. The F array has the information of which thread has taken a given triangle.

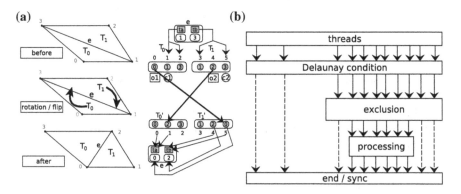

Fig. 3. (a) An example of the edge-flip procedure for e. (b) Exclusion and processing mechanism viewed as thread filters.

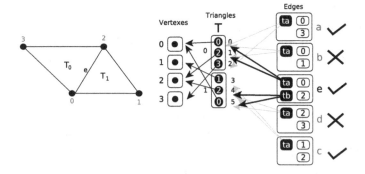

Fig. 4. Edges marked with a cross are inconsistent.

5. Update t_a, t_b and v_1, v_2:

$$E[i].t_a = [o_1, c_1]; \qquad E[i].t_b = [c_2, o_2];$$
$$E[i].v_1 = E[i].t_{a_1}; \qquad E[i].v_2 = E[i].t_{b_2};$$

The steps of this phase are summarized in Fig. 3 (right) showing how threads make their way down.

4.2 Repair

After the parallel edge-flips were done, inconsistent information can be stored on neighbor edges. Some edges can store references to triangles whom they no longer belong (obsolete t_a and t_b pairs). Figure 4 shows a simple mesh where inconsistent information appears at edges d and b after e was flipped. The information of the new triangles to whom d and b belong are in the triangles that were rotated while flipping e. Fortunately these inconsistencies can be easily identified with the following two expressions:

$$q = |v_1 - t_{a_1}| + |v_2 - t_{a_2}| \qquad (3)$$

$$w = |v_1 - t_{b_1}| + |v_2 - t_{b_2}| \qquad (4)$$

If $q > 0$ $(w > 0)$ then t_a (t_b) needs to be repaired. The rotation relations are stored at the moment of flipping an edge e using an array of rotations R[] of size m (number of triangles). The triangle that rotated with t_a and t_b is $t_{ra} = $ R$[t_{a_1}/3]$ and $t_{rb} = $ R$[t_{b_1}/3]$, respectively. Note that the indices stored in t_a and t_b point to the *Triangles* array and each triangle is defined by three consecutive vertex indices.

4.3   Handling Problematic and Worst Cases

During the first phase, there are two scenarios that require a more detailed explanation: **case (1)**; the existence of co-circular configurations and **case (2)**; the possible existence of dead-locks.

Case (1): if there are co-circular or almost co-circular configurations, our algorithm could fall into an infinite loop of edge-flips due to floating point errors. We solve this issue by using a small tolerance value in the evaluation of condition (1):

$$\lambda + \gamma \leq \pi + \epsilon \qquad (5)$$

This leads to ignoring some flips that in theory, should have been performed. That is why the generated triangulations may be quasi-Delaunay triangulations and not fully Delaunay triangulations. The ϵ value was experimentally estimated.

Case (2): a dead-lock could occur if there exists a circular chain of triangles, where all edges must be flipped and each thread can flag only one of its triangles. This kind of chain can not exist because it must have at least one edge that fulfills the Delaunay condition: the smallest edge of the chain. Note that the triangles that share the smallest edge are free to be flagged by a neighbor thread. Then, in chains like these there will always be at least one edge that can be flipped, therefore a dead-lock will never occur.

The known worst case configuration for Lawson's sequential algorithm is the one shown in Fig. 5 [5]. This worst-case triangulation has eight vertices, thirteen edges and six triangles. The algorithm executed five iterations and the number of

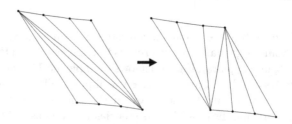

Fig. 5. A worst case for any edge-flip based method.

flips per iteration was $\{1, 2, 3, 2, 1\}$. As this triangulation gets larger, the number of triangles increases and the number of iterations also grows. However, the performance of the algorithm is better than the sequential algorithm, because under the PRAM model the cost per iteration is $\Theta(1)$ as the algorithm can do several edge flips in parallel. Experimentally, we observed that for these configurations the number of required iterations is $m - 1$, with m the number of triangles. The amount of edge-flips per iteration increases by one until the $m/2$-th iteration. Then, the number of parallel flips decreases by one until the last iteration is reached. The computational complexity is $O(n)$ (note that $m = O(n)$). This is an improvement over the sequential method, which in this case is $O(n^2)$.

5 Implementation Details

Nvidia's CUDA architecture and API were chosen to implement the kernels, while OpenGL was chosen to render the triangulations. Using C type data structures for the mesh model, it is possible to represent vertex and triangle data via the OpenGL buffer objects: the VBO (Vertex Buffer Object) and EBO (Element array Buffer Object). In addition, CUDA supports OpenGL interoperability, meaning that threads can read and write directly into the VBO and EBO arrays. As with the vertices, the edges are also sent to the GPU at mesh loading time, and they can optionally be sent back at the end if needed (for example, to save the mesh into a file). The exclusion step is handled with atomic operations available from the CUDA C API. The performance is increased by using loop unrolling, coalesced memory on per edge data, minimal branching, constant types and shared memory to reduce registry usage. The implementation is available as a functionality of *cleap*, an open source C/C++ library (http://sourceforge.net/projects/cleap/).

6 Experimental Results

In the following sections, we will refer to our implementation as MDT (Massive Delaunay Transformer). In order to analyze its performance and its behavior, we will evaluate the following aspects of the algorithm:

- Quality of the generated triangulations: how close they are to being Delaunay triangulations.
- Computational time against (a) the Triangle software and (b) the CGAL library and (c) our own implementation of Lawson's algorithm.
- Number of edges that can be flipped, number of edges that were flipped and number of edges that could not be flipped at each iteration.
- Influence of the mesh size in the number of iterations.

Table 1 shows the hardware used for the evaluation. The GPU used is the Nvidia GTX 580, it implements the *Fermi* architecture. This architecture can handle a maximum of 512 simultaneous threads and a maximum of 24,576 concurrent threads. In practice, performance is better when working concurrently

Table 1. Hardware used for testing.

Hardware	Detail
CPU	AMD Phenom I X4 9850 2.5 Ghz
GPU	Nvidia Geforce GTX 580
Mem	4 GB RAM DDR2 800 Mhz

with more than 512 threads. The reason is because the thread scheduler inside the GPU can fill up the empty pipeline of memory access and arithmetic latencies by swapping *waiting* threads with a group of *ready-to-work* threads.

For CPU based Delaunay triangulators, we have selected the algorithms available in *Triangle* and the one available in the CGAL library because they are known to generate full Delaunay meshes and cost $O(nlog\ n)$. Note that these algorithms start from a PSLG geometry and not from a given triangulation. Additionally, we have also included the Lawson algorithm based on sequential edge-flips.

6.1   Full Random 2D Triangulations

This set of tests consists of fully random bad-quality triangulations in the sense that they need a high number of edge flips to be transformed into Delaunay triangulations. These inputs are generated by placing random points inside two adjacent triangles starting from a square domain. For each new inserted point, the triangle that includes the point is divided into three smaller triangles as shown in Fig. 6. The size of the test triangulations ranges from 100 thousand to 5 million points and the smallest angle of all the meshes is practically zero (less than 10^{-6} radians). In Fig. 7(a) we present the computational time for each mesh size. It can be observed that *MDT* is approximately three times faster in these bad quality triangulations than the algorithms inside the CGAL library and the Triangle software. There is also a speedup of 50× with respect to our sequential implementation of Lawson's original edge-flip method. In Fig. 7(b) we show the quality of the generated meshes in the sense of how close they are to being full Delaunay meshes. We took the meshes generated by the CGAL library as reference triangulations. Both MDT and Triangle generate different triangles with respect to the reference triangulations. However, the missed triangles, i.e., the triangles that are in the triangulations generated by MDT and Triangle, and are not in the reference triangulations, are less than 0.05 %. The error rate is computed as the number of missed triangles with respect to the total number of triangles of the reference triangulation. Note that the triangulations generated by CGAL and Triangle are different because Triangle modifies the vertex list if two points are too close to each other. Some important aspects of the behavior of the MDT are shown in Fig. 8. Figure 8(a) shows an approximated curve that represents the number of iterations versus the mesh size. Empirically, this curve shows a complexity of $O(log\ n)$. Figure 8(b) shows how the number of edge flips

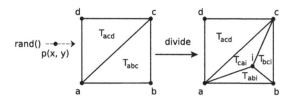

Fig. 6. Construction of a full random mesh.

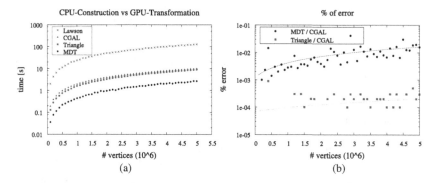

Fig. 7. (a) Computational time for all methods. (b) Differences of Triangle and MDT triangulations with respect to CGAL triangulation.

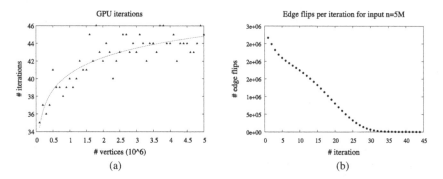

Fig. 8. (a) Number of iterations vs. problem size. (b) Number of edge-flips vs. iterations for the biggest input case (a mesh of 5 million points).

changes among the iterations while transforming the triangulation of 5 million vertices and approximately 15 million edges. We can observe that during the first half of the iterations, most of the edge-flips are done, while in the last iterations few edge flips are executed. For this input, both MDT and Lawson's edge-flip methods performed approximately 37 million edge-flips. It is worth mentioning that in all the tested triangulations, the percentage of edge flips done in parallel was more than 80 % (i.e., the excluded threads were less than 20 %).

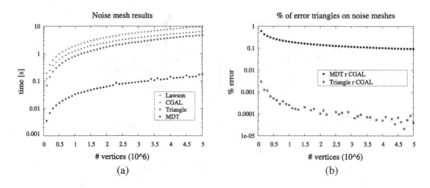

Fig. 9. (a) performance for all implementations, (b) error of MDT and Triangle with respect to CGAL.

6.2   Noise 2D Triangulations

This test consists of noise-based triangulations which are not as bad quality as the full random ones. The goal is to see how much the transformation based methods such as Lawson and MDT improve their performance in the presence of medium difficulty meshes. We define a noise triangulation as a perturbated regular square lattice with added diagonals on each square. For each vertex $v = (x, y)$ we apply the following noise function: $f(v) = (x + c_1, y + c_2)$ where $c_1 = k\ rand()r$ and $c_2 = k\ rand()sqrt(r^2 - c_1^2)$. The value r is half the distance between adjacent vertices and $rand()$ returns a random value in the range $[-1, 1]$. The noise is reduced by a constant factor $0 < k < 1$ in order to prevent duplicated vertices. In this particular case, we have used a value of $k = 0.95$. Using this rules, the noise remains inside the disk $0 \le sqrt(c_1^2 + c_2^2) < r$.

For this experiment, each test consists of measuring the time needed to transform a given noise-based triangulation G into its Delaunay form $T(G)$. For each different size the test is repeated four times, and the average value is kept. The standard error of the average measures is below 5 %. The cost of loading/saving and any initial memory movement are ignored for both CPU and GPU methods. Figure 9 presents the results for the noise based meshes.

The MDT implementation achieves a speedup of 55× with respect to Lawson's method, 36× with respect to CGAL and a up to 27× when compared to *Triangle*. The speedup values obtained over CGAL and *Triangle* are much higher than in the full random cases. As expected, both transformation methods (Lawson and MDT) are sensitive with respect to the quality of the input triangles while CGAL and *Triangle* are not, thus these last two cannot take advantage when meshes are close to their Delaunay version. Meshes similar to the noise based ones can occur in practice, even in realtime applications where meshes suffer small deformations at each time step. For all noise based tests, the amount of iterations of MDT was below 10.

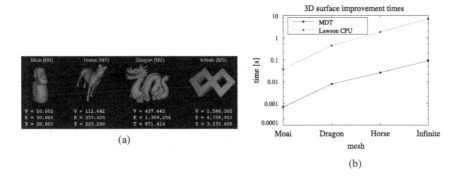

(a)

(b)

Fig. 10. (a) 3D surface test-case meshes. (b) Performance results on 3D meshes.

Table 2. Detail of effective edge-flips and parallelism ratio at each iteration for the 3d examples.

#iteration	Moai flipped	Moai excluded	Horse flipped	Horse excluded	Dragon flipped	Dragon excluded	Infinite flipped	Infinite excluded
1	1,786	3.88 %	31,453	0.08 %	106,101	6.63 %	508,502	8.62 %
2	215	1.83 %	4,376	0.21 %	22,608	4.08 %	237,340	8.48 %
3	41	4.66 %	598	1.65 %	4,455	5.86 %	95,975	3.81 %
4	3	0 %	131	4.38 %	995	1.49 %	29,568	5.95 %
5	1	0 %	33	8.34 %	207	1.43 %	7,882	4.52 %
6			10	0 %	34	0 %	2,844	1.6 %
7			4	0 %	1	0 %	762	5.81 %
8			1	0 %			195	6.25 %
9							40	0 %
10							11	0 %
Total flips	2,046		36,596		134,401		883,119	

6.3   3D Surface Triangulations

MDT was originally intended for improving the minimum angle of smooth 3D surface triangulations for the modeling of tree stem deformations. An edge e is considered for flipping only if the normal vectors of the two neighbor triangles that share e are almost parallel according to some threshold value. Figure 10 (left) shows the different test inputs with their corresponding number of vertices, edges and triangles. The dragon was taken from the Stanford Computer Graphics Laboratory, the horse from Cyberware Inc, the Moai from the GeomView examples and the Infinite was built with our custom tools. Figure 10 (right) shows the performance of the MDT and our implementation of the Lawson sequential algorithm. (The traced lines were added to connect the measurements using the same implementation.) As expected, the MDT method achieves a speedup of 80×. Table 2 shows the number of flipped-edges and the percentage of excluded threads for each iteration in the four input meshes. As in the 2D tests, the first iterations do most of the required edge-flips. The number of iterations is lower than in the 2D tests because these surface triangulations have an overall better quality.

7 Discussion and Conclusions

We have presented a GPU-based implementation for computing quasi-Delaunay triangulations. The solution is compatible with OpenGL, handles special cases such as co-circular point configurations and is free of dead-locks. The behavior of the MDT shows several interesting aspects. The amount of edge-flips per iteration quickly decreases, making the first half of the iterations much more important than the rest. We report an exclusion rate of threads under 20 % serving as a guarantee that parallelism can indeed be useful. For full random meshes, the number of iterations as a function of the mesh size grows asymptotically as $O(log\ n)$. This is a good behavior since GPU methods are aimed at addressing large problems and a small growth rate of the iterations means more parallelism. The worst behavior of the algorithm is when edge-flips can not be done in parallel. In this case the computational complexity for the sequential and parallel algorithms is the same.

We analyzed the performance of MDT under different inputs; bad-quality random 2D triangulations, noise based 2D triangulations and popular 3D surface meshes. Our experimental evaluation shows that the percentage of missed triangles of the triangulations generated by MDT with respect to the triangulations generated by CGAL was less than 0.1 % in for both random and noise based meshes. On the bad quality random meshes, MDT obtains a speedup of up to $50\times$ with respect to Lawson's $O(n^2)$ edge-flip method on CPU and a speedup of $3\times$ with respect to the 2D $O(nlog\ n)$ algorithms available inside CGAL and *Triangle*. This speedup seems to be not so impressive as we are comparing GPU with CPU implementations and quasi-Delaunay triangulations with exact ones. However, it is important to mention that the MDT implementation is sensitive to the topology of the input triangulation and the CGAL and Triangle implementations are not because they are constructive methods. Our noise based tests served as an empirical proof of such claim; MDT achieved up to $36\times$ and $27\times$ of speedup over CGAL and *Triangle*, respectively, and $55\times$ of speedup with respect to Lawson's method). In other words, if the input mesh needs little work to become Delaunay, the speedup of MDT with respect to CGAL and Triangle increases while the speedup over Lawson's method is approximately the same.

Our proposed implementation is useful for applications that need to quickly improve the minimum angle of triangulations and visualize a mesh at the same time; dynamic terrain manipulation and tree stem deformations to name some examples. The algorithm can also be implemented in parallel for multicore CPUs. In such case, the speedup S_p (with p the number of processors or cores) will be upper bounded by the number of cores, typically $S_p \leq 8$. In the near future, we will compare the in-circle test with the opposite angle test used in this implementation. We also want to test the algorithm with bad quality 3D surface meshes as well. Unfortunately, we could not compare our implementation with the parallel edge-flip methods described on the related work because different hardware was used in their results and the authors only compare their edge-flip routine against prior work of themselves.

Acknowledgements. The authors would like to thank CONICYT for supporting the PhD program of Cristóbal A. Navarro. This work was also partially supported by Fondecyt Project N° 1120495.

References

1. Antonopoulos, C.D., Ding, X., Chernikov, A., Blagojevic, F., Nikolopoulos, D.S., Chrisochoides, N.: Multigrain parallel Delaunay mesh generation: challenges and opportunities for multithreaded architectures. In: Proceedings of the 19th Annual International Conference on Supercomputing, ICS '05, pp. 367–376. ACM, New York (2005)
2. Cao, T.T.: Computing 2d Delaunay triangulation using GPU. Manuscript in preparation (2010)
3. Cervenanský, M., Tóth, Z., Starinský, J., Ferko, A., Srámek, M.: Parallel GPU-based data-dependent triangulations. Comput. Graph. **34**(2), 125–135 (2010)
4. De Berg, M.: Computational Geometry: Algorithms and Applications. Springer-Verlag TELOS, Santa Clara (2000)
5. Edelsbrunner, H.: Geometry and topology for mesh generation (Cambridge monographs on applied and computational mathematics) (2001)
6. Fortune, S.: A note on Delaunay diagonal flips. Pattern Recogn. Lett. **14**(9), 723–726 (1993)
7. Harada, T.: A parallel constraint solver for a rigid body simulation. In: SIGGRAPH Asia: Sketches, SA '11, pp. 22:1–22:2. ACM, New York (2011)
8. Healey, R.G., Minetar, M.J., Dowers, S. (eds.): Parallel Processing Algorithms for GIS. Taylor & Francis Inc., Bristol (1997)
9. Kohout, J., Kolingerová, I., Zára, J.: Parallel delaunay triangulation in e² and e³ for computers with shared memory. Parallel Comput. **31**(5), 491–522 (2005)
10. Lawson, C.L.: Transforming triangulations. Discrete Math. **3**(4), 365–372 (1972)
11. Navarro, C., Hitschfeld-Kahler, N., Scheihing, E.: A parallel GPU-based algorithm for Delaunay edge-flips. Abstracts from 27th European Workshop on Computational Geometry (EUROCG2011), Morschach, Switzerland, pp. 75–78 (2011)
12. Nvidia: NVIDIA CUDA Compute Unified Device Architecture - Programming Guide (2011)
13. Rong, G., Tan, T.-S., Cao, T.-T., Stephanus: Computing two-dimensional Delaunay triangulation using graphics hardware. In: I3D '08: Proceedings of the 2008 Symposium on Interactive 3D Graphics and Games, pp. 89–97. ACM, New York (2008)
14. Shewchuk, J.R.: Triangle: engineering a 2d quality mesh generator and Delaunay triangulator. In: ACM (ed.) First Workshop on Applied Computational Geometry, Philadelphia, Pennsylvania, pp. 124–133 (1996)
15. CGAL: CGAL, Computational Geometry Algorithms Library (2012). http://www.cgal.org
16. Tobler, R.F., Maierhofer, S.: A mesh data structure for rendering and subdivision. In: WSCG '2006: Proceedings of WSCG (International Conference in Central Europe on Computer Graphics, Visualization and Computer Vision), pp. 157–162 (2006)

Data-Aware Picking for Medical Models

Eva Monclús[⊠], Pere-Pau Vázquez, and Isabel Navazo

ViRVIG-LSI, Universitat Politècnica de Catalunya, C. Jordi Girona 1-3,
Edif. Omega, 08034 Barcelona, Spain
{emonclus,ppau,isabel}@lsi.upc.edu

Abstract. Medical doctors are often faced with the problem of selecting anchoring points in 3D space. These points are commonly used for
measurement tasks, such as lengths of bones, or dimensions of pathological structures (e.g. tumours). Since previous research indicates that
measurement tasks can be usually carried out more efficiently in VR
environments than in desktop-based systems, we have concentrated on
the development of selection tools for medical models. These models have
a set of particularities such as the presence of semi-transparencies, and
there is a lack of tools for measurement support for such models in VR
environments. Our VR-based interaction technique uses the data to automatically generate candidate anchor points, and it is specially focused
on the efficient selection of 3D points in datasets rendered using methods
with semi-transparency such as Direct Volume Rendering. We will show
that our method is effective, precise, and reduces the time and amount
of movements required to set the anchor points as compared with other
classical techniques based on clipping planes. We also provide a couple of
improvements tailored to reduce the inherent imprecision of 3D devices
due to hand vibration, and the flexibility in transfer function selection
for anchor point definition.

Keywords: 3D interaction · 3D selection · Medical visualization · Virtual reality

1 Introduction

In medical applications, the quantitative analysis of spatial relations between
structures is crucial for many tasks such as diagnosis, treatment and surgical
planning, and documentation. These measurements include, among others, the
extension of pathological structures or the distance between pathological structures and structures at risk (blood vessels). In the field of Neurosurgery, for
instance, distance between the brain surface and the ventricles is an important
parameter that may determine the surgical trajectory. However, the use of these
2D images does not facilitate the perception of the relative position of the structures, and as a consequence, it is often rough for accurately locating anchor
points and thus obtaining precise 3D magnitudes.

© Springer-Verlag Berlin Heidelberg 2014
S. Battiato et al. (Eds.): VISIGRAPP 2013, CCIS 458, pp. 50–65, 2014.
DOI: 10.1007/978-3-662-44911-0_4

Advances in volume visualization allow for the 3D reconstruction and analysis of anatomical structures from a stack of intensity-based images acquired from, usually, CT or MRI modalities. Initial algorithms identified and extracted the isosurfaces of the anatomical structures as triangle meshes. This process is time-consuming and loses contextual information. Later methods directly render the volume (Direct Volume Rendering, or DVR) by assigning color and opacity to the samples as a function of its density by using pre-defined transfer functions. Semi-transparencies provide a means to increase the amount of information visible to the users, and facilitate establishing spatial relationships between elements such as the skin and the bones. This led the development of new techniques for anchor point definition in desktop-based applications. However, occlusions still remain as a problem for the selection. This is often addressed with the introduction of clipping planes showing the volume cut mapped on them.

Reitinger *et al.* [1] found that measurement tasks can be carried out more efficiently in a Virtual Reality environment than in a desktop setup. The cost reduction of VR systems and GPUs is helping the introduction of such systems in surgical planning and diagnose. Stereo vision facilitates the perception of the relative position of anatomical structures, although occlusion remains as a research problem. It is important to note that we are not interested in selecting a concrete structure, but a point on it, without any previous surface extraction nor segmentation process. Additionally, the occlusion problem remains, as well as the fact that a VR selection environment is not familiar to medical experts.

The purpose of this paper is to provide an easy-to-use tool for the fast and accurate selection of 3D points on the implicitly defined surfaces of anatomical structures present in a volume dataset in a virtual environment. This is an extension of our previous contribution [2]. Here we include two techniques to reduce the effects of trembling hands, we include the use of the Virtual Magic Lantern [3] metaphor to increase the flexibility in transfer function usage for point selection, and we provide a broader user study on the benefits of our technique. The contributions of our paper are:

- We review DAAPMed, an anchor point selection tool suitable for medical models in VR environments. The system assists the user by automatically computing data-aware candidate anchor points (see Fig. 1).
- A series of visual cues that provide feedback on the ray position through the use of mirror views and supporting planes.
- The reduction of effects of trembling hands in picking.
- A user study analysing the accuracy and performance of the picking method.

The implementation of all these components (both GPU and CPU) guarantees real-time feedback and interaction. This is an important issue in VR environments which require rendering the model twice. We will show that the technique is effective and accurate, and reduces the amount of displacements and time required for the selection as compared with a classical clipping plane technique in a VR environment. We also introduce the use of the Virtual Magic Lantern [3] to modify the transfer function that determines the candidate points.

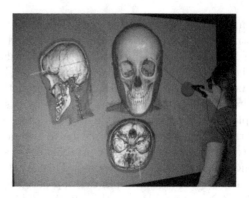

Fig. 1. User interacting with a model using the DAAPMed metaphor.

2 Related Work

In a pioneer work, Hinckley *et al.* [4] proposed a 3D user interface for pre-operative neurosurgical planning based on the physical manipulation of familiar real-world objects (head, cutting-plane and stylus-shaped props) in free space to access and manipulate a virtual model. This approach offers the possibility of selecting anchor points in a brain model. They use a clipping plane to access occluded or interior points in the brain and then select anchor points on it as the intersection of the linear trajectory defined by the stylus and the cutting-plane.

Preim *et al.* [5] introduced a set of applicable tools for the computation of distances, angles, and volumes in 3D visualizations. The tools are 3D virtual objects such as a distance line, a ruler and angular measurements that are manipulated using the mouse in a desktop-platform. They allow to determine anchor points on the surface of the pre-segmented anatomical structures. Rossling *et al.* [6] proposed a method for the automatic determination of different distance−based measures (shortest distance, diameters and wall thickness) also on segmented anatomic structures. The necessity of this kind of tool is justified by the fact that manual distance calculation is tedious and imprecise in single 2D slices, and although it is possible to achieve an accurate result in 3D, it would also be tiresome. However, completely automatic measurements are difficult to generalize due to the great variety of problems and anatomical structures. Notice that both previous approaches [5,6] work on triangle mesh representations, so a surface extraction process is needed previously to use them. Moreover, they always select the nearest visible point and they do not deal with semi-transparent models. Reitinger *et al.* [1] presented a 3D measurement toolkit developed for liver surgery especially tailored for a VR platform. Their measurements include distance, volume, and angles. Their evaluation indicated that VR-based measurement tools have a sufficient benefit compared to 2D desktop-based systems in terms of task completion time. In terms of accuracy, slightly better results in most of the tasks were achieved. The anatomical structures models (liver, vessels,...) are computed through segmentation from CT scans and they are represented by opaque triangle meshes where the user may select points by using a virtual pencil. Hagerdorn *et al.* [7] proposed a set of tools for performing measurements in a virtual reality visualization environment. A 3D Rubberbanding line for selecting *free* points in the scene is proposed. They use clipping planes for accessing interior parts of the volume dataset. Their scene is also composed by triangle meshes.

Segmentation and surface extraction are time consuming operations. To overcome this problem, Hastreiter *et al.* [8] suggest direct volume rendering of the entire data volume, giving insights to interior and superimposed information. In order to inspect interior structures, independent clipping planes provide an intuitive way to virtually cut off parts of the volume data set. Then, anchor points can be interactively placed on the clipping planes. Gallo *et al.* [9] present a VR system for the exploration of volume datasets using a Wiimote. Apart from the basic interaction techniques for navigating they propose a mechanism of selection of points based on the classical ray-casting technique adding the mechanism of *fishing reel* in which the users can move the cursor closer or farther away by using two buttons in order to accurately locate a mark. Unfortunately, points' positions are not aware of the isosurfaces and no visual cue is used to reveal the cursor when it is moved into an occluded region.

Many researchers have investigated 3D object selection techniques for general -non medical- VR applications [10]. In this area, *ray-based* techniques have shown a better performance than *point-based* techniques. These former approaches are usually based on a cone or a ray. Since our interest is on accurate anchor point selection, we only consider ray-based tools. In order to solve the inherent problem of multiple intersection candidates, several disambiguation techniques have been proposed. It is important to note that most of these VR selection metaphors are focused on selection and manipulation of objects (not points) in populated scenarios, and thus they were not specially concerned about accuracy in point selection. Grossman *et al.* [11] explored 3D selection techniques for volumetric displays and proposed new ray cursor techniques which provide disambiguation mechanisms for multiple intersected targets. The *Lock Ray* tool augments the ray cursor with a depth marker and performs the selection and disambiguation phases in a two-step process. First the user selects the ray. Once it is locked, the depth marker appears. Then, forward and backward hand movements fix the depth marker and the intersected target closest to it is highlighted in red indicating that it can be selected by releasing the button. Our approach also decouples the selection and disambiguation phases in two sequential steps, though using a cycling method for candidate selection [12]. In contrast to these previous works, we work directly with the captured volume dataset (using DVR) without any kind of costly preprocess to extract the isosurfaces.

3   DAAPMed Metaphor

Our objective is a user-friendly, efficient, accurate anchor point selection technique that facilitates getting measurements in VR environments with medical

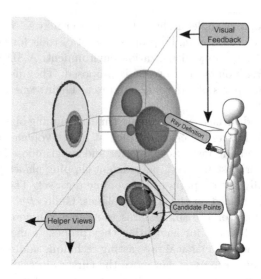

Fig. 2. DAAPMed metaphor: A ray is used for selection, and a couple of supporting planes help the user to locate it in relation to the 3D structures. Potential anchor points, represented by colored small spheres, are computed as the intersections of the ray with the isosurfaces. Finally, Helper Views provide a better perception of the ray position as well as aids disoccluding interior candidate points. Notice that Helper Views show that the large orange sphere is hollow.

models. We also require ease of use and limiting the amount of effort the user has to perform. In contrast to normal desktop environment, where working with a mouse allows users to rest the arm, in 3D environments users usually do ample arm movements and have no surface to rest. With the objective of facilitating the integration with the specialists' clinical work, we directly use the captured volume dataset rendered using DVR with a transfer function that shows semi-transparent and opaque structures (see Figs. 1 and 2).

As a first approach, we extended and adapted to 3D the classical desktop point selection using a clipping plane (see Fig. 3). However, as shown in our user study, this metaphor requires quite a long time and large movements from the user, because the correct definition of a clipping plane suitable for posterior point selection is difficult. In order to overcome these limitations we have developed a ray-based approach that uses the data information to facilitate the ray setting and point selection, reducing time and displacements.

3.1   Data Aware 3D Selection Metaphor

Studies have shown that ray-based selection techniques often result in faster selection times than hand extension techniques in VR environments [13]. Unfortunately, as commented previously, ray cursor techniques have an inherent problem: the ray may intersect multiple objects. A naïve approach simply selects the

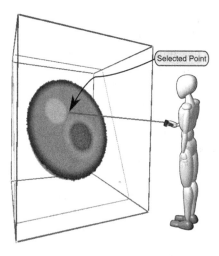

Fig. 3. Adaptation to VR of the clipping plane technique for selecting points located on it.

first target which is intersected; however, it becomes very difficult or even impossible to select occluded points. Thus a more sophisticated method is required. The DAAPMed metaphor has three main components (see Fig. 2):

- Ray cursor tool: It casts a pointing ray through the volume. The ray path visualization is enriched with the candidate selection points and its supporting planes, which provide a better insight of its position and orientation.
- Helper Views: We provide two views that help to understand the position of the ray inside the volume. This extra-visualization is inspired by the Magic Mirrors View [14], but, instead of showing the whole model, our view shows the model clipped by a plane that enables the possibility of showing the ray trajectory without any occlusion.
- Disambiguation mechanism: Once the ray is locked, we may select among the different intersections of the ray with the isosurfaces in the model. We adopt the same solution as Hinckley [12] cycling from one target to the next.

The key difference with previous selection methods is the ability to work with volumetric models by automatically generating candidate points through a rapid isosurface detection. Moreover, we also add visual cues that facilitate the understanding of the ray position and orientation, and disocclude inner intersection points.

Figure 2 shows all the components involved in the metaphor. In this example, the dataset consists of four spheres of different materials. The metaphor works as follows: when the user presses the back button of the input device, the *selection task* starts and the ray is painted with a gradient color from red to yellow (in this way we provide users with a visual cue of the depth of the ray). Throughout this process, the system continuously computes the proper set of candidate points. This set is composed by all the intersections of the ray with the implicitly defined isosurfaces. Upon button release, the last ray shown is locked, meaning that the selection phase has finished and the disambiguation task begins. The nearest candidate point is marked in orange (default selection) and the rest of the points are in white. The joystick provided by the input device allows the user to cycle between all the candidate points. This is convenient because it reduces movements. Since candidate points may have a random distribution, tracking the user's movement to reach all the candidate points without a large arm movement (as proposed in [11]) would be difficult and might result in large varying patterns for different rays of the same volume.

As the 3D ray is painted over the volume, it is sometimes difficult to interpret how the volume is traversed. In order to give the user a second cue on the intersection of the ray with the volume, we provide the Helper Views. These showed to be of great utility, since some candidate points are usually occluded by other parts of the volume (Fig. 1 shows a snapshot of our technique). We augment the visualization of the volume model with a wireframe representation of the cutting planes used in the Helper Views in order to provide the users with a visual feedback of the placement of such planes.

3.2   Implementation Details

In this section we give some details on how the isosurfaces are detected in real time as well as on how the Helper Views are created. One key difference with other anchor point selection methods is the automatic detection of isosurfaces on-the-fly along the pointing ray. Since we have a non-segmented model, this isosurfaces must be determined in real-time, as they depend on the transfer function. Throughout all the process we use a DVR method using a GPU-based ray casting.

Ray - Isosurface Intersection Detection. Volumetric models can be seen as a 3D scalar function $f : V \subseteq \Re^3 \rightarrow \Re$ (e.g. density value of a material). Let $TF : \Re \rightarrow \Re^4$ be the transfer function used in the volume rendering algorithm, that assigns color and opacity to a scalar property. First of all, we have to define the conditions that a point p of the volume dataset V must fulfill to be considered a boundary-surface candidate point. These are:

1. p must belong to a visible material. This condition can be expressed formally as $opacity(TF(f(p))) > 0.0$
2. p must belong to the boundary of a well-defined isosurface. This condition is satisfied if:
   (a) The gradient at point p, $\nabla f(p)$, has to be well defined. This means that $\|\nabla f(p)\|$ is larger than a certain threshold. This threshold is automatically set by a previous analysis of the range of the magnitudes of the gradient.
   (b) There exists a change in the sign of the direction of the gradient at p at the neighborhood of p. This property expresses the fact that the boundary passes through p.

Since the detection of the boundary condition (2.b) may not be real-time in a VR environment, the information necessary to test this condition is precomputed. This is carried out by applying a 3D edge detection process [15] to the volume V and storing the result in a 3D texture which consists of a value per voxel that indicates if the voxel is being crossed by the boundary of a surface. Our system guarantees testing at least a point for each voxel intersected by the ray, thus the accuracy of our approach is related to voxel's size. As shown in Sect. 4, we obtain an accuracy comparable to the clipping plane selection approach. We also compared the accuracy with a desktop-based approach (using the raycasting paradigm for the nearest point selection) which works with a triangle mesh obtained using the Marching Cubes algorithm from the same volume dataset than in our VR-based metaphor. We obtained errors that did not differ significantly, which demonstrates that we may achieve comparable results in a VR environment. In both cases, the error performed was below the voxel size.

Helper Views. The goal of Helper Views is to provide additional information on the exact position of the ray inside the volume. These views are drawn on two fixed planes, located to the left (YZ) and bottom (XZ) of the volume dataset (see Fig. 2). Images displayed on these views are generated with the same algorithm used for rendering the volume dataset but clipping it by the plane that contains the ray and is the most parallel to each of the image planes YZ and XZ, respectively. This has a main advantage: it shows the candidate points that lie inside the volume, therefore facilitating ray selection without previous manipulation of the volume (i.e. clipping). The visualization of the cut volume dataset is enhanced with an illustrative motif: view-dependent contours computed by using a Sobel kernel, highlighting the silhouette of the clipped region.

4   Evaluation and Results

We have conducted a formal user study to evaluate the accuracy, efficiency and ease of use of our approach. We take as a reference an implementation of the Clipping Plane (CP) selection method, since it is a technique that has been widely used in medical applications. We have found that the users required far less movement with our system than with CP, moreover DAAPMed technique was more accurate than the CP technique. We performed the user study in an immersive virtual reality setup composed of a 2.7×2 m passive stereo Power-Wall. Users were tracked using an Intersense IS-900 Motion Tracking System device consisting on a Head Tracker and a MiniTrax Wanda with a joystick and five programmable buttons.

4.1   Design Details of the Clipping Plane Technique in Virtual Reality

In order to compare our selection technique with the classical approach for anchor point selection using clipping planes (CP), we ported this metaphor the following way. Two buttons of the input device allows the user to set the action to be performed: rotate or translate the clipping plane. While the user is pressing the selected button, the clipping plane is rotated or translated accordingly to the user's hand movement. Once the plane is fixed, the user can select a point on it using the ray-cursor paradigm. By pressing another button, the user indicates the desired point, so every point inside the volume, belonging to the plane, could be a candidate point to be selected. However, due to changes in the holding forces done by users when pressing or releasing a button, called Heisenberg effect [16], the accuracy of the selection may be affected. In order to solve this problem, we enhanced the visualization of the ray with a freezing timer.

4.2   Test Design

Medical doctors often address two different point selection problems: selection of well-established anatomical points and distance measurement.

As a consequence, we decided to test two different tasks: the selection of individual points (T_1), and the measurement of distances (T_2). In order to get more information on the performance of our method, we added an extra experiment tailored to determine the accuracy of point selection (T_3). The processes of each task were defined as:

- In T_1 task, users had to introduce two anchor points $(P_1$ and $P_2)$ at positions which were marked in the model with the use of a cone representation.
- To solve T_2, it was required to take a measure (calculated as a distance between two anchor points).
- T_3 consisted of locating, as accurately as possible, a set of points with the helping of a image shown in the bottom left corner of the screen.

We performed two sessions: one consisted of T_1 and T_2 (we called this session as $Test_1$) and the other called $Test_2$ conformed by task T_3.

Data Preparation. Regarding $Test_1$ we prepared two different datasets. The first one was used for training, while the other was used for the test. The training model consisted of a set of four spheres of different materials (Fig. 4-left). The second model consisted of a typical CT dataset in volume visualization, a tooth, using a transfer function which shows the outside and inner shape of it (Fig. 4-middle). The anchor points used in task T_1 were chosen between external and internal characteristics of the model (see Fig. 4).

The model used in $Test_2$, was taken from a medical dataset. Figure 4-right shows the helping image presented to users in task T_3.

We recorded the following indicators for each task:

- Task completion time (TCT): We measured the amount of time devoted to complete each task.
- Input Device Footprint (IDF): We measured the length of the total path followed by the device to complete each task.

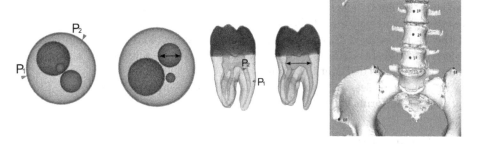

Fig. 4. The datasets involved in the user study. The left images show the training dataset used in $Test_1$. The testing dataset in $Test_1$ is shown in the center block images. Each figures block show the description of the tasks T_1 and T_2. The right image shows the model used in T_3 task and the set of points users have to select as accurately as possible.

– User footprint (UF): It measures the user displacement inside the VR environment done while carrying out the task.
– Accuracy (Ac): This value measures the error in the selection with respect to the reference points, taking into account the dimension of the voxel dataset as a metric of the error made. The model used in T_1 and T_2 task has a resolution of $256 \times 256 \times 256$ and a voxel dimension of $1.0 \times 1.0 \times 1.0\,\mathrm{mm}$. The model used in T_3 task has a resolution of $512 \times 512 \times 369$ and a voxel dimension of $2.042 \times 2.042 \times 3.56\,\mathrm{mm}$.

Subjects and Procedure. 17 subjects participated in the evaluation; 13 male and 4 female, ranging between 23 and 63 years old. Subjects were asked to classify (as Low, Medium or High) their experience in a VR setup, experience with input devices and expertise in 3D application. All of the participants were people from our department: computer scientists at different levels of studies (master and PhD students) and faculty staff.

All the subjects participated in $Test_1$. In $Test_2$, only a subset of it participated (13 subjects: 10 male and 3 female, ranging between 23 and 40 years old). Every user performed each test once.

Before the first test started, a complete training (using the spheres dataset) was performed for the users to get familiar with the two interaction techniques to evaluate. Each test was divided into two blocks, one for each technique. The order of the blocks was chosen randomly in order to avoid skewing one of the techniques with a learning effect.

As said before, $Test_1$ consisted of two kind of tasks: selecting two predefined points (T_1), and measuring a certain distance (T_2). For T_1, we asked the users to introduce two anchor points (P_1 and P_2) at positions that were marked in the model with the use of a cone representation (see Fig. 4). Once completed, we stopped tracking the movements of the user until he or she was ready for the next task. T_2 consisted of taking a measure (calculated as a distance between two anchor points). The specification of this task was accompanied with different descriptions and pictures of the goal (we used the ones shown in Fig. 4). None of the users involved in the experiment had any problem understanding the objective of the task. Users were allowed to repeat the selection of a point as many times as needed, until the point was validated.

In the $Test_2$ session, we proceed in the same way as the first one. Each participant performs the test once.

4.3 Statistical Results

A repeated measures within subjects design was used. The independent variable was the technique and the dependent variables were the set of tracked variables. A one-way analysis of variance (ANOVA) comparing both techniques was used.

Table 1 summarizes the statistical analysis of the relevant variables for test $Test_1$. For each variable the mean and the standard deviation are shown. Task T_1 is tagged as P_1 and P_2, corresponding to the two anchor points.

Regarding *Completion Time*, there is significant evidence in all the experiments that DAAPMed performed better than CP. For P_1 ($p = 0.028$, $F = 5.83$), for P_2 ($p = 0.008$, $F = 9.35$) and for T_2 ($p = 0.044$, $F = 4.79$). Figure 5-left shows the total time for each technique.

Regarding *Input Device Footprint*, we measured the length of the total path which the device took to complete the experiment. We have found a significant effect on the *Input Device Footprint* variable for P_1 ($p = 0.036$, $F = 5.24$) and for P_2 ($p = 0.004$, $F = 11.70$). Figure 5-right illustrates the effect of the reduction of the footprint for DAAPMed technique. The reduction of footprint is especially important since a handheld 6-DOF device is being used, which can lead to fatigue with extended use [17].

We also measured the movement carried out by the user. In all cases, our system requires a lower amount of movement by the user. The analysis shows that the movement done in DAPPMed is significantly less than CP for P_2 ($p = 0.009$, $F = 8.72$) and for T_2 ($p = 0.03$, $F = 5.62$).

Table 1. The overall statistical results of the evaluation shown as means and standard deviations of the variables measured for test $Test_1$. Regarding the mean and the standard deviation, DAAPMed is superior to CP. The one-way ANOVA analysis will show which differences were statistically significative.

	CP			DAAPMed		
	P_1	P_2	T_2	P_1	P_2	T_2
Ac	0.76 ± 0.23	0.93 ± 1.37	1.15 ± 0.81	0.56 ± 0.23	1.37 ± 3.13	1.08 ± 0.79
TCT	62.42 ± 34.08	73.8 ± 47.1	119.8 ± 65.5	43.07 ± 36.5	41.1 ± 25.7	84.1 ± 43.4
IDF	3.711 ± 2.75	4.86 ± 4.8	7.92 ± 5.57	2.33 ± 3.26	1.88 ± 1.46	5.42 ± 3.31
UF	1.94 ± 1.53	2.41 ± 2.33	4.281 ± 3.23	1.33 ± 1.87	1.26 ± 1.04	2.83 ± 1.79

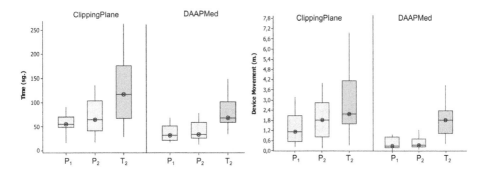

Fig. 5. Results of the completion task timings (left) and the Input Device footprint (right) for test $Test_1$. The boxes show the interquartile range with the median as the horizontal bar. The whiskers extend to the minimum and maximum of the data. CP exhibits longer selection times. Regarding the Input device footprints, it is clear that DAAPMed method performed significantly better than CP.

Table 2. The overall statistical results of the evaluation for the test $Test_2$ shown as means and standard deviations of the tolerance error. We can clearly see how the DAPPMed metaphor provides better results for all the tasks than the CP method.

	P_1	P_2	P_3	P_4	P_5	P_6
CP	2.94 ± 1.30	3.02 ± 1.49	3.17 ± 1.73	2.34 ± 0.88	2.07 ± 1.09	2.07 ± 1.17
DAAPMed	1.29 ± 0.67	1.70 ± 0.70	1.60 ± 0.50	1.77 ± 0.57	1.79 ± 0.42	0.28 ± 0.08
p,F	$0.002 - 16.55$	$0.011 - 9.01$	$0.005 - 11.58$	$0.19 - 1.96$	$0.38 - 0.81$	$0.001 - 17.42$

Table 2 summarizes the statistical analysis of the relevant variables for test $Test_2$. The first and second rows show the mean and the standard deviation for both techniques. The third row shows the statistical significance information (p and F). For all the points introduced (except P_4 and P_5), the DAAPMed technique shows significant statistical difference with respect CP. Figure 6 shows a boxplot for all the performed tasks.

4.4   Post-questionnaire Results

To complete the information, we also asked the subjects to fill some questionnaires, to know the preferences of the users between the two techniques. All responses in the post-questionnaire were measured on a Likert scale of 1–5, where 1 meant the worst value and 5 was the best value. The results are shown in Fig. 7. The answers seem to indicate that DAAPMed metaphor is more suitable than the CP technique.

The users noted two major problems with respect to our technique. The first one is the inherent jittering of the tracker, that made selection affect user performance. Only two users agreed in that it seems to produce a more relevant effect to the ray-based selection than to the plane-based. Furthermore, in all the experiments, the ray-based approach showed a better behavior than the

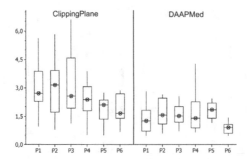

Fig. 6. Accuracy by technique. The boxes show the interquartile range with the median as the horizontal bar. The whiskers extend to the minimum and maximum of the data.

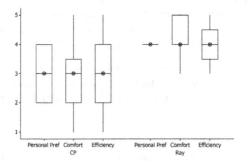

Fig. 7. Results obtained from a personal preference evaluation questionnaire. These results show that the users' perceptions are quite positive with our tool.

clipping-planes system. The second issue was the lack of ray refinement: most users suggested that a fine tuning of the ray, after its initial positioning would be welcome. We let this work for future improvements.

5   Picking Optimizations

Working with 3D input devices require a steady hand in order to obtain an accurate selection due to the inherent jittering of the tracker. However, due to changes in the holding forces done by users when pressing or releasing a button, called Heisenberg effect [16], the accuracy of the selection may be affected. In order to solve this problem, we enhanced the visualization of the ray with a freezing timer. Though providing better feedback to the user, there are still some users that shake their hands inadvertently and this often affects the selection accuracy.

5.1   Shake Filtering

In order to reduce the effect of quivery hands, we combine the use of the freezing time with an averaging of the captured position. Trembling hands affect the overall performance and produce a bad sensation of using this kind of input devices and on account of this a complete refusal of the use of virtual reality. Our algorithm filters the selection position by taking the average of the last 20 captured positions by the tracker. Moreover, we further check whether the final position falls within a maximum tolerance range from the position at which the selection button was initially pressed.

Although not a full user study has been performed, we took two of the users that showed a bad steady hand, and they experimented with the improved method. In one case, the results were similar (with a precision improvement of around the 10 %), but the second showed an increase in precision of around the 40 %. These results look promising, but further tests have to be carried out.

5.2   Extending the Selection Candidates Using VML

In Volume Rendering, it is difficult to simultaneously visualize interior and exterior structures because the structures are commonly quite complex and it is easy to lose the context. The *Virtual Magic Lantern* [3] (VML) is a specialized interaction tool tailored to facilitate the inspection of a volume dataset in VR environments. It addresses the occlusion management problem, facilitating the inspection of inner structures without the total elimination of the exterior structures, offering in this way, a context-based visualization of the overall structures. We have made more powerful the DAAPMed technique increasing its capabilities coupling it with the VML metaphor. In this sense, we build the VML through the use of the 3D pointer device that casts a cylinder onto the model. The axis of the cylinder is defined from the orientation of the 3D pointer device. The volume not intersected by the cylinder is rendered using the original transfer

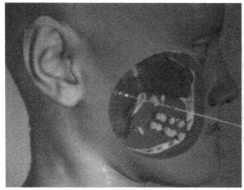 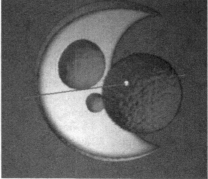

Fig. 8. These images illustrate the integration of both techniques. The left image shows a head where the outside of the VML consists of the skin, while its interior shows the air-cavities in the body. The right image shows one of the models from the user study. The most exterior sphere is visualized with a blue opaque material, while the transfer function inside the VML is the same transfer function that was used in the user study.

function while the volume intersected by it is rendered using the second transfer function (see Fig. 8). Regarding DAAPMed, the *Ray cursor tool* fit in the axis of the cylinder. The set of candidate selection points are calculated taking into account the transfer function used inside the cylinder. In this way, the user can pick points inside a volume dataset without losing the overall context provided by the other transfer function.

6   Conclusions

We have presented a new interaction technique for picking points in a volume dataset. This selection technique follows the *ray casting* paradigm, enhanced with an automatic calculation of the set of suitable points of interest by an on-the-fly determination of the isosurfaces along the ray path. The feedback with the interaction is enhanced with a meaningful visualization called *Helper Views* that provides context for the ray selection and shows occluded detected candidate points that would be otherwise invisible to the user without posterior and ad-hoc volume manipulation.

The user study showed that our technique is easy to learn and to use. Despite the limited precision of the 3D input devices, our technique achieves a precise 3D interaction thanks to the automatic anchor point calculation provided by the system. Users felt more comfortable and achieved better results with our system than with the clipping plane technique.

Acknowledgements. The authors want to thank all the participants involved in the user study. This work has been supported by the project TIN2010-20590-C01-01 of the Spanish Government.

References

1. Reitinger, B., Schmalstieg, D., Bornik, A., Beichel, R.: Spatial analysis tools for virtual reality-based surgical planning. In: 3D User. Interfaces, pp. 37–44 (2006)
2. Monclús, E., Vázquez, P.P., Navazo, I.: DAAPMed: a data-aware anchor point selection tool for medical models in VR environments. In: VISIGRAPP - International Joint Conference on Computer Vision, Imaging and Computer Graphics Theory and Applications, pp. 308–317 (2013)
3. Monclús, E., Díaz, J., Navazo, I., Vázquez, P.P.: The virtual magic lantern: an interaction metaphor for enhanced medical data inspection. In: VRST '09: Proceedings of the 16th ACM Symposium on Virtual Reality Software and Technology, pp. 119–122. ACM, New York (2009)
4. Hinckley, K., Pausch, R., Goble, J.: A three-dimensional user interface for neurosurgical visualization. In: The SPIE Conference on Medical Imaging, pp. 126–136. SPIE (1994)
5. Preim, B., Tietjen, C., Spindler, W., Peitgen, H.O.: Integration of measurement tools in medical 3D visualizations. In: Visualization '02, pp. 21–28. IEEE Computer Society (2002)

6. Rössling, I., Cyrus, C., Dornheim, L., Boehm, A., Preim, B.: Fast and flexible distance measures for treatment planning. Int. J. Comput. Assist. Radiol. Surg. **5**, 633–646 (2010)
7. Hagedorn, J., Joy, P., Dunkers, S., Peskin, A.: Measurement tools for the immersive visualization environment: steps toward the virtual laboratory. J. Res. Nat. Inst. Stan. Technol. **112**, 257–270 (2007)
8. Hastreiter, P., Rezk-Salama, C., Tomandl, B., Eberhardt, K.E.W., Ertl, T.: Fast analysis of intracranial aneurysms based on interactive direct volume rendering and CTA. In: Wells, W.M., Colchester, A.C.F., Delp, S.L. (eds.) MICCAI 1998. LNCS, vol. 1496, pp. 660–669. Springer, Heidelberg (1998)
9. Gallo, L., De Pietro, G., Marra, I.: 3D interaction with volumetric medical data: experiencing the wiimote. In: Proceedings of the 1st International Conference on Ambient Media and Systems, pp. 14:1–14:6 (2008)
10. Bowman, D., Kruijff, E., LaViola, J., Poupyrev, I.: 3D User Interfaces: Theory and Practice. Addison-Wesley, Pearson Education (2004)
11. Grossman, T., Balakrishnan, R.: The design and evaluation of selection techniques for 3D volumetric displays. In: Proceedings of the Symposium on User Interface Software and Technology, pp. 3–12. ACM (2006)
12. Hinckley, K., Pausch, R., Goble, J., Kassell, N.: A survey of design issues in spatial input. In: Proceedings of the Symposium on User Interface Software and Technology, pp. 213–222. ACM (1994)
13. Bowman, D.A., Johnson, D.B., Hodges, L.F.: Testbed evaluation of virtual environment interaction techniques. In: Proceedings of the ACM Symposium on Virtual Reality Software and Technology, pp. 26–33 (1999)
14. König, A.H., Doleisch, H., Gröller, E., Brain, T.H.: Multiple views and magic mirrors - fmri visualization of the human brain (1999)
15. Monga, O., Deriche, R., Malandain, G., Cocquerez, J.P.: Recursive filtering and edge closing: two primary tools for 3-d edge detection. In: Faugeras, O. (ed.) ECCV 1990. LNCS, vol. 427, pp. 56–65. Springer, Heidelberg (1990)
16. Bowman, D.A., Wingrave, C.A., Campbell, J.M., Ly, V.Q., Rhoton, C.J.: Novel uses of pinch gloves for virtual environment interaction techniques. Virtual Reality **6**, 122–129 (2002)
17. Ware, C., Slipp, L.: Using velocity control to navigate 3D graphical environments: a comparison of three interfaces. In: Human Factors and Ergonomic Studies (HFES) Meeting, pp. 25–32 (1991)

Information Visualization Theory
and Applications

An Interactive Visualization for Tabbed Browsing Behavior Analysis

Daniel Cernea[1,2]([⊠]), Igor Truderung[1], Andreas Kerren[2], and Achim Ebert[1]

[1] Computer Graphics and HCI Group, University of Kaiserslautern,
P.O. Box 3049, 67653 Kaiserslautern, Germany
{cernea,i_truder,ebert}@cs.uni-kl.de
[2] Computer Science Department, ISOVIS Group, Linnaeus University,
Vejdes Plats 7, 35195 Växjö, Sweden
andreas.kerren@lnu.se

Abstract. Web browsers are at the core of online user experience, enabling a wide range of Web applications, like communication, games, entertainment, development, etc. Additionally, given the variety and complexity of online-supported tasks, users have started parallelizing and organizing their online browser sessions by employing multiple browser windows and tabs. However, there are few solutions that support analysts and casual users in detecting and extracting patterns from these parallel browsing histories. In this paper we introduce *WebComets*, an interactive visualization for exploring multi-session multi-user parallel browsing logs. After highlighting visual and functional aspects of the system, we introduce a motif-based contextual search for enabling the filtering and comparison of user navigation patterns. We further highlight the functionality of WebComets with a use case. Our investigations suggest that parallel browser history visualization can offer better insight into user tabbed browsing behavior and support the recognition of online navigation patterns.

Keywords: Tabbed browsing behavior visualization · Parallel browsing history · Time series · Glyph-based techniques

1 Introduction

From the beginnings of the Internet, the most important client-side software that users employed to navigate online was the Web browser. However, in the last decades the tasks that users could execute on the Web have greatly increased in complexity, thus influencing the range of features that today's Web browsers incorporate. As a result, users now employ the browser in extremely diverse scenarios, ranging from checking e-mails, chatting and streaming media, to playing games, managing schedules and even developing software [17].

To further support this development many browsers started implementing *tabs* to support parallel browsing. Tabs allow users to access and explore multiple Web pages simultaneously. The importance of tab-based operations can be

© Springer-Verlag Berlin Heidelberg 2014
S. Battiato et al. (Eds.): VISIGRAPP 2013, CCIS 458, pp. 69–84, 2014.
DOI: 10.1007/978-3-662-44911-0_5

further supported by the work of Miyata et al. [19], where the presence of foreground and background tasks and their interconnection in the user's mind are emphasized from the perspective of cognitive psychology. As such, Web browser tabs are specifically designed to follow this principle and allow users to distribute their attention based on this model. At the same time, the logging features of Web browsers, called *browser histories*, have the ability to reflect user interests and activity. However, most current browser histories do not consider the additional dimensions introduced by tabbed browsing behavior and fail to capture and adequately represent this parallel navigation information.

In this paper, we address the problem of designing an interactive visualization tool for Internet browser histories that supports intuitive search operations based on content and context information, and that allows the tool user to more quickly find, compare and analyze parallel navigation behavior based on a set of existing—e.g., those described in [14]—and novel metrics. This work extends the research presented in [6].

The remainder of the paper is organized as follows: First, we focus on research that is relevant to the topic at hand and continue with a requirement analysis. This is followed by a detailed discussion of the design decisions and the featured interactions of our proposed visualization. This is further complemented by a use case highlighting how WebComets works in a particular scenario. In order to validate our approach we then describe an evaluation of our tool, and lastly we offer our conclusions.

2   Related Research

Maybe the most common approach for visually encoding browsing histories are tree representations. Tools like MosaicG [11], PadPrints [13], Organic Bookmark Management [21], WebMap [9] and Domain Tree Browser [12] use one or multiple vertical or horizontal 2D trees to represent the domain-structure of the navigated Web sites. In some cases, these tree views are coupled with additional list views that highlight the temporal order of visit, as the tree representations do not reflect the temporal succession of events. Additionally, in many cases screenshots of the Web pages are used as thumbnails embedded in the nodes to support the recognition process [11,13,21]. Still, all these approaches represent a Web page only once in the tree, even if it is visited multiple times.

An alternative 2D graph representation focuses on capturing and visualizing the branching events in the navigation path [25]. These visualizations manage to capture the sequential aspect of the browsing process, as each accessed page is drawn as an additional node in the graph. If the user navigates back and accesses a different Web site, the resulting branch will be accordingly represented in the visualization.

A slightly different 2D space-filling solution is offered by the Trails plug-in [27] that supports a hierarchical, chronological and group-based representation of the visited pages. Furthermore, it offers a statistical overview of the most often visited Web sites. Another method for representing browser histories is highlighted by solutions that employ one [15] or multiple [7] interconnected linear views that are enhanced by graphical elements (e.g., thumbnails).

Besides 1D and 2D solutions, Web browser histories that employ multiple dimensions or intuitive metaphors have been developed. VISVIP [8] is a 3D representation of a navigation log, where two dimensions are used for drawing the Web site structure, while the third one encodes the temporal information. On the other hand, the combo WebBook and WebForager [5] use the concept of a book to give an overview of the Web sites as well as offer an intuitive information-space for the user.

A special class of browser histories is represented by the statistical summary histories. Tools like SlifeWeb [2], RescueTime [1] or Eyebrowse [17] are mainly focused on time management and analytics, and allow users to generate their own statistic view about how they—or others—navigate the Internet.

However, browser histories are not the only type of data revolving around complex, interconnected temporal events. Other time-series visualizations employing similar visual concepts to our approach include World Lines [24], a visualization technique for exploring the alternative paths of heterogeneous simulation runs, and LeadLine [10], a visual analytics tool for identifying and representing meaningful events in news and social media data.

While diverse and functional, none of these methods focuses on the complex parallel browsing habits of today, where tabs and windows have become means for the user to organize his thoughts, actions and accessed information [14]. The importance of a tool for visualizing, analyzing and comparing parallel browser behavior is further highlighted in [4], since users tend to use multiple windows and tabs as means for backtracking (e.g., users abandon the use of in-browser back operations in favor of opening new tabs and switching between them) and multitasking (e.g., users interact with one tab while Web pages are being loaded and processed in others). Similarly, findings from [22, 26] suggest that users often employ parallel browsing in Web search tasks for reasons like comparing search results, executing multiple queries, interacting with a page while others are being loaded, etc.

3   Requirement Analysis

To support flexible search and analysis efforts, all control and interaction elements that users employ to organize complex and parallel browsing sessions—such as windows / tabs and back-forward operations—need to be recorded and graphically represented in a first step (cp. Subsect. 4.1). The captured data organized into a set of different user profiles will be at the core of the later visualization. It has to embed rich meta-information that could be of interest for the user of WebComets, i.e., for researchers in information retrieval, behavioral sciences and related fields (called tool user or analyst in this paper). Following the study described in [14], typical research questions for a better understanding of parallel browsing behavior on the Web are for example: *When and to what extent are users parallel browsing on the Web? What affects parallel browsing behavior during interaction with Web search results?*

Another possible research question is to identify reasons why users revisit pages—for example, because of monitoring pages [3,16]—and how this is typically done in a multi-tab browser environment. For supporting such studies and for finding answers to such questions, a visualization tool has to offer specific functionalities. We have composed a list of requirements that need to be satisfied by a browser history visualization based on preliminary studies, user feedback about browser histories and their limitations, and information about the nature of parallel browsing behavior from the previously referenced publications. Fundamental requirements for the visualization of the captured data are:

- The visualization should offer an *overview* of the loaded data and *support detailed investigations*. This can be achieved by means of tailored interactions and methods like "detail-on-demand".
- The *temporal flow* of the visualized navigation sessions needs to be clearly distinguishable. While most Web browsers only display a chronologically sorted list of the accessed Web pages, it is important that the temporal dependencies are visually and relationally highlighted.
- For each visited Web page, *additional meta-data* needs to be captured like the duration of each visit or the duration of interacting with the Web page. While many solutions already count the number of executed accesses to each Web page, it is important to visualize the temporal sequence of events related to any sequence of navigated pages because documents may be inspected more often and for longer periods.
- *Web site categories*, like search engines or news Web sites, should be introduced and represented. Current browsers support bookmarking of Web pages, which implies saving the Web page's address while at the same time tagging it with the help of keywords or categories, which. These operations increase the retrievability of stored bookmarks and should also be offered by our system.
- The visualization should clearly represent which *navigation path*—or sequence of visited Web pages—the users have followed during their browsing sessions. This includes information about what browser windows and tabs have been opened and closed. Thus, it will be possible to reconstruct the steps that lead to the opening of a particular Web page—a missing feature in many related solutions.

Requirements that improve scalability (with respect to log size and number of user profiles) and analysis possibilities:

- *Visualizing multiple browsing histories* at the same time should be supported in order to allow comparison and analysis operations (e.g., detect if multiple users have similar interests).
- *Connections between similar Web sites* should be emphasized as these might be relevant alternatives in search and analysis tasks.
- Our tool users should be able to *search for particular Web pages* based on content (e.g., title or category) and context information (e.g., pages accessed prior to the one in question). While content-based search is present in all history lists, a search for the context is not supported in most cases.

- Equally important for the analysis of parallel browsing behavior is the *search for navigation patterns*, i.e., finding specific structures (motifs) in the navigation graph which results from branching out from a linear navigation behavior by using tabs or additional browser windows.

4   WebComets

WebComets is a system for the interactive visualization of extended, tab-based browser histories. It was implemented in Adobe Flash ActionScript, with both online and standalone capabilities. The representation and interaction metaphors it incorporates satisfy the requirements highlighted in the previous section. Figure 1 shows a screenshot of our tool.

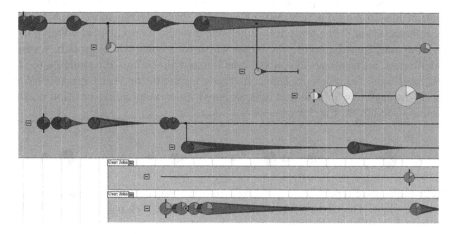

Fig. 1. WebComets visualization of the parallel browsing histories of two users (light-brown and light-grey background). Each horizontal line represents the timeline of a tab that the user has opened, while vertical branches highlight new tabs that have been created by clicking a hyperlink in the parent tab. The comet glyphs encode loaded Web sites and their color coding represents topics. Their position on the time axis depends on the moment when they were accessed (Color figure online).

To achieve the required functionality and analysis capabilities, WebComets cannot solely rely on information gathered by standard logging systems. For example, browsers like Mozilla Firefox or Internet Explorer do not record the duration for which a user has actively interacted with a Web page. More importantly, browsers do not focus on capturing the parent-child relationships between accessed Web pages and even less the connections between opened tabs or windows. Other researchers have also encountered this difficulty when investigating the parallel browsing behavior of Internet users [14]. The unavailable information included, among others, missing source tabs for branching operations and no information on how a tab or window was created (new tab, hyperlink click).

To address this, we developed a Mozilla Firefox browser add-on with the help of Javascript and libraries like jQuery and Kinetic. The add-on incorporates the ability of recording and saving an Extended Browser History (EBH) inside an SQLite database. The information collected in this manner can be subsequently accessed and visualized for multiple browsing sessions and users. For any current user profile, the extension saves the navigated URLs together with relevant additional information, representing a combination of a subset of the metrics employed in [14] and a set of additional metrics relevant to the analysis and comparison of parallel browsing habits. Additional details about the EBH data are highlighted in our related publication [6].

4.1 Design

In order to satisfy the requirements highlighted in Sect. 3, the WebComets visualization has to consider a variety of aspects. Probably the most important is the representation of the temporal dimension and the mapping of the Web pages to a time axis. In order to use the larger width to height ratio of modern screens (widescreen), a visualization concept was devised that maps the timeline to the horizontal axis, from left to right. In this representation, each accessed Web page is displayed as a circle and gets assigned its corresponding position on the timeline (x-axis), cf. Fig. 2.

Fig. 2. Conceptual representation of a tab-line that maps the flow of time from the left to the right. The circles on the line represent visited Web pages. Their diameter may represent different attributes.

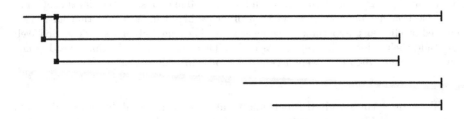

Fig. 3. Conceptual representation of the tab hierarchy. Each horizontal line represents a single tab. Tabs that are connected through a vertical line suggest a parent-child relationship between the tabs and, respectively, between the Web pages loaded in the tabs at that point in time.

The encoding of the parallel navigation that the users are involved in by using multiple browser windows and tabs is another important aspect of the visualization. WebComets represents each browser tab as a separate horizontal line segment that is parallel to the time axis (Fig. 3). This combination of patches and parallel segments is similar to the representation of a parallel browsing session in [14], as well as to [18] where multiple time-series are visualized through a comparable solution.

As tabs can be opened manually or by clicking a link in another tab, this can result in a tree-like structure that also suggests connections in terms of hyperlinks, but possibly also themes between various Web sites. This parent-child relationship is represented in the visualization as two horizontal lines connected by a vertical one (Fig. 3). At the same time, if the user opens a tab manually, there is no clear way of connecting the first Web page of this tab to any other already opened pages. Therefore, a new tab line is shown as disconnected from the rest of the tabs that were already loaded.

At the same time, multiple opened browser windows are visually encoded as framed rectangular areas, where each rectangle contains a tree-like structure of tabs that reflects the opened tabs in each window during the user session.

Comet-Like Glyphs. The representation of a visited Web page has at its core a pie chart enriched with additional graphical elements encoding multiple EBH attributes as shown in Fig. 4. These circular glyphs are mapped on the horizontal axis to the moment in time when the corresponding Web page was loaded, while the vertical positioning identifies the tab in that the Web page was loaded. There are two different visual encodings for the accessed Web pages. While both are based on pie chart representation, there are differences that need to be highlighted.

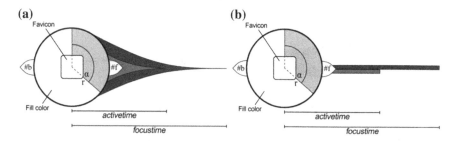

Fig. 4. Circular glyph representation of a visited Web page. The figure highlights two versions of representing the focus and active times of the visited Web pages: as a comet tail (left) or as beams (right). Active time is represented in light-blue, whereas focus time is in dark-blue (Color figure online).

Encoding 1. The first design focuses on representing the visit counts through the pie charts. More precisely, the radius of each circular representation encodes the number of visits (c_{site}) the user executed in the current session to a particular domain, e.g., www.google.com. To correctly visualize this, the maximum visit counts (c_{max}) are computed for each domain in the EBH. Also, tool users have the option of setting and storing the minimum and maximum size for the pie chart radii (r_{min} and r_{max}). Based on these values, the radius of each Web page circle is computed as:

$$r = \frac{(r_{max} - r_{min})(c_{site} - c_{max})}{c_{max} - 1} + r_{max} \tag{1}$$

As a result, pages that are part of domains that are visited more often will have a larger pie chart than those that have domains that are visited rarely.

At the same time, the pie chart representation is divided into two sectors. The first sector to the right captures the ratio of visit counts for the current Web page compared to the overall visit count for the domain. For example, if the domain *google.com* has been accessed six times in total and the current Web page (www.google.com/search?q=conference) only two times, then the pie chart will encode a sector of 1/3. This is computed by the following formula where c_{link} represents the number of accesses executed to the current link:

$$\alpha = \frac{360 \cdot c_{link}}{c_{site}} \tag{2}$$

As mentioned in Subsect. 4.1, the EBH includes three time intervals for every Web page: total, focus and active time. Note that the focus time stores the amount of time the Web page was in the foreground and active time captures the duration for which there the user was clearly present and interacting with the Web page, e.g., by mouse movements or key strokes. Therefore, the following relationship is valid for any visited Web page:

$$total\_time \geq focus\_time \geq active\_time \tag{3}$$

Fig. 5. Example of a Web page glyph employing the first encoding.

In all visual encodings, the total time for a Web page is represented by the horizontal segment between its pie chart representation and the position of the pie chart for the following Web page on the same tab. Because of Eq. 3, the focus and active times are visualized as subsegments of the total time. This is achieved by two representations that resemble a comet tail and a beam that follow the pie chart on the right side (Figs. 4 and 5). Both intervals have their origin at the loading time of the current Web page. The length along the timeline is computed by Eq. 4, where t_{enter} and t_{quit} are the timestamps for the begin and end of the session, $x_{rightEdge}$ is the rightmost x position and Δt is the focus time and active time, respectively.

$$l = \frac{x_{rightEdge} \cdot \Delta t}{t_{quit} - t_{enter}} \tag{4}$$

Encoding 2. While this encoding is similar to the previously highlighted one, there are two important differences: complexity and attribute mapping. This representation is simpler as not all attributes are encoded in the glyph, and attributes like active time and visit count are neglected. At the same time, the visual elements now encode other attributes of the EBH: the radius of the pie chart is now proportional to the total time of the Web page. This is achieved by using Formula 5 for the radii r, where r_{min} and r_{max} are selected by the tool user, Δt is the total time for the current Web page, and Δt_{min} and Δt_{max} represent the time interval for the shortest and the longest Web page visit.

$$r = \frac{(r_{max} - r_{min})(\Delta t - \Delta t_{max})}{\Delta t_{max} - \Delta t_{min}} + r_{max} \tag{5}$$

Additionally, the focus time is encoded as a sector of the Web page pie chart, where:

$$\alpha = \frac{360 \cdot focustime}{\Delta t} \tag{6}$$

This approach eliminates the need for a comet tail or beam representation, thus freeing up screen space and simplifying the visualization at the cost of removing information. The tool users have the possibility to seamlessly switch between the two encodings in the WebComets visualization.

Further glyph features, like category colors, favicons and back-forward operations, have been extensively highlighted in [6] and will not be detailed in this paper.

4.2   Interaction

Besides the already presented features of the approach, tool users have additional possibilities to customize and interact with WebComets. The current configuration can be stored inside an option window and includes—but is not limited to—the following: switching between comet tail and beam representations, customizing min and max values for the pie chart radii, enabling or disabling elements like favicons or back-forward arrows, and selecting the EBH attributes to be displayed.

Visual Exploration. A set of interaction metaphors complement the visualization's abilities by addressing topics like flexibility, scalability or detail-on-demand. The WebComets interface supports pan and zoom operations, similar to modern interactive maps. While the panning operation is self-evident, there are two zooming approaches implemented in the tool: one is a regular 2D zoom that allows tool users to inspect the details in a certain area, while the other is a 1D horizontal zoom along the timeline that stretches the horizontal axis.

When a Web page is selected, WebComets searches the browser history to check for similar Web pages. By default, only pages with the same domain are considered to be similar, but more complicated rules for interconnection can be generated, e.g. pages containing a keyword, pages that have an active time of

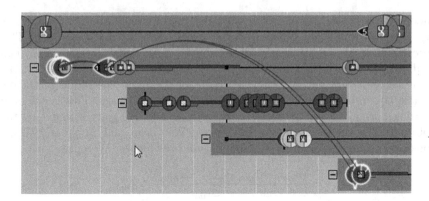

Fig. 6. Connections between the selected Web pages and other glyphs highlighted through continuous curved lines.

similar length, etc. These are highlighted by adding links between each selected element and its counterpart. The curved lines (Fig. 6) are used for showing the presence of similar Web pages to the selected ones, possibly in areas of the visualization that are not currently visible. Curves can be easily perceived as they contrast with the overall orthogonal representation of our approach. To avoid clutter, curves are drawn in such a way that the probabilities of intersecting curves and a curve intersecting a glyph are reduced.

It might occur that multiple glyphs are partially or almost totally overlapping. Even if the tool user has the possibility to execute timeline zoom commands to compensate for this and clearly separate the overlapping glyphs, this is a vital scalability issue. To deal with this, WebComets displays partially overlapping pie charts by positioning the glyph of the Web page that has been accessed later over the top of the previous one. To further compensate, the tool user can move the mouse pointer over a set of densely grouped circles. By doing so, the glyph with the center closest to the pointer will be moved to the foreground.

Content and Motif-Based Filtering. Highlighting different elements in a browser history is closely coupled with searching for Web pages or navigation patterns. Most Web browsers support a text-based search of their records that limits their ability to detect context information. This functionality is also supported by WebComets. Tool users can search for terms and keyword combinations (e.g., *apple+pc*), strict phrases (by using quotes, e.g., *"apple pc"*) or even exclude words from their query (by using the minus sign, e.g., *apple-pc*).

Besides the possibility to execute a text-based search of the extended browser history's informational content, supporting the detection, analysis and comparison process of temporal patterns in the navigation graph requires a different approach. Thus, WebComets offers a motif search window (Fig. 7) that allows users to define, store and search for custom information and patterns of navigation. Inspired by the building blocks concept in [20,23], motifs in WebComets

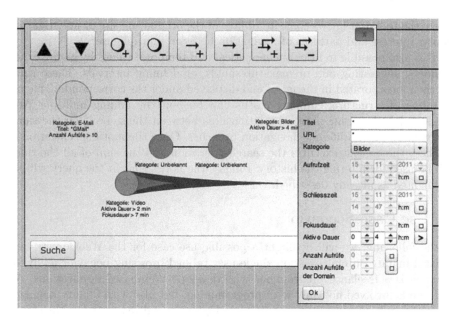

Fig. 7. The motif window that helps users construct, save and search for custom motifs based on Web page attributes and context information.

are predefined subgraph structures that can be used to filter the current history. Compared to other approaches, the WebComets motif search has the advantages of allowing logical combinations of sought patterns (e.g. find all node groups that satisfy motif A and do not satisfy motif B), as well as the possibility to model a large set of node and internode attributes.

These subgraphs can be generated in two ways: either by mining substructures from the currently opened history log files or by manually defining a motif and its corresponding rules. In the first case, the tool user would look through the visualized browser histories and select any subset of glyphs that could be at the core of a parallel browsing behavior. When all relevant elements are selected, the generated motif can be edited further in the motif window to generalize or particularize the final structural pattern. Contrary to this, in the second approach the analyst would start generating a motif by directly building it in the motif window, adding node after node and customizing their attributes based on his experience and assumptions.

As such, tool users analyzing an EBH can not only look for topics of the visited pages, but also detect navigation motifs. For example, the motif search could detect that in 72 % of the cases when an Internet user accesses his e-mail account, he also opens a Web page from the category "video" in a new tab originating from his e-mail page. This might suggest that he receives much e-mail with links to video content. Thus, filtering the browser history based on structural aspects can have many applications, for example, detecting a Web page where the tool user knows some attributes of the originating site or investigating similar interest and patterns of navigation between multiple users.

It is also possible to filter out numerical and temporal values by giving exact numbers, suggesting min or max thresholds, or defining intervals. These rules are then incorporated in the motif and displayed under the corresponding pages. In terms of structure, complex motifs can be built by adding multiple Web pages and highlighting existing relationships between them, be it on the same tab/window or on different navigation branches. Once the motif specification is finished, the analyst executes the search operation and the sum of all the rules will be used for filtering the history. Finally, the nodes that fit the query will be highlighted as already described.

5   Use Case Scenario

In the following, we will highlight a possible use case for the WebComets tool focused mainly on multi-session single-user tabbed browsing behavior analysis. Thomas is a freelance programmer who develops Web-based applications. As such, he is involved not only with programming, but also with quality management and even customer support for some highly specialized modules. His attention is currently focused on an application he is developing in a programming team as well as answering written queries from former customers. For all these operations, Thomas uses mainly online tools: online chat rooms, online documentation, and even an online PHP editor inside his Web browser. Additionally, in order to have a close collaboration with his team, he spends some time on *fonie.de*, where he has periodical online conferences about implementation ideas and concept ambiguities.

After some workdays, Thomas notices that while he spends more then his daily eight hours in front of the computer, he still does not manage to finalize his tasks during the designated timeframe. He is aware that he takes short breaks now and then from writing code in order to inspect documentation, read e-mails, or simply to disconnect for a few minutes. Still, he does not believe that these interruptions are the sole reason for his reduced efficiency. Thus, he decides to use WebComets to examine the extended browser history for the last nine hours he was working (Fig. 8).

Initially, Thomas is trying to obtain an overview and recognizes that he has been distracted multiple times on the day in question. At the beginning of the day, he opened the online PHP editor and accessed his project files to continue coding. Immediately after, a conference call interrupted his work and lasted over an hour, much longer than initially intended (Fig. 9). Furthermore, Thomas notices that he read multiple PHP articles before noon that also resulted in a couple of visits to news Web sites. After the lunch break, he accessed his project files again and continued programming. This time, a piece of information about PHP distracted him and he ended up watching a set of YouTube videos related to coding practices and later entertainment. Soon afterwards, he had to participate in an online conference with a customer. Towards the end of the day, he inspected a set of Web pages with PHP articles and documentation.

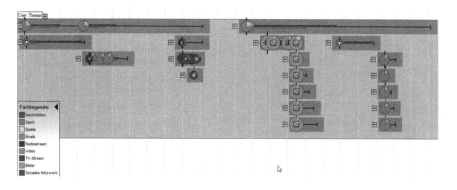

Fig. 8. WebComets representation of Thomas' browser history for today.

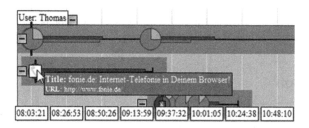

Fig. 9. Conference call executed by Thomas in the morning.

Thomas wants to find out exactly how his navigation time is distributed over the various Web sites, in terms of actual time investment. Also, he would like to know how much percent of his working time actually flowed into the project development. From the times of the navigated Web pages, he is only interested in the focus time, because only during these periods the pages were in the foreground. To find out how much time he spent on particular Web pages, he selects the corresponding glyphs. He can inspect an information box for additional overview or detail information. By executing a mouse over operation in the left-top corner of the box, he finds the convoluted values for the focus times on each domain (Fig. 10 (left)).

Thomas notices that he has worked on the project only 48 % of the eight hours he was supposed to. Instead, approximately one quarter of the time he has spent speaking with colleagues or customers. Furthermore, he has spent 13 % of his time watching videos and another 10 % on inspecting PHP documentation. To illustrate the result again, Thomas selects all pages by executing a search without search terms. He then sorts the list of all pages presented in the information box based on the focus time (Fig. 10 (right)). He now can see a clear distribution of the times spent on various Web sites and Web pages.

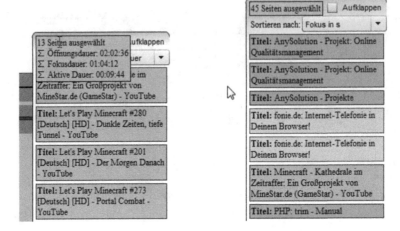

Fig. 10. Information box with the summed durations (open, focus and active time) for every accessed site (left). List of accessed Web pages sorted by focus time (right).

6 Evaluation

A brief evaluation of the WebComets visualization approach has been executed in order to capture advantages and disadvantages. The aim of the study was to compare the performance and accuracy of tool users when inspecting and comparing patterns in multiple parallel browsing histories. For this purpose, the participants would interact with the same EBH log files by two different approaches: the WebComets visualization and a list-based browser history.

The evaluation involved 20 participants with experience in knowledge exploration as well as with extensive background in using diverse Web browsers and accessing a variety of online applications. An initial step in the evaluation process was to randomly divide the participants into two groups and attribute a task to them. Each member of the first group would have to solve the task using the WebComets visualization, while the members of the second group used a list-based history.

The scenario involved the analysis of two browsing sessions from different users. An initial assumption was made that the users have participated at an online conference call where they suggested relevant Web sites to each other. This collaborative browsing approach is frequently used in cases where one party tries to highlight some information to the other. A simple example for this would be the collaboration between two students that are preparing for an exam at remote locations. As a result, both users would access multiple similar or identical Web pages in the same time interval. The test persons had to determine if the initial assumption of collaboration is supported by the browser histories, and if so, what Web pages might have been involved and in what time interval this collaboration took place.

The results were evaluated by inspecting the total time each participant took to find a solution and the time frame he/she reported as part of the conference session. On average, users managed to find a solution more than twice as fast with the WebComets visualization than with the text-based representation of the navigation history. Further, the subjects that used the WebComets tool have identified the correct time frame in almost 100 % of the cases, while the group using the list-based browser history has reported a lower success rate with only a 71 % average overlap of the detected collaboration time frame. Based on these findings and the results of the post-task questionnaire given to the participants, WebComets seems to address the issues raised by our requirement analysis. Additional details of the evaluation are presented in [6].

7   Conclusions

In this paper we presented WebComets, an interactive visualization for tabbed browser histories. After discussing related work and functional requirements, we focused on the interactive features and filtering capabilities of our tool. Web-Comets allows its users to more efficiently search for patterns in parallel browsing sessions by means of motif-based filtering as well as compare and analyze the tabbed browsing behavior of Internet users. This functionality is further highlighted by a use case. Finally, an evaluation confirmed that our approach has met the initial requirements, and our users were able to quickly filter navigational information and detect patterns in the online sessions they were exploring.

References

1. Rescuetime (2013). http://www.rescuetime.com
2. Slife labs time management software (2013). http://www.slifeweb.com
3. Adar, E., Teevan, J., Dumais, S.T.: Large scale analysis of web revisitation patterns. In: 26th Annual SIGCHI Conference on Human Factors in Computing Systems, CHI '08, pp. 1197–1206. ACM, New York (2008)
4. Aula, A., Jhaveri, N., Kaki, M.: Information search and reaccess strategies of experienced web users. In: 14th International Conference on World Wide Web (WWW '05), pp. 583–592 (2005)
5. Card, S.K., Robertson, G.G., York, W.: The Webbook and the Web Forager: an information workspace for the World Wide Web. In: Human Factors in Computing Systems (CHI 96), pp. 111–117 (1996)
6. Cernea, D., Truderung, I., Kerren, A., Ebert, A.: WebComets: a tab-oriented approach for browser history visualization. In: Conference on Information Visualization Theory and Applications (IVAPP), pp. 439–450. SciTePress (2013)
7. Cockburn, A., Greenberg, S., Jones, S., McKenzie, B., Moyle, M.: Improving web page revisitation: analysis, design and evaluation. IT Soc. **1**(3), 159–183 (2003)
8. Cugini, J., Scholtz, J.: VISVIP: 3D visualization of paths through websites. In: International Workshop on Web-Based Information Visualization (WebVis 99), Florence, Italy, pp. 259–263 (1999)
9. Doemel, P.: Webmap - a graphical hypertext navigation tool. In: 2nd International World Wide Web Conference, vol. 28(1–2), pp. 85–97 (1995)

10. Dou, W., Wang, X., Skau, D., Ribarsky, W., Zhou, M.X.: LeadLine: interactive visual analysis of text data through event identification and exploration. In: IEEE Conference on Visual Analytics Science and Technology (VAST), pp. 93–102 (2012)
11. Eric, M., Ayers, E.Z., Stasko, J.T.: Using graphic history in browsing the world wide web. In: International WWW Conference, pp. 1–7 (1995)
12. Gandhi, R., Girish, K., Bederson, B.B., Shneiderman, B.: Domain name based visualization of web histories in a zoomable user interface. In: International Workshop on Database and Expert Systems Applications (DEXA), pp. 591–598 (2000)
13. Hightower, R.R., Ring, L.T., Helfman, J.I., Bederson, B.B., Hollan, J.D.: Graphical multiscale web histories: a study of padprints. In: 11th Annual ACM Symposium on User Interface Software and Technology, pp. 58–65 (1998)
14. Huang, J., White, R.W.: Parallel Browsing behavior on the web. In: 21st ACM Conference on Hypertext and Hypermedia (HT), pp. 13–18 (2010)
15. Kaasten, S., Greenberg, S.: Integrating back, history and bookmarks in web browsers. In: Extended Abstracts of ACM Conference of Human Factors in Computing Systems (CHI), pp. 1–2. ACM Press (2000)
16. Kellar, M., Watters, C., Inkpen, K.M.: An exploration of web-based monitoring: implications for design. In: SIGCHI Conference on Human Factors in Computing Systems, CHI '07, pp. 377–386. ACM, New York (2007)
17. Kleek, M.V., Xu, C., Moore, B., Karger, D.R.: Eyebrowse: real-time web activity sharing and visualization. In: CHI 2010 Extended Abstracts on Human Factors in Computing Systems (CHI EA), pp. 3643–3648. ACM, New York (2010)
18. Krstajic, M., Bertini, E., Keim, D.: Cloudlines: compact display of event episodes in multiple time-series. IEEE Trans. Visual Comput. Graph. **17**(12), 2432–2439 (2011)
19. Miyata, Y., Norman, D.: Psychological issues in support of multiple activities. In: Norman, D.A., Draper, S.W. (eds.) User Centered System Design, pp. 265–284. Lawrence Erlbaum, Hillsdale (1986)
20. Reeder, J., Reeder, J., Giegerich, R.: Locomotif: from graphical motif description to RNA motif search in bioinformatics. Bioinformatics **23**(13), 392–400 (2007)
21. Shen, S.-T., Prior, S.D., Chen, K.-M.: A solution to revisitation using organic bookmark management. In: Marcus, A. (ed.) HCII 2011 and DUXU 2011, Part II. LNCS, vol. 6770, pp. 46–52. Springer, Heidelberg (2011)
22. Spink, A., Park, M., Jansen, B.J., Pedersen, J.: Multitasking during web search sessions. Inf. Process. Manage. **42**(1), 264–275 (2006)
23. von Landesberger, T., Rehner, R., Gorner, M., Schreck, T.: A system for interactive visual analysis of large graphs using motifs in graph editing and aggregation. In: Vision Modeling Visualization Workshop (VMV), pp. 331–340 (2009)
24. Waser, J., Fuchs, R., Ribicic, H., Schindler, B., Blšschl, G., Gršller, E.: World lines. IEEE Trans. Visual Comput. Graph. **16**(6), 1458–1467 (2010)
25. Waterson, S., Hong, J.I., Sohn, T., Heer, J., Matthews, T., Landay, J.: What did they do? Understanding clickstreams with the webquilt visualization system. In: Advanced Visual Interfaces, pp. 94–102 (2002)
26. Weinreich, H., Obendorf, H., Herder, E., Mayer, M.: Off the beaten tracks: exploring three aspects of web navigation. In: 15th International Conference on World Wide Web (WWW'06), pp. 133–142 (2006)
27. Yu, W., Ingalls, T.: Trails–an interactive web history visualization and tagging tool. In: Marcus, A. (ed.) HCII 2011 and DUXU 2011, Part II. LNCS, vol. 6770, pp. 77–86. Springer, Heidelberg (2011)

The Landscape Metaphor for Visualization of Molecular Similarities

Martin Gronemann[1]([⊠]), Michael Jünger[1], Nils Kriege[2], and Petra Mutzel[2]

[1] Institut für Informatik, Universität zu Köln, Cologne, Germany
{gronemann,mjuenger}@informatik.uni-koeln.de
[2] Department of Computer Science,
Technische Universität Dortmund, Dortmund, Germany
{nils.kriege,petra.mutzel}@tu-dortmund.de

Abstract. Clustered graphs are a versatile representation formalism for expressing relations between entities, and simultaneously, reflecting their hierarchical structure. This makes clustered graphs well-suited to model complex structured data. However, obtaining appealing drawings of clustered graphs is a challenging task. We employ the landscape metaphor to visualize clustered graphs in a cheminformatics application. In order to browse chemical compound libraries in a systematic way, we consider two different molecular similarity concepts. Combining the scaffold-based cluster hierarchy with molecular similarity graphs allows for new insights in the analysis of large molecule libraries. Here, like in certain other application domains, the cluster hierarchy does not necessarily reflect the underlying graph structure. We improve the approach taken in [1] by applying a modified treemap algorithm for node positioning that takes the edges of the graph into account. Experiments with real-world instances clearly show that the new algorithm leads to significant improvements in terms of the edge lengths.

Keywords: Graph drawing · Clustered graphs · Landscape metaphor · Topographic maps · Drug discovery · Molecule libraries

1 Introduction

Drug discovery is a tedious and expensive process that typically involves the experimental evaluation of large compound libraries by high-throughput screening in order to identify promising small molecules that bind to a specific biological target. These compounds may serve as a starting point for chemical modifications, e.g., with the aim to reduce side effects or to increase potency. A guiding principle during this process is to elucidate and exploit the relationship between the structure of a molecule and its biological properties.

In the course of the drug discovery process typically structural information on compounds as well as experimental results are generated. Supporting the

---

Research supported by the German Research Foundation (DFG), priority programme "Algorithm Engineering" (SPP 1307).

S. Battiato et al. (Eds.): VISIGRAPP 2013, CCIS 458, pp. 85–100, 2014.
DOI: 10.1007/978-3-662-44911-0_6

drug discovery process based on this data by adequate computational methods like, e.g., largely automated data mining algorithms, is a fundamental task in cheminformatics [2]. However, only recently several sophisticated visual analysis tools for this domain have been developed [3–7] with the aim to allow the user to explore the chemical space and make decisions based on his expert knowledge. These tools often represent sets of molecules and their structural relations by means of graphs, and they rely on graph drawing techniques for visualization. Since structural relations are rather complex, different approaches have been developed, some of which organize molecules in a tree-like hierarchy while others are based on pairwise similarities. The complexity of structural relations, the amount of data and the different perspectives, which chemists from different branches of chemistry may have, make it difficult to find an approach that satisfies all needs.

Irwin recently summarized the problem as follows: "In principle, one would like to be able to organize and browse large chemical datasets [. . .] as easily as one can today browse maps on the internet" [8]. This comparison gives the impetus for our approach to represent molecule sets by clustered graphs, which are then visualized as topographic maps based on a method recently proposed [1]. The use of clustered graphs allows us to model different aspects of structural similarity between compounds in a single graph and to visualize them in one picture in which similar molecules appear close to each other. Clustered graphs have not yet been applied to visualize chemical compounds, the most likely reason is that drawing them is difficult. This is caused by the requirement to generate an appealing drawing of the underlying graph that simultaneously represents the hierarchy of nested subsets of its nodes. The issue becomes especially challenging when the cluster hierarchy does not reflect the "natural" clusters of the underlying graph. This problem arises with our representation of molecular data sets by clustered graphs and was not addressed in [1]. Therefore we develop a new partitioning procedure that exploits the degrees of freedom in the algorithm with the goal to obtain shorter edges. In order to meet the requirements of the application domain, our procedure also supports the display of structural formulae of compounds and the superimposition of a heat map that allows the representation of property values.

2   Related Work

Recently several sophisticated tools for the visualization of compound sets have been developed. Many of these represent chemical compounds by means of graphs: In [9] the concept of 'Network-like Similarity Graphs' was introduced to study structure-activity relationships of small molecules. Here, compounds are represented by nodes and two nodes are connected by an edge if their compounds exceed a certain similarity threshold. These graphs are then visualized using the force-directed Fruchterman-Reingold layout algorithm [10]. In addition, similarities are used to derive a hierarchical clustering of all nodes. However, for visualization only a single clustering is selected instead of displaying the full hierarchy.

The approach was implemented by the open-source application SARANEA [5] based on the framework JUNG[1]. A different application, also based on pairwise molecular similarities, is HiTSEE [6]. This tool maps compounds on the plane trying to preserve distances derived from similarities by Multidimensional Scaling (MDS). Several concepts to organize compounds via hierarchical classification schemes have been proposed [11]. These are, e.g., based on clustering algorithms or on domain specific methods based on rules incorporating chemical knowledge. An approach of the second category is the so-called scaffold tree [12] on which the visual analysis tool Scaffold Hunter [4,7] is based. For visualization, a radial style tree drawing algorithm is used. The tool MolWind [3] is also based on the scaffold tree concept, but uses NASA's World Wind engine to map scaffolds to a virtual globe. Structure-activity landscapes [13] are a general concept relating structural differences of molecules to differences in potency. Several techniques for visualization have been proposed including the depiction as 3D landscapes [14]. While MolWind and structure-activity landscapes are not directly related to graph drawing, we take up the idea to map chemical information to intuitively understandable geographic representations, and realize it in the realm of clustered graph drawing.

While clustered graph drawing is a lively research topic in graph drawing [15,16] (see, e.g., in GDEA[2]), only few approaches exist for drawing clustered graphs as maps. Gansner et al. have suggested the use of geographic maps for enhancing clusters and visualizing similarities [17,18]. They first compute a partition of the nodes by applying a cluster algorithm, then use a force-directed method or MDS to compute a layout, and finally use both to create a colored map. The combination of the layout and clustering methods used for generating the map, plays an important role regarding the visual shape of the clusters in the final layout. In order to obtain a map where the countries form compact areas, requires that the result produced by the layout algorithm matches the partitioning of the clustering step. Otherwise, the partitions are visually scattered, this problem is referred to as *fragmentation*.

An alternative approach for visualizing hierarchically clustered graphs as topographic maps has been suggested recently in [1]. Topographic maps have a long history in information visualization. Mostly used for visualizing point distributions, they offer a natural way to explore data. In [19] the effect of using topographic maps as metaphor is studied. They confirm the usage of elevation levels as an effective way to encode similarities. Gronemann and Jünger propose to represent the complete hierarchy of a clustered graph by elevation levels. The elevation model is defined such that nodes in different subtrees are separated by a valley. In other words, nodes in the same cluster are placed together on a plateau. This simple idea requires that the layout algorithm generates compact areas for all clusters.

By using a treemap approach for the layout the problem of fragmentation is avoided. Several methods for generating treemaps exist in the literature. Starting

---

[1] http://jung.sourceforge.net
[2] Graph Drawing E-Print Archive, http://gdea.informatik.uni-koeln.de/.

with the work of [20], where a hierarchy is mapped on a space filling curve, most algorithms are based on a rectangular subdivision scheme. A good overview over the vast amount of treemap techniques can be found in [21].

3   Compound Libraries and Clustered Graphs

A *clustered graph* is a tuple (G, T), where $G = (V, E)$ is a graph and $T = (V_T, E_T)$ is a rooted tree such that the leaves of T are the nodes in V. Each inner node v of T corresponds to a *cluster* of G comprising all leaves of the subtree rooted at v. Therefore the inner nodes of T are called *cluster nodes*, T is referred to as *cluster tree* and defines a hierarchy of nested subsets of V.

Approaches to explore chemical compound libraries typically allow the user to navigate between regions of molecules with a similar structure. We combine two orthogonal concepts from cheminformatics to derive clustered graphs that represent two different aspects of structural similarity.

3.1   Molecular Similarity Graph

A set of compounds with pairwise similarities can be represented by a graph: Molecules are associated with nodes and two nodes are connected by an edge if their similarity exceeds a certain threshold. This approach is applied in [5,9], for example. We additionally annotate edges with the corresponding similarity values. For a given set of molecules M we define a *similarity graph* $G(M) = (V, E)$ with edge weights w according to $V = M, E = \{(u, v) \in V \times V \mid \text{sim}(u, v) \geq t\}$, and $w((u, v)) = \text{sim}(u, v)$ for all $(u, v) \in E$, where $\text{sim}(\cdot, \cdot)$ is a similarity measure defined on molecules and t is a threshold value with direct influence on the density of the graph.

While computing adequate structural similarity measures for molecules is a wide and challenging research topic on its own [22], we rely on standard techniques often used in practice: Molecules are represented by so-called *fingerprints*, i.e., binary vectors of constant size, where bits encode the presence or absence of certain fragments [2]. We employ the path-based hash-key fingerprint provided by the cheminformatics toolkit CDK [23]. The fingerprints are then compared with each other by computing the Tanimoto coefficient in order to obtain pairwise similarities.

3.2   Scaffold-Based Cluster Hierarchy

A different approach to organizing chemical compound sets is based on a hierarchical classification scheme representing molecules by their core structures referred to as *scaffolds*. The scaffold tree algorithm [12] builds a tree-like hierarchy of scaffolds. It essentially proceeds as follows: For each molecule in the dataset its scaffold is created by pruning all terminal side chains. Then the scaffold is successively simplified by removing a single ring in each step such that the resulting parent scaffold stays connected. The procedure stops when a one-ring

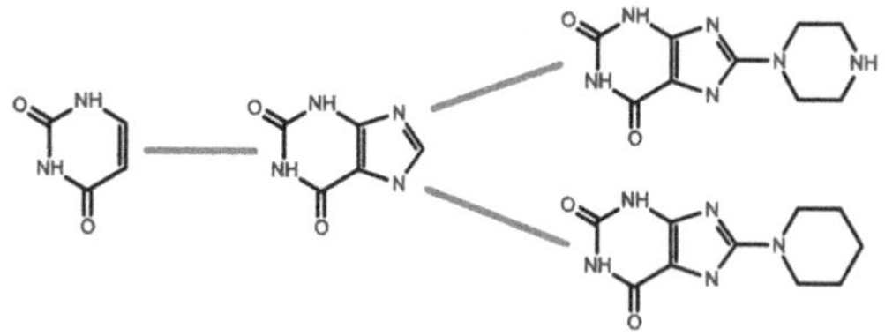

Fig. 1. A branch of a scaffold tree.

scaffold is obtained. Since in each step multiple rings can be removed, a unique parent scaffold is selected by a set of rules incorporating chemical knowledge with the aim to preserve the most characteristic ring structure. When the procedure is applied to a set of molecules, typically some have the same scaffold and several scaffolds share the same parent scaffold. A scaffold tree is obtained by merging these multiple scaffolds and connecting all one-ring scaffolds to a virtual root. Figure 1 shows four scaffolds and their relation in a scaffold tree branch.

Generating the scaffold tree for a set of molecules M and connecting all molecules to their scaffold yields a valid cluster tree for the similarity graph $G(M)$. While the scaffold tree concept has been successfully applied to various research tasks [7,24], an obvious conceptual weakness is that side chains are not taken into account although they may constitute key functional groups [8]. Therefore, the combination with a similarity graph based on a whole-molecule structural similarity measure may help to alleviate this drawback.

4   Edge-Aware Drawing of Clustered Graphs

Visualizing the hierarchy provided by the scaffold tree and drawing edges of the similarity graph at the same time turned out to be a challenge. The main problem is that the hierarchy is not related to the similarity graph, because nodes contained in a cluster are not necessarily similar. When the original method proposed in [1] is applied to these graphs, the results are rather unpleasant. Especially on very sparse graphs, edge clutter occurs. In [1], where a clustering method is applied to the input, and thus the clusters are consistent with the placement algorithm, nodes that are well connected are placed close to each other, while nodes with higher graph theoretic distance are located in different subtrees. Before we present two improvements, we sketch the outline of the original method. First, the input graph is clustered using the algorithm of [25] to obtain a cluster hierarchy with the aforementioned properties. Then a tree mapping approach called *fat polygon partitioning*, based on [26], is used. The nodes are placed inside their partition that form a nested structure of convex polygons representing the hierarchy. The layout is then transformed into a triangle mesh by applying a Delaunay triangulation. This mesh serves both as a basis for drawing a topographic map and as a routing network for edge bundling. For more details, see [1].

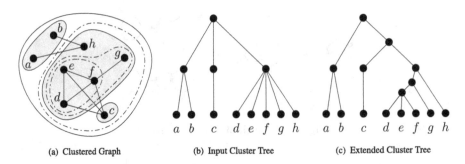

(a) Clustered Graph   (b) Input Cluster Tree   (c) Extended Cluster Tree

Fig. 2. Example of a clustered graph (a) with cluster tree (b). The extended cluster tree (c) contains dummy nodes determined by betweenness based clustering. Dashed shapes in (a) depict the clusters representing these dummy nodes.

In the following we present two improvements of the original method. First, we suggest to extend the input hierarchy by adding virtual clusters without changing the nested structure of the input. These new clusters help to place highly connected groups of nodes together. Second, the fat polygon partitioning is modified to optimize edge length and to place clusters based on an arbitrary edge set, while still generating good polygons. The goal is to make the tree map algorithm aware of the edges and exploit the degrees of freedom offered by the input hierarchy and the polygon partitioning. Finally, we evaluate the modifications based on the instances of our application area.

4.1 Extending the Input Hierarchy

The inner nodes of the scaffold tree usually contain many children, while the fat polygon partitioning requires a binary tree. Therefore, a non-binary tree has to be transformed into a binary one as described in [1]. However, since the provided input hierarchy is not edge-aware, the subdivision procedure may result in edge clutter. This is due to the fact that highly connected child clusters are placed in distant subtrees. In order to solve this problem, we use edge betweenness clustering to extend the input hierarchy. The algorithm proposed in [25] is rather simple. For all edges, the betweenness score is calculated and the edges with the highest score are removed. This procedure is repeated until the graph becomes disconnected. The connected components serve as clusters on which the method recurses.

This method can easily be adapted to work on an existing hierarchy. We traverse the input hierarchy top-down. For each cluster C with children $C_1, \ldots, C_n$, $n > 2$, we construct a graph $G(C)$ induced by the underlying edge set E and the children of C. Let $V(C_i)$ denote the graph nodes contained in the subtree rooted at C_i. Let $E(C_i, C_j) = E \cap (V(C_i) \times V(C_j))$ denote the edges having one end point in C_i and the other in C_j. The obvious way to obtain the inter-cluster edge weights $w(C_i, C_j)$ is to sum up the 'cluster-parallel' edge weights according to

$$w(C_i, C_j) = \sum_{e \in E(C_i, C_j)} w(e).$$

The original algorithm is then used to obtain a hierarchy for this graph, which we can insert into the existing subtree. The leaves of the obtained hierarchy correspond to the children of the cluster node C, which can be replaced by the root of the hierarchy.

In Fig. 2 a small example is displayed. The dashed shapes are the newly inserted clusters after the algorithm has decomposed as much as possible without violating the nested structure of the input hierarchy. The newly created clusters are used as "ghost clusters", which are not visible on the final map. Their only purpose is to group tightly connected components together. In case that the result is not a binary tree, the transformation used in [1] is applied. Notice that the extended hierarchy is based on intra-cluster adjacency only and does not take external edges into account. This issue is addressed in the following section.

4.2   Edge-Aware Polygon Partitioning

In this section we investigate the degrees of freedom of the polygon partitioning and how to exploit them to minimize the length of edges between clusters.

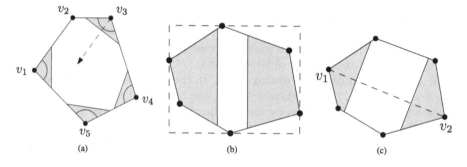

Fig. 3. Enumeration of allowed cuts. In (a) we only want to cut off a small part of the polygon. The two choices when choosing an axis-aligned cut and a cut perpendicular to the diameter defined by v_1, v_2 are shown in (b) and (c), respectively.

A tree map based on fat polygon partitioning follows the same principle as most tree map algorithms. The idea is to recursively subdivide a convex polygon in order to obtain a nested structure of polygons representing the cluster tree. Starting with the root which represents the boundary polygon the algorithm proceeds in a top-down manner: At each cluster node, the associated polygon is split into two convex subpolygons which represent the subtrees rooted at the two children. The cutting line is chosen, such that the area of the subpolygons is proportional to the number of leaves in the corresponding subtrees. We place the graph nodes, i.e., the leaves of the tree, in the centroid of the associated polygon computed by the partitioning.

The basic problem in the individual steps of the partitioning algorithm can be summarized as follows: We are given a convex polygon P with k vertices

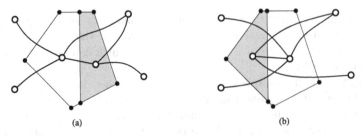

(a)   (b)

Fig. 4. Example for two possible partitions of a polygon with adjacencies to external clusters. In (a) the total edge length is less compared to the partition in (b).

and a parameter $0 < a \leq \frac{1}{2}$, where a is the fraction of the area we require for the smaller child. Let area(P) denote the area of P and diam(P) its diameter, i.e., the maximum distance between two vertices of P. We want to find a direction for a cutting line that partitions P into two subpolygons P_1 and P_2, such that area(P_1) = $a \cdot$ area(P) and area(P_2) = $(1 - a) \cdot$ area(P). When given a cut direction, we choose the orientation of the cutting line perpendicular to this direction. In general finding such a cut is easy for a convex polygon. However, a convenient property of the greedy algorithm proposed in [26] is that it yields polygons with bounded aspect ratios, where the aspect ratio is defined as asp(P) = diam(P)^2/area(P). We want to preserve this property without unnecessarily restricting the number of allowed cuts.

In [26] two main cases are distinguished: In the first case, when we want to cut off a small piece, that is when $a \leq 1/k^2$, the bisector at the vertex with the smallest interior angle is taken as the cut direction. However, the guarantee of the small aspect ratio only relies on the fact that the smallest interior angle of a convex polygon is bounded by $\pi \cdot (1 - \frac{2}{k})$ [26]. Thus, we are allowed to choose any other bisector as long as the interior angle at the corresponding vertex is small enough. In Fig. 3(a) an example is given, where we are allowed to choose every bisector, except the one at v_2, which is not small enough.

In the second case, when $a > 1/k^2$, the aspect ratio of the boundary polygon must be considered. When P has a good aspect ratio, i.e., asp(P) $\leq k^6$, we are allowed to choose any direction for a cut [26]. In this case and when $a > \frac{1}{3}$ holds, our implementation chooses an axis-aligned cut perpendicular to the longest side of the bounding rectangle for aesthetic reasons, see Fig. 3(b). Otherwise, when asp(P) > k^6 or $1/k^2 < a \leq \frac{1}{3}$ holds, we choose the direction of the line representing the diameter of the polygon. This is the line that connects any two vertices of P with maximum distance to each other, cf. Fig. 3(c).

The key idea is to enumerate all allowed cuts for a given polygon and a parameter a in each step of the partitioning procedure and to take the one that minimizes the edge length. That is, we try to place the polygon of a child cluster in the direction of clusters to which it is highly connected. Figure 4 illustrates the idea. We will apply this procedure in a top down manner to obtain a partitioning that is optimized for edge length. However, there is no accurate information

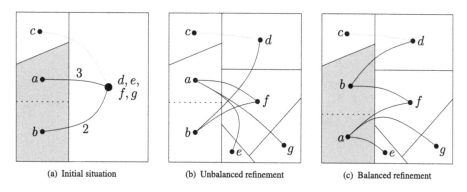

(a) Initial situation   (b) Unbalanced refinement   (c) Balanced refinement

Fig. 5. Example of layouts obtained for different refinement strategies.

available as to where these adjacent clusters are located because the corresponding polygon has not been computed yet. Therefore, we propose a heuristic to decide which cut to use based on the partial knowledge of the surrounding clusters.

The available information on node positions depends on the current state of the subdivision process. While the cluster tree is typically traversed in a depth-first fashion, we propose a different procedure to achieve a more balanced level of refinement: The subdivision process always splits the polygon covering the larger area first. We keep all cluster nodes whose polygons still have to be partitioned in a priority queue Q ordered by area requirement. These nodes, together with the leaves that have been processed, form a layer L of nodes with associated polygons that we call *active*. The polygons of all active nodes cover the entire boundary polygon and realize the preliminary layout on which the selection of an allowed cut is based.

Figure 5 exemplifies the influence of the refinement order. When partitioning the gray polygon containing a and b in Fig. 5(a) there is no accurate information available on the positions of d, e, f, g. Therefore, the polygon of a is placed in the middle since minimizing the distance representing the length of three inter-cluster edges is prioritized. The result of this bad decision is displayed in Fig. 5(b). When polygons are partitioned in order of decreasing size the information on neighboring polygons is more accurate. This typically results in a better final layout. Figure 5(c) shows the cut that would be chosen after the large right polygon has been refined.

We introduce additional notation to precisely define the criterion we use to assess the potential of a cut to minimize edge lengths. Let C be a node of the cluster tree. We use $\mathrm{ctr}(C)$ to refer to the centroid of the associated polygon; $\mathrm{awc}(C)$ denotes the average weighted center of the centroids of active polygons adjacent to C weighted by inter-cluster edges, i.e.,

$$\mathrm{awc}(C) = \frac{1}{w(C, L)} \sum_{P \in L} \mathrm{ctr}(P) \cdot w(C, P),$$

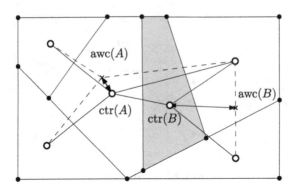

Fig. 6. Edge-aware cut selection.

where $w(C, L) = \sum_{P \in L} w(C, P)$. The value of awc($C$) can be considered as the preferred location of (the centroid of) the polygon associated with C.

Consider an active node $C \in Q$ with children C_1 and C_2. Each allowed cut assigns a subpolygon to the two children, cf. Fig. 3. The idea is to choose the cut that minimizes the distance between the centroids of the subpolygons and their preferred positions according to the average weighted center. We define the distance between the two points associated with a node C as

$$\text{dist}(C) = \begin{cases} \|\text{awc}(C) - \text{ctr}(C)\| & \text{if } w(C, L) \neq 0, \\ 0 & \text{otherwise.} \end{cases}$$

Note that in the second case there are no edges leaving the cluster C and the position of the polygon has no effect on edge lengths. We choose the cut that minimizes

$$\sum_{i \in \{1,2\}} \text{dist}(C_i) \cdot w(C_i, L), \qquad (1)$$

where the factor $w(C_i, L)$ reflects the impact of the individual children. Figure 6 illustrates the method for a given cut. Putting all the above steps together, we can outline the algorithm: We start with the root of the tree, assign it the boundary polygon given as input and add it to Q. Then we repeat the following steps until all leaves have been processed.

1. Pop a node C with its boundary polygon P from the queue Q.
2. If C is a leaf, add it to the active nodes and go to the first step, otherwise C must be partitioned.
3. Compute the fraction a of the area required for the smaller child of C and check which case applies based on a and P.
4. Enumerate all allowed cuts and choose the cut that minimizes Eq. (1).
5. Enqueue the two children in Q.

Notice that neither C nor its children are active during the cut enumeration phase.

5   Results and Application

In this section, we report on an experimental evaluation of the proposed techniques to minimize edge length and introduce several domain-specific extensions.

5.1   Evaluation of Edge Length

In order to determine the effect on the layout, we tested our approach on real-world datasets. The instances were derived from a publicly available pyruvate kinase high-throughput screening dataset[3], which has previously been used in [7] and consists of $51,415$ compounds. We generated 20 subsets by randomly selecting 200, 400, 600 and 800 compounds, respectively. For each subset we created clustered graphs according to the graph model described in Sect. 3 with varying densities by selecting suitable threshold parameters. We report the average weighted edge length of these instances drawn in the unit square. Figure 7 displays the results for different densities. It is clearly visible that the two presented approaches affect the edge length in a positive way. As expected, the effect is less when the density increases. Interestingly, the changes made to the fat polygon partitioning are significant even for higher densities, unlike the extension of the cluster hierarchy. The latter performs well on the sparse instances, while the result is slightly worse for the highest density in comparison to the edge-aware fat polygon partitioning.

The runtime[4] for the largest instance with $|V| = 800$ and $|E| = 6400$ is about 7 s for the cluster extension and 0.6 s for the edge-aware fat polygon partitioning.

Figure 8 shows an example which illustrates the effectiveness of the proposed techniques. Note that in Fig. 8(a) there are several long edges, some of which even cross the entire drawing area connecting nodes in the bottom left corner (cluster A) to nodes in the top right corner (cluster E). In such cases edges are bundled

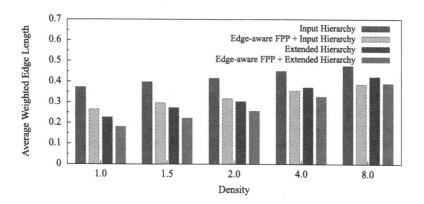

Fig. 7. Comparison of the average weighted edge length.

---

[3] Available from PubChem BioAssay, AID 361.
[4] Machine with Core i7 2.7 GHz and 8 GB RAM.

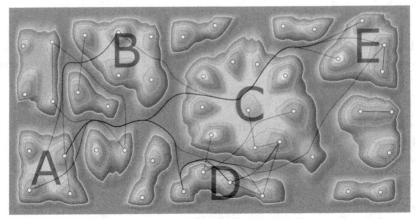

(a) Without improvements

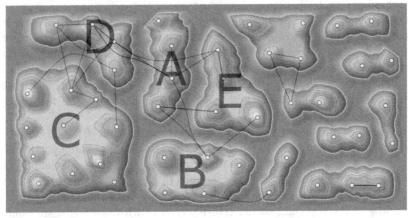

(b) Extended hierarchy and edge-aware partitioning

Fig. 8. Visual comparison of the layout generated by the original approach (a) and the proposed method (b). Letters indicate corresponding main clusters.

to avoid visual clutter. However, a downside of edge bundling is that individual edges become difficult to identify. In Fig. 8(b) the same instance is drawn using the proposed optimization techniques. Here, the layout leads to short edges and individual connections are easily recognizable. Since highly similar molecules are placed close to each other, this drawing is also clearly preferable from the application point of view.

5.2   Representation of Chemical Information

In this section we report on the application of our approach to a real-world dataset and describe several extensions we incorporated to meet requirements of the application area. To focus on relevant molecules we filtered the dataset used

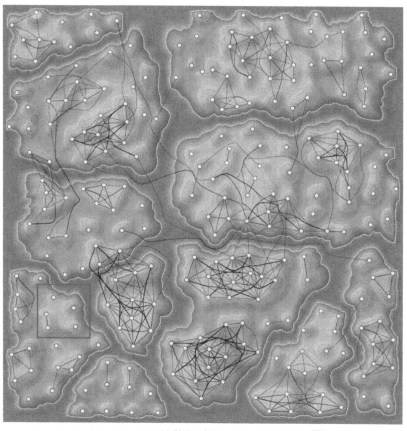

(a) Real-world instance

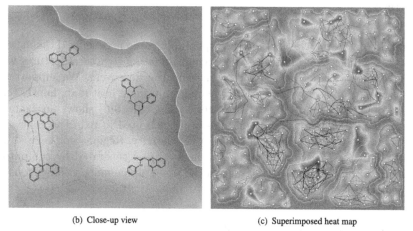

(b) Close-up view   (c) Superimposed heat map

Fig. 9. Visualization of the real-world instance consisting of 256 molecules (a) and the same map with property annotations (c). In (b) a close-up view of the region highlighted in red shows five molecules represented by structural formulae.

in Sect. 5.1 for active compounds with $AC_{50} \leq 10\,\mu M$ and decreasing activity direction, which yields a dataset with 432 compounds. From this subset we selected all molecules associated with scaffold tree branches containing at least 10 compounds. The threshold for the similarity graph was set to $t = 0.5$. While our approach also works smoothly with larger datasets, we decided to use this small focused dataset consisting of 256 compounds to provide screen shots.

The resulting topographic map is shown in Fig. 9(a). Since the water level is chosen such that each scaffold tree branch is represented by one island, this overview directly conveys to what extent branches are populated by compounds. With our approach the altitude represents the number of rings compounds have and whenever two molecules are located on the same hill, they share a common scaffold (according to the scaffold tree) whose number of rings is represented by the elevation level of the hill. While edges often connect molecules on the same islands, there are also edges connecting molecules placed on different islands (see, e.g., the central island on the left hand side and the small island southeast) indicating the presence of highly similar molecules in different branches of the scaffold tree. Placing these molecules near each other helps to generate continuous regions of highly similar molecules and is achieved by our heuristic approach. Furthermore, we support additional annotations to specifically foster the application in drug discovery.

Depiction of Structural Formulae. The most widely used representation of chemical compounds are 2D depictions of their structure. To allow a detailed investigation of structural relationships, we support displaying structural formulae. Figure 9(b) shows a close-up view of a region of an island. The shown molecules are placed on the same elevated plateau indicating their common two-ring scaffold. The two molecules on the left hand side even share a scaffold with three rings.

Mapping of Properties. While the topographic map is generated taking only structural similarity of molecules into account, relating structural features with certain properties is of utmost importance in drug discovery. We support the visualization of molecular properties by superimposing a heat map, faintly reminiscent of a temperature related weather map. Figure 9(c) shows an example where regions of highly active molecules are highlighted in red. The color gradient from red to green represents decreasing activity. Regions not colored are populated by less active molecules. The heat map is generated by computing a Delaunay triangulation and, similar to the topographic map, visualized using color encoded levels based on the property values.

6   Conclusions and Outlook

Organizing compound libraries by structural similarity in a way that allows for intuitive navigation for chemical tasks is challenging. We proposed a clustered graph model and adapted a technique to draw them as topographic maps. We have already received some first positive feedback from domain experts, and the representation as topographic map has been well accepted. However, a large-scale systematic evaluation of the method based on a wide range of datasets and different chemical workflows is out of the scope of this article, but an important future task.

The goal to place similar molecules near each other while respecting the cluster hierarchy leads to the graph drawing problem to minimize edge length in the known approach [1]. To achieve this goal we proposed a heuristic that exploits the degrees of freedom in the polygon partitioning procedure in order to avoid long edges. The effectiveness of the method has been demonstrated by an experimental evaluation using real-world instances.

Acknowledgements. We would like to thank Claude Ostermann and Philipp Thiel for their valuable feedback and for sharing their chemical knowledge.

References

1. Gronemann, M., Jünger, M.: Drawing clustered graphs as topographic maps. In: Didimo, W., Patrignani, M. (eds.) GD 2012. LNCS, vol. 7704, pp. 426–438. Springer, Heidelberg (2013)
2. Brown, N.: Chemoinformatics - an introduction for computer scientists. ACM Comput. Surv. **41**, 1–38 (2009)
3. Herhaus, C., Karch, O., Bremm, S., Rippmann, F.: MolWind - mapping molecule spaces to geospatial worlds. Chem. Cent. J. **3**, P32 (2009)
4. Klein, K., Kriege, N., Mutzel, P.: Scaffold hunter: facilitating drug discovery by visual analysis of chemical space. In: Csurka, G., Kraus, M., Laramee, R.S., Richard, P., Braz, J. (eds.) VISIGRAPP 2012. CCIS, vol. 359, pp. 176–192. Springer, Heidelberg (2013)
5. Lounkine, E., Wawer, M., Wassermann, A.M., Bajorath, J.: SARANEA: a freely available program to mine structure-activity and structure-selectivity relationship information in compound data sets. J. Chem. Inf. Model. **50**, 68–78 (2010)
6. Strobelt, H., Bertini, E., Braun, J., Deussen, O., Groth, U., Mayer, T.U., Merhof, D.: HiTSEE KNIME: a visualization tool for hit selection and analysis in high-throughput screening experiments for the KNIME platform. BMC Bioinform. **13**(suppl. 8), S4 (2012)
7. Wetzel, S., Klein, K., Renner, S., Rauh, D., Oprea, T.I., Mutzel, P., Waldmann, H.: Interactive exploration of chemical space with Scaffold Hunter. Nat. Chem. Biol. **5**, 581–583 (2009)
8. Irwin, J.J.: Staring off into chemical space. Nat. Chem. Biol. **5**, 536–537 (2009)
9. Wawer, M., Peltason, L., Weskamp, N., Teckentrup, A., Bajorath, J.: Structure-activity relationship anatomy by network-like similarity graphs and local structure-activity relationship indices. J. Med. Chem. **51**, 6075–6084 (2008)
10. Fruchterman, T.M.J., Reingold, E.M.: Graph drawing by force-directed placement. Softw. Pract. Exper. **21**, 1129–1164 (1991)
11. Schuffenhauer, A., Varin, T.: Rule-based classification of chemical structures by scaffold. Mol. Inform. **30**, 646–664 (2011)

12. Schuffenhauer, A., Ertl, P., Roggo, S., Wetzel, S., Koch, M.A., Waldmann, H.: The scaffold tree - visualization of the scaffold universe by hierarchical scaffold classification. J. Chem. Inf. Model. **47**, 47–58 (2007)

13. Guha, R.: The ups and downs of structure-activity landscapes. In: Bajorath, J. (ed.) Chemoinformatics and Computational Chemical Biology. Methods in Molecular Biology, vol. 672, pp. 101–117. Humana Press (2011)

14. Peltason, L., Iyer, P., Bajorath, J.: Rationalizing three-dimensional activity landscapes and the influence of molecular representations on landscape topology and the formation of activity cliffs. J. Chem. Inf. Model. **50**, 1021–1033 (2010)

15. Sugiyama, K., Misue, K.: Visualization of structural information: Automatic drawing of compound digraphs. IEEE Trans. SMC **21**, 876–892 (1991)

16. Huang, M.L., Eades, P.: A fully animated interactive system for clustering and navigating huge graphs. In: Whitesides, S.H. (ed.) GD 1998. LNCS, vol. 1547, pp. 374–383. Springer, Heidelberg (1999)

17. Gansner, E.R., Hu, Y., Kobourov, S.G., Volinsky, C.: Putting recommendations on the map: visualizing clusters and relations. In: Proceedings of the ACM Conference on Recommender Systems, pp. 345–348 (2009)

18. Gansner, E.R., Hu, Y., Kobourov, S.G.: GMap: Visualizing graphs and clusters as maps. In: Pacific Visualization Symposium (PacificVis), pp. 201–208. IEEE (2010)

19. Fabrikant, S.I., Montello, D.R., Mark, D.M.: The natural landscape metaphor in information visualization: The role of commonsense geomorphology. J. Am. Soc. Inf. Sci. Technol. **61**, 253–270 (2010)

20. Johnson, B., Shneiderman, B.: Tree-maps: a space-filling approach to the visualization of hierarchical information structures. In: Proceedings of the 2nd Conference on Visualization, pp. 284–291 (1991)

21. Schulz, H.J.: Treevis.net: A tree visualization reference. IEEE Comput. Graphics Appl. **31**, 11–15 (2011)

22. Maggiora, G.M., Shanmugasundaram, V.: Molecular similarity measures. Methods Mol. Biol. **672**, 39–100 (2011)

23. Steinbeck, C., Hoppe, C., Kuhn, S., Floris, M., Guha, R., Willighagen, E.L.: Recent developments of the chemistry development kit (CDK) - an open-source java library for chemo- and bioinformatics. Curr. Pharm. Des. **12**, 2111–2120 (2006)

24. Bon, R.S., Waldmann, H.: Bioactivity-guided navigation of chemical space. Acc. Chem. Res. **43**, 1103–1114 (2010)

25. Girvan, M., Newman, M.E.J.: Community structure in social and biological networks. Proc. Natl. Acad. of Sci. **99**, 7821–7826 (2002)

26. de Berg, M., Onak, K., Sidiropoulos, A.: Fat polygonal partitions with applications to visualization and embeddings. CoRR abs/1009.1866 (2010)

Computer Vision Theory
and Applications

Facial Landmarks Localization Estimation by Cascaded Boosted Regression

Louis Chevallier[1]([✉]), Jean-Ronan Vigouroux[1], Alix Goguey[1,2], and Alexey Ozerov[1]

[1] Technicolor, Cesson-Sévigné, France
{louis.chevallier,jean-ronan.vigouroux,alexey.ozerov}@technicolor.com
http://www.technicolor.com
[2] Ensimag, Saint-Martin d'Hères, France

Abstract. Accurate detection of facial landmarks is very important for many applications like face recognition or analysis. In this paper we describe an efficient detector of facial landmarks based on a cascade of boosted regressors of arbitrary number of levels. We define as many regressors as landmarks and we train them separately. We describe how the training is conducted for the series of regressors by supplying training samples centered on the predictions of the previous levels. We employ gradient boosted regression and evaluate three different kinds of weak elementary regressors, each one based on Haar features: non parametric regressors, simple linear regressors and gradient boosted trees. We discuss trade-offs between the number of levels and the number of weak regressors for optimal detection speed. Experiments performed on three datasets suggest that our approach is competitive compared to state-of-the art systems regarding precision, speed as well as stability of the prediction on video streams.

Keywords: Face landmarks localization · Boosted regression

1 Introduction

Facial landmarks detection is an important step in face analysis. Indeed, performance of face recognition or characterization systems [1] greatly depends on the accuracy of this module. Accordingly, much work has been devoted to the problem of accurate and robust localization of facial landmarks. The importance of the required accuracy level depends on the final application. For example, for applications requiring a fine analysis of faces like lips-reading, a very precise localization of landmarks is needed. Typically, such high precision performance is required on near frontal faces; non-frontal positions are less likely to be subjected to these analyzes. Moreover, when this analysis involves motion video, temporal tability at a given precision rate is useful.

Most of state of the art landmark detectors [2–6] are formulated as optimization or regression problems in some high-dimensional space (e.g., dozens of thousands of features). Thus, the precision of these approaches is limited by feature

© Springer-Verlag Berlin Heidelberg 2014
S. Battiato et al. (Eds.): VISIGRAPP 2013, CCIS 458, pp. 103–115, 2014.
DOI: 10.1007/978-3-662-44911-0_7

resolution. Using higher feature resolution (i.e., a feature space of much higher dimension), will in general not lead to improved precision due to limited training data, but instead entail over-fitting problems. We propose a new approach that allows increased feature resolution while keeping the feature space dimension unchanged, leading to higher landmark detection accuracy. This is achieved by using a cascade of boosted regressors, where the features used at each cascade level are extracted from a restricted area surrounding the corresponding landmark estimated by the previous levels of the cascade. We also discuss trade-offs between the number of cascades and the number of weak regressors for an optimal detection speed/precision ratio.

Our main contributions are:

1. A fast and accurate landmark position estimation algorithm, based on boosted weak regressors and Haar features extracted from the surrounding area, and a cascaded estimation scheme iterating on narrowing areas around each landmark.
2. A comprehensive assessment of the proposed estimator with regards to standard benchmarks, databases and state of the art landmark estimators, including an evaluation of its spatial stability. This is a new feature to our knowledge which is of great importance for the applications we are considering.
3. The flexibility of the proposed approach allows adjustment of the accuracy vs. computational load by simply varying the number of cascades.

The paper is organized as follows: related work and the proposed approach are described respectively in Sects. 2 and 3. Sections 4 and 5 are devoted to evaluation of performance and temporal stability. Some conclusions are drawn in Sect. 6.

2   Related Work

The problem of predicting the location of facial landmarks consists in estimating the vector $S = [x_1, y_1, ...x_i, y_i, x_N, y_N]^T$ comprising N pairs of 2D coordinates based on the appearance of the face. To minimize $||S - \hat{S}||_2$, where $\hat{S}$ denotes an estimate, most of the existing approaches use optimization techniques [3,7] where the prediction is obtained as a solution of some optimization criterion, or regression techniques [5,8] where a function directly produces the prediction. Our approach follows the second direction.

Regarding data modeling, most approaches rely on both shape modeling representing a priori knowledge about landmarks locations and texture modeling corresponding to values of pixels surrounding the landmarks in the image itself, i.e., the posterior observations.

Active Shape Models (ASM) [9] is a popular hybrid approach that uses a statistical model describing the shape (set of landmarks) of faces together with models of the appearance (texture) of landmarks. The prediction is iteratively updated to fit an example of the object in a new image. The shapes are constrained by the Point Distribution Model (PDM) [10] to vary only in ways seen in a training set of labeled examples. Active Appearance Models (AAM) [2] are an extension of the ASM approach. In AAM, a global appearance model is used to optimize the shape parameters. Among the weaknesses frequently pointed out for this approach are the need for images of sufficiently high resolution, and the sensitivity to initialization. Our regression approach using Haar features computed over the face area, can, on the contrary, work with small images–in theory as small as the grid used for defining the set of Haar features–in our case 17×17, yielding 13920 features. Moreover, as a regression approach there is no iterative search process to be initialized.

A straightforward approach to landmark detection is based on using independently trained detectors for each facial landmark. For instance the AdaBoost based detectors and its modifications have been frequently used [11]. If applied independently, the individual detectors often fail to provide a robust estimate of the landmark positions because of the weakness of local evidence. This can be solved by using a prior on the geometrical configuration of landmarks.

Valstar et al. [8] proposed transforming the detection problem into a regression problem. They define a regression algorithm, based on Support Vector Regression, BoRMan, to estimate the positions of the feature points from Haar features computed at locations with maximum a priori probabilities. A Belief Propagation algorithm is used to improve the estimation of the target points, using a Markov Random Field modeling the relative positions of the points. Series of estimations are performed, by adding Gaussian noise to the current target estimation, and retaining the median of the predictions as the final estimation.

In [1], a facial landmark detector is described which is based on the independent training of a local appearance model and the deformation cost of the Deformable Part Model–a structure which captures spatial relation between landmarks. The former relies on an AdaBoost classifier using Haar like features. The latter consists of a generative model using a mixture of Gaussian trees. In our evaluation section, we use an implementation of this system, which represents an optimization based solution to landmark detection.

Another approach based on regression for determining landmarks localization is described in [4]. In this work, explicit multiple regression is used to directly predict landmarks localization. All landmarks coordinates (the shape) are predicted simultaneously by the regressor. The design relies on a cascaded structure: a top level boosted regressor uses weak regressors that are themselves boosted. These primary regressors use weak fern regressors: regression trees with a fixed number of leaves. In contrast with this system, our system consists of as many regressors as landmarks to be predicted. While [4] described a hierarchical structure, the structure of our system is a true cascade of regressors similar to the classifiers cascade proposed by [11] in their face detector.

3   Landmark Position Estimation by Cascaded Boosted Regression

We propose to estimate the position of the landmarks by using boosting and cascading techniques that lead to a fast and accurate result. The prediction of

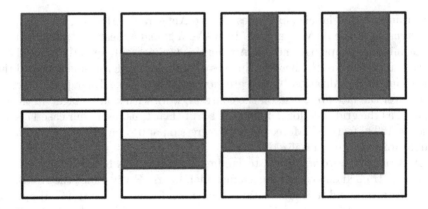

Fig. 1. The eight Haar features used.

the coordinates (x, y) of each landmark is done using a boosted regressor, based on Haar features computed on the detected face. A more precise localization is obtained using cascaded predictors. Each landmark is predicted independently of the others, instead of using a shape-based approach, as in [2,3,7,12], and for each landmark the x and y coordinates are predicted independently. Actually, even if each landmark is predicted independently, a shape constraint is implicitly taken into account by the first regressor since the features used by this regressor are extracted from the totality of the face area. A final test could be made to detect and correct grossly erroneous landmarks. We believe that this approach is robust to partial occlusion, since variability of one landmark does not perturb the position of the others.

In contrast to [8] we do not regress from different starting points, and take the median position as an estimator. We build a series of estimations of the positions of the landmarks, designed to converge to the sought landmark with high precision. At each step the regressor operates on increasingly narrow windows.

The image measurements used in our system are Haar features. This choice has the advantage that integral representations of images were readily available since they are typically required by the ubiquitous Viola and Jones face detector [11] we are using. The Haar features are defined based on a regular grid mapped on the shrinking image area to be analyzed. We set the size of the grid to 17×17 cells and we use eight Haar feature shapes (see Fig. 1). Scaling and translating them results in a total of 13,920 Haar features.

3.1   The First Level Regressor

The first level regressor is a boosted regressor, using the algorithms described in [13].

For the clarity of presentation we consider the case where we have only one coordinate of one landmark to predict for each image. Let G be a set of N images, and y_i be the coordinate of the landmark on image i; the coordinates

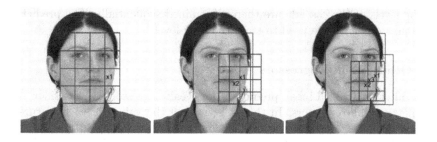

Fig. 2. Three successive steps of regression for the *Left Mouth Corner*.

are measured in pixels from the top-left corner of the detection box. We have at our disposal a set of measurements (Haar features) on each image, used by the *weak regressors* and we want to create the most efficient *strong predictor* of the landmark coordinate, from a linear combination of weak predictors. Here the weak predictors consist of least-square fitted linear predictors using Haar features computed on the detected face [11].

The strong predictor is built iteratively as follows. Let F be a matrix such that F_{ij} is the value of the feature F_j on image i. Let $Y^{(n)}$ be a vector containing the values to be predicted at iteration n. At first step $Y^{(1)}$ is initialized to the coordinates to predict: $Y^{(1)} = Y$, i.e., the vector of all the y_i. We predict $Y^{(n)}$ from F_j using a standard linear predictor: $\widehat{Y^{(n)}} = a_j F_j + b_j$. The prediction error is $E_j^{(n)} = Y^{(n)} - \widehat{Y^{(n)}} = Y^{(n)} - a_j F_j - b_j$, and the mean error is $e_j^{(n)} = \frac{1}{N}\|E_j^{(n)}\|$. The feature minimizing this error, F_{j_n} is selected as n^{th} weak predictor. The predictions are subtracted from the value to predict, with a given weight w_n set between 0.1 and 1, and the new value to predict is thus:

$$Y^{(n+1)} = Y^{(n)} - w_n \left(a_{j_n} F_{j_n} - b_{j_n}\right).$$

This is iterated p times and results in a Linear strong predictor of the form:

$$P^{(p)}(i) = \sum_{k=1}^{p} w_k \left(a_{j_k} F_{j_k} + b_{j_k}\right).$$

3.2 Next Regression Levels

The estimation of the position of a landmark can be improved by using the first estimation to re-center a window around the landmark of interest. This is the basis of our cascading process (see Fig. 2).

The prediction window on the first level is the window detected by the face detector. In the second and subsequent levels it is a smaller window centered on the landmark position predicted by the previous level. For the size of the successive windows we use a decreasing ratio applied to the original face bounding box : 1.0, 0.8, 0.6, 0.4 for the four first levels.

The levels of the cascade are therefore trained sequentially. The predictions of the previous level are used to train the next level.

3.3   Other Weak Regressors

As an alternative to Linear predictors for weak regressors we consider Non-Parametric weak-regressors. In this case, we bin the values of each feature F_j and we estimate y_i by the mean of Y for the images falling in the same bin as F_{ij}. The boosting algorithm is applied as previously on the residual. This is somewhat equivalent to ferns [14] using only one feature.

We have also experimented with gradient boosted trees (GBT) as weak regressors. Those regressors combining many Haar features were expected to provide more expressive power. Given the number of training image samples – ca. 5,000 – compared to the number of features (13,920), the challenge was to prevent over-fitting. Optimal parameters were found through cross validation and we set the number of trees and maximal depth so that the total number of leaves (Haar features) were the same as in the two previous methods. In this experiment we are using 30 Haar features per weak regressor. The training time per landmark with 4 cascades is 8 min on an octo-core 3 GHz Intel processor.

We compare the merit of these three boosted weak regressors by testing them on the BioID database [15] using four cascades (see Table 1).

Table 1. Percentage of tested images below error threshold on BioID dataset with three different weak regressors predicting the right of mouth corner.

Percent. of tested images	25 %	50 %	75 %
GBT	2.2 %	3.4 %	5.0 %
Linear	2.7 %	4.2 %	6.5 %
Non parametric	3.0 %	4.8 %	8.4 %

We notice that GBT clearly outperforms the two other approaches.

3.4   Parameters Settings

Our approach uses two important parameters for training: the number of weak regressors and the number of cascade levels. In order to find the optimal choice we have tested several trade-offs presented in Table 2. Of course the greater the computation effort, the lower the error, but for a given computation load (i.e., the total number of Haar features which is proportional to the product $numberOfWeaks \times numberOfLevels$), say 90, we can see that two levels and 45 weak regressors is the best choice.

Table 2. Error threshold at 50 % of tested images on BioID dataset with respect to weak regressors number and cascade levels.

# weaks # levels	15	30	45	60
1	0.057	0.044	0.041	0.038
2	0.047	0.039	**0.036**	0.034
3	0.042	0.037	0.034	0.032
4	0.040	0.037	0.033	0.032

4   Evaluation of Performance

4.1   Evaluation Methodology

The models trained as described in the previous section were applied on three publicly available data sets with a manually labeled ground truth:

1. BioID [15] is a very popular dataset containing 1,521 frontal face images with moderate variations in light condition and pose.
2. The PUT [16] dataset has 9,971 faces. The main source of face appearance variations comes from changes in poses and expressions.
3. The MUCT [17] dataset has 3,755 faces. It provides some diversity of lighting, age and ethnicity.

The set of landmarks provided by these databases are all different, so we retained a set of nine landmarks found on all three datasets and for which there is a good agreement regarding actual landmark positions: right and left corners of mouth, inner and outer corners of eyes, nose and nostrils (see Fig. 3).

Our evaluation methodology consists of training our system with half of the images of each dataset and testing it on the rest. We use an evaluation metrics proposed in [2] and defined as follows:

$$m_e = \frac{1}{ns} \sum_{i=1}^{n} d_i \tag{1}$$

where d_i is the Euclidean distance between the ground truth landmark and the predicted one and s is the inter-ocular distance. $n = 9$ is the number of landmarks.

4.2   Results

The systems against which we benchmarked our system are *FLandmark* [3], *Oxford* [1], *CLM* [7], *Kumar* [18], *Valstar* [8] and *Cao* [4]. The INRIA system is a variant of [1] trained with a different training dataset.

We compare our system with recent systems for which the implementation was available[1]. For some others, we use the figures reported in corresponding

---

[1] We did some tests with an implementation of [8], but it gave results very different to what was reported in the paper, thus we do not present them.

papers on the same datasets: In the curves on Figs. 4 and 5 the error curve corresponds to the average error and to the maximum error observed on all the landmarks.

The obtained precision on PUT and MUCT images (Fig. 5) are not as good as on BioID (Fig. 4) because the pose of faces varies much more (Table 3).

Table 3. Percentage of tested images below the average error threshold on BioID dataset.

Percent. of tested images	25 %	50 %	75 %
FLandmark	5.4 %	5.5 %	7.0 %
Our system	2 %	2.6 %	3.2 %
CLM	2.5 %	4.5 %	6.5 %
Valstar	1.5 %	3 %	5 %

5   Evaluation of Temporal Stability

5.1   Motivation

In practice, the accuracy of landmark prediction is limited by the modeling restriction, noise in the annotation and inherent ambiguity of the localization of facial landmark. 3 % seems to be a performance that will be difficult to outperform.

If a perfect accuracy cannot be reached, for some applications, it is important that the detector be as stable as possible. For example, the output of a landmark detector might be used as input of a *speaking/non-speaking* classifier, which

Fig. 3. The nine landmarks used for the experiments.

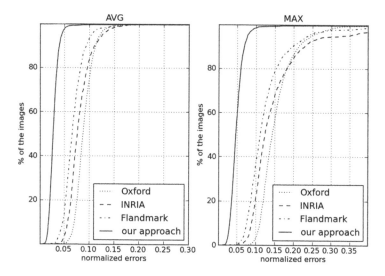

Fig. 4. Cumulative distribution of point to point error measure on the BioID test set.

decides whether or not a visible face is currently speaking. Thus, if the landmarks are used to analyze the face (evolution of the mouth height or width), the noise due to the predictor should be kept as small as possible. If the accuracy is not good because of a constant bias, the prediction can still be useful.

Temporal stability of landmarks prediction has rarely been evaluated in the literature. We approach the problem by analyzing the normalized error over time. We propose to evaluate stability using auto-correlation of the vectors of normalized errors corresponding to landmarks estimated for each frame of a video sequence. For this purpose, we have created our own ground truth of annotated frames. This dataset is comparable to the FGNET[2] database but we found that we required more precision in the position of the landmarks than available in the latter for our comparison.

The auto-correlation vector $ACor$ was calculated, using function Cor, as follows. x and y are two vectors and $N = Card(x) = Card(y)$, the cardinality of x and y. s is the shift index. Therefore, $ACor(x) = (Cor(x,x)_s)_{s \in [\![1-N;N-1]\!]}$.

$$Cor(x,y)_s = \begin{cases} Cor_A(x,y)_s & s \in A = [\![0, N-1]\!] \\ Cor_B(x,y)_s & s \in B = [\![1-N, -1]\!] \end{cases} \qquad (2)$$

where

$$Cor_A(x,y)_s = \frac{\sum_{i=0}^{N-s}(x_{i+s} - \bar{x}_s)(y_i - \bar{y}_s)}{\sqrt{\sum_{i=0}^{N}(x_i - \bar{x}_s)^2 \sum_{i=0}^{N}(y_i - \bar{y}_s)^2}} \qquad (3)$$

and

---

[2] http://www-prima.inrialpes.fr/FGnet/data/01-TalkingFace/talking_face.html

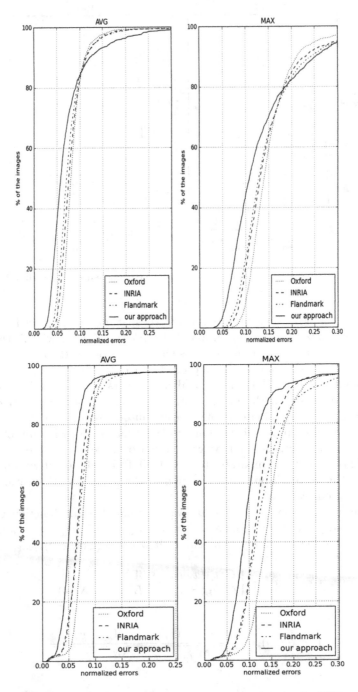

Fig. 5. Cumulative distribution of point to point error measure on the PUT and MUCT test set.

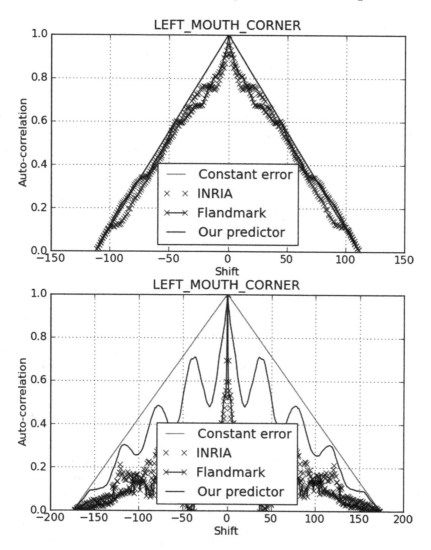

Fig. 6. Auto-correlation of the normalized error vector of a *non-speaking* video sequence (upper graph) and a *speaking* one (lower graph).

$$\bar{x}_s = \frac{1}{2*N-s} \sum_{i=0}^{N-s} x_{i+s}$$

$$\bar{y}_s = \frac{1}{2*N-s} \sum_{i=0}^{N-s} y_i$$

Similarly:

$$Cor_B(x,y)_s = Cor_A(y,x)_{-s} \tag{4}$$

5.2 Results

In the two graphs represented in Fig. 6, we plot the auto-correlation of a constant error vector (as a baseline) and the normalized errors vector computed by three different detectors. The more stable a detector is, the closer to the baseline the corresponding curves should be.

We present here the results for two types of video streams: one with a speaker (whose head and lips are moving) and another with a quiet listener (who remains still). In each case, we show the graph corresponding to the *left corner of mouth* landmark error. The results show that our system has a better stability compared to the others in both types of video streams. The curve oscillations observed in the lower graph of Fig. 6 are due to a repetitive movement of the speaker lips. In the upper graph, the described feature does not have a repetitive pattern. This behavior can be regarded as an illustration of the superiority of regression techniques over optimization based techniques.

6   Conclusions

We have presented a technique of cascaded regression for direct prediction of facial landmarks. The algorithm consists of predicting successive 2D locations of the landmarks in a coarse to fine manner using a series of cascaded predictors, conferring robustness to the approach. Indeed predicting landmarks independently results in high precision since failure to find the good location of one of the landmarks does not propagate to the others. The regressors at each level of the cascade are based on gradient boosting. Three kinds of weak regressors have been assessed: linear regressors, non-parametric regressors and regression trees. The gradient boosted trees have the best performance. This simple scheme has proved to be very efficient compared to other tested approaches in terms of location errors. This approach is also very fast: it takes 8 ms to compute the locations of 20 landmarks (not counting the computation of the integral image which is typically required for the detection of the face).

As possible extensions of the approach, we could consider applying a post-processing to the predicted landmarks by enforcing shape consistency [18]. An attractive capability of our model is to make it possible to trade precision against speed by traversing only a suitable number of levels of the cascade.

We believe that this generic approach could be applied to other problems involving regression where features derive from measurements from the signal e.g., to detection and localization of more generic objects using part based models.

Acknowledgements. This work was partially funded by the QUAERO project supported by OSEO and by the European integrated project AXES.

References

1. Everingham, M., Sivic, J., Zisserman, A.: Hello! my name is...Buffy – Automatic naming of characters in TV video. In: Proceedings of the British Machine Vision Conference, vol. 2 (2006)
2. Cootes, T.F., Edwards, G.J., Taylor, C.J.: Active appearance models. IEEE Trans. Pattern Anal. Mach. Intell. **23**, 681–685 (2001)
3. Uřičář, M., Franc, V., Hlaváč, V.: Detector of facial landmarks learned by the structured output svm. In: Proceedings of the 7th International Conference on Computer Vision Theory and Applications, VISAPP '12 (2012)
4. Cao, X., Wei, Y., Wen, F., Sun, J.: Face alignment by explicit shape regression - to appear. In: Proceedings of CVPR'12 (2012)
5. Dantone, M., Gall, J., Fanelli, G., Van Gool, L.: Real-time facial feature detection using conditional regression forests. In: Computer Vision and Pattern Recognition (CVPR) (2012)
6. Vukadinovic, D., Pantic, M.: Fully automatic facial feature point detection using gabor feature based boosted classifiers. In: Proceedings of IEEE International Conference Systems, Man and Cybernetics (SMC'05), Waikoloa, Hawaii, pp. 1692–1698, October 2005
7. Cristinacce, D., Cootes, T.: Automatic feature localisation with constrained local models. Pattern Recogn. **41**, 3054–3067 (2008)
8. Valstar, M., Martinez, B., Binefa, X., Pantic, M.: Facial point detection using boosted regression and graph models. In: Proceedings of IEEE International Conference Computer Vision and Pattern Recognition (CVPR'10), San Francisco, USA, pp. 2729–2736, June 2010
9. Cootes, T.F., Taylor, C.J., Cooper, D.H., Graham, J.: Active shape models - their training and application. Comput. Vis. Image Underst. **61**, 38–59 (1995)
10. Kass, M., Witkin, A., Terzopoulos, D.: Snakes: active contour models. Int. J. Comput. Vision **1**, 321–331 (1988)
11. Viola, P.A., Jones, M.J.: Rapid object detection using a boosted cascade of simple features. In: Computer Vision and Pattern Recognition (CVPR), pp. 511–518 (2001)
12. Lanitis, A., Taylor, C.J., Cootes, T.F.: Automatic interpretation and coding of face images using flexible models. IEEE Trans. Pattern Anal. Mach. Intell. **19**, 743–756 (1997)
13. Friedman, J.H.: Greedy function approximation: a gradient boosting machine. Ann. Stat. **29**, 1189–1232 (2001)
14. Dollár, P., Welinder, P., Perona, P.: Cascaded pose regression. In: Computer Vision and Pattern Recognition (CVPR), pp. 1078–1085 (2010)
15. Jesorsky, O., Kirchberg, K.J., Frischholz, R.W.: Robust face detection using the hausdorff distance. In: Bigun, J., Smeraldi, F. (eds.) AVBPA 2001. LNCS, vol. 2091, pp. 90–95. Springer, Heidelberg (2001)
16. Kasiński, A., Florek, A., Schmidt, A.: The PUT face database. Image Process. Commun. **13**, 59–64 (2008)
17. Milborrow, S., Morkel, J., Nicolls, F.: The MUCT landmarked face database. Pattern Recognition Association of South Africa (2010)
18. Belhumeur, P.N., Jacobs, D.W., Kriegman, D.J., Kumar, N.: Localizing parts of faces using a consensus of exemplars. In: The 24th IEEE Conference on Computer Vision and Pattern Recognition (CVPR), June 2011

A Video Retargeting Technique
for RGB-D Camera

Huei-Yung Lin[1]([✉]), Chin-Chen Chang[2], and Jhih-Yong Huang[1]

[1] Department of Electrical Engineering,
National Chung Cheng University, Chiayi 621, Taiwan
hylin@ccu.edu.tw, t901108@hotmail.com
[2] Department of Computer Science and Information Engineering,
National United University, Miaoli 360, Taiwan
ccchang@nuu.edu.tw

Abstract. This paper presents a content aware video retargeting technique with the help of an RGB-D camera based on the detection of saliency objects. The content aware image resizing algorithm requires some energy terms to separate the main contents and the background. In this work, we use the scene depth information, gradient information, visual saliency and saliency object to create an image on the visual focus of the energy map. The experimental results show that the proposed approach performs well in terms of the resized quality.

Keywords: Image retargeting · RGB-D Camera · Feature map · Depth map

1 Introduction

Numerous and varied devices for displaying multimedia contents exist, from CRTs to LCDs, and from plasma to LEDs. Display device has moved from the two-dimensional plane toward 3D TV. To meet various demands, changing display content has facilitated the development of a highly dynamic range of display devices. Regarding display screen size, two commonly used display specifications (aspect ratios) are 4:3 and 16:9. These display specifications are applied to displays as large as billboards and as small as mobile phone screens. Display devices, however, have only one screen aspect ratio. This aspect ratio causes upper and lower black bands to appear when multimedia contents are displayed on screens.

Apart from the two screen aspect ratios described above, nonstandard screen aspect ratios will be applied more extensively because of cellular phones, portable multimedia players and so on. In such cases, different image sizes are required to adapt to the display devices. Scaling and cropping are two standard methods for resizing images. Scaling resizes the image uniformly over an entire image. However, when the display screen is too small, the image loses some of its detail in adjusting to the limitations of the display screen. Cropping resizes the image by discarding boundary regions and preserving important regions. This method

© Springer-Verlag Berlin Heidelberg 2014
S. Battiato et al. (Eds.): VISIGRAPP 2013, CCIS 458, pp. 116–131, 2014.
DOI: 10.1007/978-3-662-44911-0_8

provides a close up of a particular image section, but prevents users from viewing the rest of the image.

Recently, several retargeting techniques [1–5] for resizing image based on image contents has been proposed. These methods require a certain understanding of image content and do not adjust the size of the image as a whole. Retargeting preserves important regions and discards less important regions, to achieve a target image size.

In this paper, a novel image retargeting approach for ranging cameras is proposed. The proposed approach first extracts three feature maps: depth map, saliency map, and gradient map. Then, the depth map and the saliency map are used to compute a map of saliency objects. After that, the proposed approach constructs an importance map which combines the four feature maps by the weighted sum. Based on the importance map, the important regions are preserved and less important regions are discarded. Finally, the proposed approach constructs the target image using the seam carving method [1] based on the importance map. The experimental results show that the proposed approach resizes image effectively.

2   Related Works

Avidan and Shamir [1] proposed a method for adjusting image size based on image content. They analyzed the relationships of energy distribution in the image and compared methods of image resizing. The proportion of residual energy after image resizing indicated the quality of the resizing. Moreover, they proposed a simple method for image processing using seams, which are 8-connected lines that vertically or horizontally cross images. By iteratively adding or removing seams, their approach can alter the size of images. However, because the content of images is often complex, how to determine the correct subject position according to image features is a goal for future research.

Kim et al. [3] used the adaptive scaling function, utilizing the importance map of the image to calculate the adaptive scaling function, which indicated the reduction level for each row of the original image. Kim et al. [4] used Fourier analysis for image resizing. After constructing the gradient map, they divided the image into strips of various lengths, and then used Fourier transform to determine the spectrum of each strip. The spectrums were then used as a low-pass filter to obtain an effect similar to smoothing. The level of horizontal reduction for each strip was then determined according to the influence of the filter.

Detecting visually salient areas is a part of object detection. The traditional method for determining the most conspicuous objects in an image is to set numerous parameters and then use the training approach to determine image regions that may correspond to the correct objects [6–9]. However, the human eye is capable of quickly locating common objects. Various approaches have proposed for simulating the functions of the human eye; for instance, Saliency ToolBox [10] and Saliency Residual (SR) [11]. The Saliency ToolBox requires a large amount of computation. By comparison, SR is the fastest algorithm. SR transforms the image into Fourier

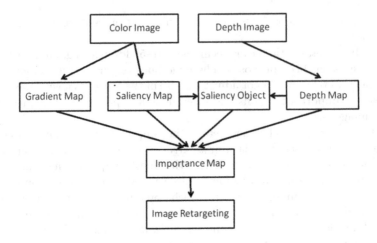

Fig. 1. The flowchart of the proposed approach.

space and determines the difference between the log spectrum and averaged spectrum of the image. The area, which shows the difference, is the potential area of visual saliency.

Hwang and Chien [2] used a neural network method to determine the subject of images. They also used face recognition techniques to ensure the human faces within images. For ratios that could not be compressed using the seam carving method, they used proportional ratio methods to compress the subject of images. Rubinstein et al. [12] proposed a method of improvement for the procedure of seam carving. This method utilized techniques of forward energy and backward energy to reduce discontinuity in images.

Wang et al. [13] proposed a method that simultaneously utilized techniques of stereo imaging and inpainting. This method had the capacity to remove image objects that caused occlusion, restoring original background image and depth information. They also presented a warping approach for resizing images and preserving visually features. The deformation of the image is based on an importance map that is computed using a combination of gradient and salience features.

Achanta et al. [14] proposed an approach for detecting salient regions by using only color and luminance features. Their approach is simple to implement and computationally efficient. It can clearly identify the main silhouettes. Also, this approach outputs saliency maps with well-defined boundaries of salient objects. Goferman et al. [15] proposed an approach which aims at detecting the salient regions that represent the scene. The goal is to either identify fixation points or detect the dominant object. They presented a detection algorithm which is based on four principles observed in the psychological literature. In image retargeting, using their saliency prevents distortions in the important regions.

3   The Proposed Approach

The flowchart of the proposed approach is shown in Fig. 1. First, the proposed approach extracts three feature maps, namely, a depth map, a saliency map, and a gradient map from an input color image and a depth image. Then, the depth map and the saliency map are used to compute a map of saliency objects. After that, the proposed approach integrates all the feature maps to an importance map by the weighted sum. Finally, the proposed approach constructs the target image using the seam carving method [1].

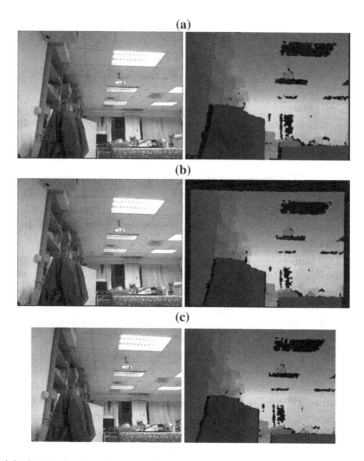

Fig. 2. (a) Original color image and corresponding depth image captured by the Kinect; (b) Original color image and adjusted depth image by an official Kinect SDK; (c) Cropped color image and cropped depth image.

Fig. 3. Original image (left), saliency map by [14] (middle), saliency map by [15] (right).

3.1 Important Map

The importance map E_{imp} is defined as

$$E_{imp} = \begin{cases} 1 & \text{if } E_o = 1 \\ \alpha_1 E_d + \alpha_2 E_s + \alpha_3 E_g & \text{if } E_o = 0 \end{cases}$$

where α_1, α_2, and α_3 are the weights for the depth map E_d, the saliency map E_s, and the gradient map E_g, respectively; E_o is the saliency object map.

Depth Map. The Kinect camera is used to extract depth information from an input color image. The camera uses a 3D scanner system called Light Coding using near-infrared light to illuminate the objects and determine the depth of the image. Figure 2(a) shows a color image and the corresponding depth image captured by the Kinect.

From Fig. 2(a), pixel positions of the color image and the corresponding pixel positions of the depth image are not consistent. This problem can be adjusted by an official Kinect SDK, as shown in Fig. 2(b). Hence, the pixel positions of the color image and the corresponding pixel positions of the depth image are consistent. However, the range covered by the depth image becomes smaller. Therefore, the original depth image of size 640×480 is cropped into a new depth image of size 585×430 by removing the surrounding area of the original depth image without the depth information and leaving the area with the usable depth, as shown in Fig. 2(c). Also, as shown in Fig. 2(c), black blocks in the cropped depth image are determined and the depth values of these blocks are set as 0. They cannot be measured by the Kinect due to strong lighting, reflected light, outdoor scenes, occlusions, and so on. Therefore, the depths of these regions are negligible since these areas in the whole depth image are very small.

Saliency Map. Visual saliency is an important factor for human visual system. Therefore, the proposed approach extracts a saliency map from the input color image. The computer vision [1,12] tries to imitate the possible visual perception of the human eye, from object detection, object classification to object recognition. Recently, Achanta et al. [14] proposed an approach for detecting salient regions by using only color and luminance features. Goferman et al. [15]

proposed an approach which aims at detecting the salient regions that represent the scene. Figure 3 shows the comparison of the two previous approaches [14, 15]. When a scene is complex, the approach of Achanta et al. cannot identify salient areas effectively and the method of Goferman et al. can obtain better results. Therefore, in the proposed approach, the technique of Goferman et al. is applied to complex environments for extracting a saliency map. The main concepts of the approach of Goferman et al. are described as the following.

For each pixel i, let p_i be a single patch of scale r centered at pixel i. Also, let $d_{color}(p_i, p_j)$ be the distance between patches p_i and p_j in CIE Lab color space, normalized to the range $[0, 1]$. If $d_{color}(p_i, p_j)$ is high for each pixel j, pixel i is salient. In the experiment, r is set as 7. Moreover, let $d_{position}(p_i, p_j)$ be the distance between the positions of patches p_i and p_j, which is normalized by the larger image dimension. A dissimilarity measure between a pair of patches is defined as

$$d(p_i, p_j) = \frac{d_{color}(p_i, p_j)}{1 + c \cdot d_{position}(p_i, p_j)},$$

where c is a parameter, In the experiment, c is set as 3. If $d(p_i, p_j)$ is high for each j, pixel i is salient.

In practice, for each patch p_i, there is no need to evaluate its dissimilarity to all other image patches. It only needs to consider the K most similar patches $\{q_k\}_{k=1}^{K}$ in the image. If $d(p_i, p_j)$ is high for each $k \in [1, K]$, pixel i is salient. For a patch p_i of scale r, candidate neighbors are defined as the patches in the image whose scales are $R_q = \{r, \frac{1}{2}r, \frac{1}{4}r\}$.

The saliency value of pixel i at scale r is defined as

$$s_i^r = 1 - \exp\{-\frac{1}{K} \sum_{k=1}^{K} d(p_i^r, q_k^{r_k})\},$$

where $r_k \in R_q$ and K is set as 64 in the experiment. Furthermore, each pixel is represented by the set of multi-scale patches centered at it. Thus, for pixel i, let $R = \{r_1, r_2, \ldots, r_M\}$ be the set of patch sizes. The saliency of pixel i is defined as the mean of its saliency at different scales

$$\bar{S}_i = \frac{1}{M} \sum_{r \in R} S_i^r.$$

If the saliency value of a pixel exceeds a certain threshold, the pixel is attended. In the experiment, the threshold is set as 0.8. Then, each pixel outside the attended areas is weighted according to its distance to the closest attended pixel. Let $d_{foci}(i)$ be the positional distance between pixel i and the closest focus of attention pixel, normalized to the range $[0, 1]$. The saliency of a pixel i is redefined as

$$\hat{S}_i = \bar{S}_i(1 - d_{foci}(i)).$$

Gradient Map. The human visual system is sensitive to edge information in an image. Therefore, the proposed approach extracts a gradient map from the input color image to represent edge information.

The Sobel calculation on original image I results in the gradient map. The operators of X direction and Y direction of Sobel are defined by

$$Sobel_x = \begin{bmatrix} -1 & 0 & 1 \\ -2 & 0 & 2 \\ -1 & 0 & 1 \end{bmatrix}$$

and

$$Sobel_y = \begin{bmatrix} 1 & 2 & 1 \\ 0 & 0 & 0 \\ -1 & -2 & -1 \end{bmatrix}$$

The horizontal operators, which are shown as a vertical line on the image, are used to find the horizontal gradient of the image, while the vertical operators, which are shown as a horizontal line, are used to find the vertical gradient of the image. The gradient map is defined as

$$E_{gradient} = \sqrt{(Sobel_x * I)^2 + (Sobel_y * I)^2}.$$

Using the Sobel operator can easily detect gradients of an image. However, the detected gradients do not fit the gradients perceived by the human eye. Therefore, a bilateral filter [4] is used to reduce borders that are not visually obvious and keep borders that vary largely. The bilateral filter is a nonlinear filter and smoothes noises effectively and keeps important edges. A Gaussian smoothing is applied to an image in both spatial domain and intensity domain at the same time. The definition of the Gaussian smoothing is as follows:

$$J_s = \frac{1}{k(s)} \sum_{p \in \Omega} f(p - s) \cdot g(I_p - I_s) \cdot I_p,$$

where J_s is the result after processing pixel s by the bilateral filter. I_p and I_s are intensities of pixels p and s, respectively. Ω is the whole image. f and g are Gaussian smoothing functions for the spatial and intensity domains, respectively. $k(s)$ is a function for normalization and its definition is given by

$$k(s) = \sum_{p \in Omega} f(p - s) \cdot g(I_p - I_s).$$

Therefore, in the proposed approach, the input color image is filtered by the bilateral filter. Then, the resulting image is filtered by Sobel filter to compute the final gradient map. The proposed approach can effectively remove gradients with small changes and reserve gradients with large variations in an image. The gradients are close to human visual perception. In the experiments, the spatial domain parameters are set as 10 and the intensity domain parameters are set as 100.

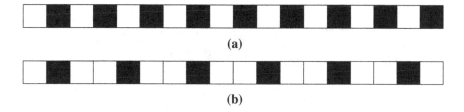

(a)

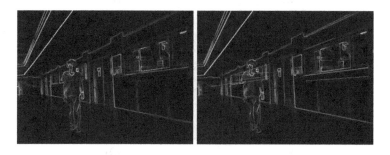

(b)

Fig. 4. (a) Periodic weights of (1,0); (b) Periodic weights of (1,0,1).

Fig. 5. (a) Original gradient map; (b) Improved gradient map.

Gradient information can keep the consistency of a line in the image. However, when the gradient in the image has a certain percentage of length, the use of seam carving can pass through the gradients. The gradients will be broken or distorted. Therefore, it is necessary to improve gradients for a certain length of gradients. The improved approach first uses Canny edge detection to detect edges in an image and then uses Hough transform to find a certain length of a line. After finding straight lines by Hough transform, weights are assigned to the straight lines. When the input image is reduced to less than half of the original image, the periodic weights $(1,0)$ are used for the weighting. When an input image is reduced to more than half of the original image, the periodic weights $(1,0,1)$ are used for the weighting. See Fig. 4 as an illustration.

After improving gradients, seam carving can cut gradients uniformly. Removing gradients with weight 0 can retain the gradients with weight 1. It can maintain the existing continuity and is less likely to remove the same area resulting in clear discontinuities. Figure 5 shows the original gradient map and the improved gradient map.

Salient Object. In an image, the human visual eye may have one or more attentions that have the greatest saliencies. Therefore, the most salient objects in the image are identified for retargeting. The salient objects are defined as the visually indistinguishable components. Since each pixel of a salient object is not necessarily a high value, image segmentation is used to find main partitions to obtain salient objects.

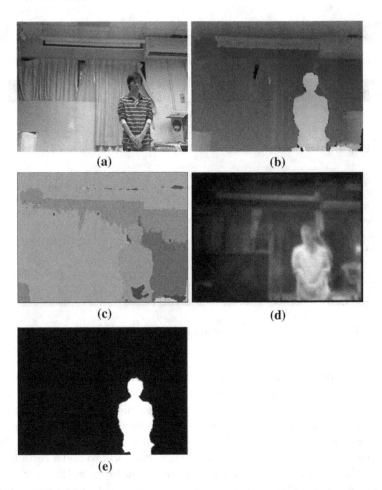

Fig. 6. (a) Original image; (b) Depth map; (c) Depth regions; (d) Saliency map; (e) Saliency object.

The depth image is segmented into depth regions. The depths are classified based on depth similarity of the scene. The image pyramids are used to split depth regions. The image pyramids down-sample the image into different scales. If pixels of i-th layer and farther pixels of the adjacent layer have similar colors, the father pixels and the pixels of i-th layer are merged into a connected component. In the same layer, if the adjacent components are too similar, they are merged into a larger connected component. After processing layer by layer, the depth image (Fig. 6(b)) of an input image (Fig. 6(a)) is segmented into depth regions (Fig. 6(c)).

The advantage of using the image pyramids to determine depth regions is that thresholds can be easily used for adjustment. Each component representing pixels in this region has similar depths. The depth regions segmented by the

Fig. 7. Original image, depth map, saliency map, gradient map, saliency object, and importance map from left to right and top to bottom, respectively.

image pyramids and the saliency map (Fig. 6(d)) are combined to obtain salient objects. If the salient value of a region is above a certain threshold, this region is defined as an indistinguishable object, as shown in Fig. 6(e). In the experiment, if the salient object is too small, it is ignored.

3.2 Image Retargeting

The proposed approach applied the method of Avidan and Shamir [1] for image retargeting. Let I be an $n \times m$ image and the vertical seam is defined as

$$s^x = \{s^x_i\}^n_{i=1} = \{(x(i), i)\}^n_{i=1}, \text{ s.t.} \forall i, |x(i) - x(i-1)| \leq 1,$$

where x is a mapping $x : [1, \cdots, n] \to [1, \cdots, m]$.

A vertical seam is an 8-connected line. Every row only contains a single pixel. Carving the seam interactively is considered an advantage because it can prevent horizontal displacement during the deleting process. Horizontal displacement appears if the number of deleted pixels in each row is different, resulting in changes in the shape of the object. Therefore, the route of the vertical seam is indicated as $I_s = \{I(S_i)\}^n_{i=1} = \{I(x(i), i)\}^n_{i=1}$. All pixels will move leftward or upward to fill the gaps of deleted pixels.

Horizontal reduction can be equated with deleting the vertical seam; the energy map is used to select seams. Given an energy function e, the energy $E(s) = E(I_s) = \sum^n_{i=1} e(I(s_i))$ of a seam is determined by the energy occupied by the positions of each pixel. When cutting a particular image horizontally, deleting the seam with the lowest energy $s^* = \min_s E(s) = \min_s \sum^n_{i=1} e(I(s_i))$ first is essential.

Dynamic programming can be employed to calculate s^*. The smallest accumulated energy M is calculated with every possible point on the seam (i, j) from

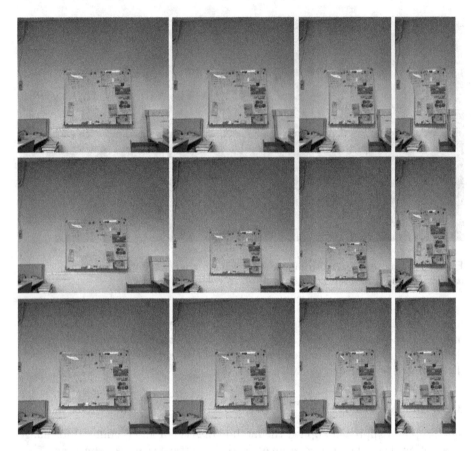

Fig. 8. Resized images by [1] (top); resized images by [5] (middle); resized images by the proposed approach (bottom).

the second to the last row of the image as

$$M(i, j) = e(i, j)$$
$$+ \min\{M(i - 1, j - 1), M(i, j - 1), M(i + 1, j - 1)\}$$

Then, the backtracking method was adopted to iteratively delete the seams with relatively weak energy by gradually searching upward for the seams with a minimum energy sum from the point with the weakest energy in the last row.

4   Results

Several experiments were conducted to evaluate the effectiveness of the proposed approach. The proposed algorithm was running on a laptop with a 2.40 GHz Core2 Quad CPU and 3.0 GB of memory. The camera used in this experiment was a Microsoft Kinect. If E_{object} is $0, a_1, a_2$, and a_3 are set as 0.1, 0.5, 0.4, respectively. If the Kinect cannot detect depths, a_1 and a_2 are both set as 0.5. The size of the original image is 585×430. Without loss of generality, a source image is resized in the horizontal direction only to make a target image. The extension for resizing in the vertical direction is straightforward. Therefore, the sizes of the resized images are 500×430, 400×430, 300×430, and 200×430. Moreover, the proposed approach was compared to the two previous approaches [1,5].

The first image is an indoor environment. There is no salient object and the depths are similar. The importance map is mainly dominated by saliency map and gradient map. Figure 7 shows the original image, the depth map, the saliency map, the gradient map, the salient object and the importance map, respectively, from left to right and top to bottom. Figure 8 shows the resized results of Avidan and Shamir (the top row), of Wang et al. (the middle row), and of the proposed approach (the bottom row). For the resized images of 500×430 and 400×430, the results of the proposed approach are similar to those of the two previous approaches. However, for the resized images of 300×430 and 200×430, the results show that the proposed approach performs better than the two previous approaches. There is a serious distortion in the results of Avidan and Shamir. The size of the whiteboard in the results of Wang et al. is over reduced.

The second image is an indoor environment. There is a salient object. Figure 9 shows the original image, the depth map, the saliency map, the gradient map, the salient object and the importance map, respectively, from left to right and top to bottom. Figure 10 shows the resized results of Avidan and Shamir (the top row), of Wang et al. (the middle row), and of the proposed approach (the bottom row). For the resized images of 500×430 and 400×430, the results of the proposed approach are similar to those of the two previous approaches. However, for the resized images of 300×430 and 200×430, the results of the proposed

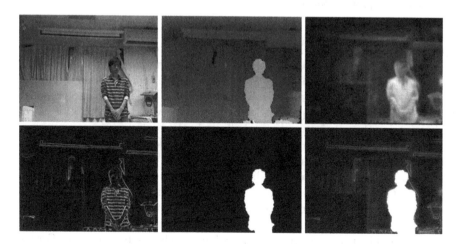

Fig. 9. Original image, depth map, saliency map, gradient map, saliency object, and importance map from left to right and top to bottom, respectively.

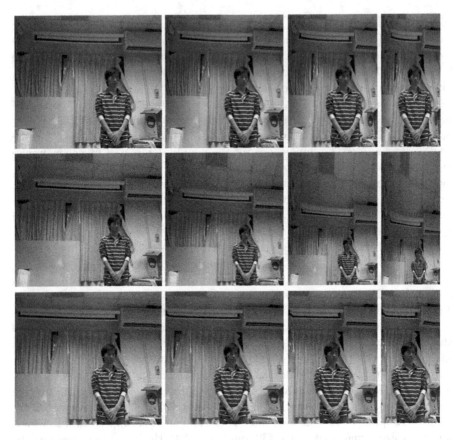

Fig. 10. Resized images by [1] (top); resized images by [5] (middle); resized images by the proposed approach (bottom).

approach are better than those of the previous approaches. The gradients are preserved well such that gradient density is too high in the results of Avidan and Shamir. There is distortion in the face of the person. For the results of Wang et al., the difference between the salient objects and non-salient background is too large. Conversely, the proposed approach preserves the salient object well and maintains the gradient and visual effects in the background.

The final image is an outdoor environment. The depth map is not complete. Since there are strong lighting and reflected light, the Kinect cannot detect the depths well and the detected salient object is not complete. Figure 11 shows the original image, the depth map, the saliency map, the gradient map, the salient object and the importance map, respectively, from left to right and top to bottom. Figure 12 shows the resized results of Avidan and Shamir (the top row), of Wang et al. (the middle row), and of the proposed approach (the bottom row). For the

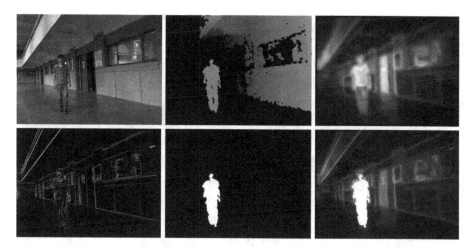

Fig. 11. Original image, depth map, saliency map, gradient map, saliency object, and importance map from left to right and top to bottom, respectively.

resized images of 500×430 and 400×430, the results of the proposed approach are similar to those of the two previous approaches. However, for the resized images of 300×430 and 200×430, the proposed approach performs better than the previous approaches. The gradients are preserved well such that gradient density is too high in the results of Avidan and Shamir. There is distortion in the body of the person. The visual effects in the background are not consistent. For the results of Wang et al., the difference between the salient objects and non-salient background is too large. The legs of the salient object and the floor have similar colors such that the energy is not enough and there is distortion in the salient object. For the proposed approach, although the salient object is not complete, it can still maintain the integrity of the salient object. However, since the environment is more complex, it is difficult to achieve good visual effects for the resized results of 200×430.

From the above results, the approach of Avidan and Shamir puts more emphasis on gradient information. For making large adjustments to an image, the gradients can still be preserved well. However, gradient density is too high and the visual effects are not consistent. For the approach of Wang et al., it has good continuity for image resizing. However, for making large adjustments to an image, the salient object is too small and non-salient areas are too large. In the proposed approach, making large adjustments to an image, it can preserve the salient object well. Also, it can keep the surrounding area of the salient object on the background and remove the gradients of background far away the salient object to avoid over-concentration of the gradients. It can protect the salient object from being destroyed by the seam carving algorithm.

Fig. 12. Resized images by [1] (top); resized images by [5] (middle); resized images by the proposed approach (bottom).

5   Conclusions

This paper has proposed a novel image retargeting method for ranging cameras. Several analyses were conducted, including the energy of depth, gradient, and visual saliency. Then, the depth map and the saliency map are used to determine a map of saliency objects. Moreover, different types of energy were integrated as importance maps for image retargeting. Unlike previous approaches, the proposed approach preserves the salient object well and maintains the gradient and visual effects in the background. Moreover, it protects the salient object from being destroyed by the seam carving algorithm. Therefore, a perfect protection of the subject was achieved.

References

1. Avidan, S., Shamir, A.: Seam carving for content-aware image resizing. ACM Trans. Graph. **26**(3), 10 (2007)
2. Hwang, D.S., Chien, S.Y.: Content-aware image resizing using perceptual seam carving with human attention model. In: 2008 IEEE International Conference on Multimedia and Expo, pp. 1029–1032, 23–26 April 2008
3. Kim, J., Kim, J., Kim, C.: Image and video retargeting using adaptive scaling function. In: Proceedings of 17th European Signal Processing Conference (2009)
4. Kim, J.S., Kim, J.H., Kim, C.S.: Adaptive image and video retargeting technique based on fourier analysis. In: IEEE Conference on Computer Vision and Pattern Recognition, CVPR 2009, pp. 1730–1737, June 2009
5. Wang, Y.S., Tai, C.L., Sorkine, O., Lee, T.Y.: Optimized scale-and-stretch for image resizing. In: SIGGRAPH Asia '08: ACM SIGGRAPH Asia 2008 papers, pp. 1–8. ACM, New York (2008)
6. Fergus, R., Perona, P., Zisserman, A.: Object class recognition by unsupervised scale-invariant learning. In: Proceedings of the 2003 IEEE Computer Society Conference on Computer Vision and Pattern Recognition, vol. 2, pp. II-264–II-271, June 2003
7. Itti, L., Koch, C., Niebur, E.: A model of saliency-based visual attention for rapid scene analysis. IEEE Trans. Pattern Anal. Mach. Intell. **20**(11), 1254–1259 (1998)
8. Gao, D., Vasconcelos, N.: Integrated learning of saliency, complex features, and object detectors from cluttered scenes. In: IEEE Computer Society Conference on Computer Vision and Pattern Recognition, CVPR 2005, vol. 2, pp. 282–287, June 2005
9. Liu, T., Sun, J., Zheng, N. N., Tang, X., Shum, H. Y.: Learning to detect a salient object. In: IEEE Conference on Computer Vision and Pattern Recognition, CVPR '07, pp. 1–8, June 2007
10. Walther, D., Koch, C.: Modeling attention to salient proto-objects. Neural Netw. **19**(9), 1395–1407 (2006). Brain and Attention
11. Hou, X., Zhang, L.: Saliency detection: A spectral residual approach. In: IEEE Conference on Computer Vision and Pattern Recognition, CVPR '07, pp. 1–8, June 2007
12. Rubinstein, M., Shamir, A., Avidan, S.: Improved seam carving for video retargeting. ACM Trans. Graph. **27**(3), 1–9 (2008)
13. Wang, L., Jin, H., Yang, R., Gong, M.: Stereoscopic inpainting: Joint color and depth completion from stereo images, pp. 1–8, June 2008
14. Achanta, R., Hemami, S., Estrada, F., Susstrunk, S.: Frequency-tuned salient region detection. In: IEEE Conference on Computer Vision and Pattern Recognition, CVPR 2009, pp. 1597–1604, June 2009
15. Goferman, S., Zelnik-Manor, L., Tal, A.: Context-aware saliency detection. In: 2010 IEEE Conference on Computer Vision and Pattern Recognition (CVPR), pp. 2376–2383, June 2010

A Robust Least Squares Solution
to the Calibrated Two-View Geometry
with Two Known Orientation Angles

Gaku Nakano[✉] and Jun Takada

Information and Media Processing Laboratories, NEC Corporation,
1753 Shimonumabe, Nakahara-ku, Kawasaki, Kanagawa, Japan
g-nakano@cq.jp.nec.com, j-takada@bc.jp.nec.com

Abstract. This paper proposes a robust least squares solution to the calibrated two-view geometry with two known orientation angles. Using the knowledge reduces the degrees of freedom (DoF) from five to three: one from a remaining angle and two from a translation vector. This paper determines that the three parameters are obtained by solving a minimization problem of the smallest eigenvalue containing the unknown angle. The proposed solution minimizes a new simple cost function based on the matrix determinant in order to avoid the complicated eigenvalue computation. The estimated parameters are optimal since the cost function is minimized under three DoFs. Experimental results of synthetic data show that the robustness of the proposed solution is up to $1.5°$ angle noise, which is approximately three times that of a conventional solution. Moreover, 60 point correspondences, fewer than half those in conventional solutions, are sufficient to reach the performance boundary.

Keywords: Two-view geometry · Relative pose problem · Essential matrix · Structure from motion · Two known orientation angles

1 Introduction

The calibrated two-view geometry is an estimation problem of the relative pose between two cameras capturing the same scene from different positions. It is the most basic theory for an image based 3D reconstruction. "Calibrated" means that the intrinsic camera parameters, e.g., the focal length, are assumed to be known.

The relative pose is generally expressed by five parameters, i.e., three orientation angles and a 3D translation vector up to scale. The absolute scale factor cannot be estimated without any prior knowledge about the scene. One point correspondence in the two images gives one constraint between the correspondence and the relative pose. Therefore, the calibrated two-view geometry is solved by at least five point correspondences. Many solutions based on point correspondences have been proposed, which are called the 5-point [1–7], 6-point [8], 7-point [9] and 8-point [9] algorithms.

© Springer-Verlag Berlin Heidelberg 2014
S. Battiato et al. (Eds.): VISIGRAPP 2013, CCIS 458, pp. 132–145, 2014.
DOI: 10.1007/978-3-662-44911-0_9

Meanwhile, a restricted relative pose problem has been raised in which two orientation angles are known. Two orientation angles are obtained by an internal measurement unit (IMU) sensor or a vanishing point. Using the known angles brings two great benefits. The one is that an angle measured by high accurate sensors is more reliable than that obtained by the point correspondence based algorithms. The other is that the relative pose problem becomes simpler since the total degrees of freedom (DoF) is reduced from five to three. Therefore, the relative pose problem is solved by at least three point correspondences. This reduces the computational cost of the pose estimation and also reduces the number of iterations of RANSAC [10].

Actual IMU sensors in many consumer products do not have the high accuracy needed in those solutions due to noise caused by camera shake and temperature change. Therefore, pragmatic solutions to the restricted pose problem must provide robustness to not only image noise but also sensor noise.

Although some solutions are proposed for using two known orientation angles, they are neither robust nor able to estimate the optimal pose. Kalantari et al. proposed a solution to the 3-point minimal case [11]. They formulate the problem as a system of multivariate polynomial equations and solve it by using a Gröbner basis method. Since the Gröbner basis method for that formulation requires large matrix decompositions, Kalantari et al.'s solution is difficult to extend to the least squares case in which the degree of polynomial equations becomes higher and the size of matrices becomes much larger. Fraundorfer et al. proposed three kind of solutions [12]. One is for the minimal case, and the others are for the least squares case of four and more than five point correspondences, respectively. Fraundorfer et al. show that the minimal solution is efficient for a RANSAC scheme. However, the two least squares solutions are neither optimal nor robust to noise because they do not exactly satisfy the nonlinear constraints that express three DoFs.

This paper proposes a robust least squares solution to the calibrated two-view geometry with two known orientation angles. The problem is formulated as a minimization problem of the smallest eigenvalue of a 3×3 matrix containing the unknown angle. The proposed solution minimizes a new simple cost function based on the matrix determinant in order to avoid the complicated eigenvalue computation. The unknown angle and translation vector are obtained as the root of an eighth degree univariate polynomial and the eigenvector corresponding to the smallest eigenvalue, respectively. Since the cost function is minimized under three DoFs, the proposed solution is optimal and robust to noisy data.

2   Problem Statement

This section describes the calibrated two-view geometry with two known orientation angles. Figure 1 shows an example such that the two orientation angles are obtained by the gravity direction g.

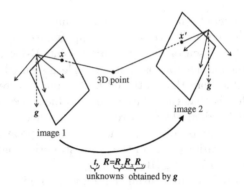

Fig. 1. Calibrated two-view geometry with two known orientation angles.

Let x and x' be point correspondences represented by 3D homogeneous coordinates in images 1 and 2, respectively. Then, the calibrated two-view geometry is written in the form

$$x'^{T}[t]_\times R_z R_y R_x x = 0. \tag{1}$$

where $t = [t_x, t_y, t_z]^T$ denotes a 3D translation vector up to scale, $[\ ]_\times$ denotes a 3×3 skew symmetric matrix representation of the vector cross product, and R_x, R_y, and R_z are 3×3 rotation matrices around x, y, and z-axis, respectively. Equation (1) has five DoFs (two from t and three from R_x, R_y and R_z.)

Let ϕ, ψ, and θ be the orientation angles around x, y, and z-axis, respectively. R_x, R_y, and R_z are expressed as

$$R_x = \begin{bmatrix} 1 & 0 & 0 \\ 0 & \cos\phi & \sin\phi \\ 0 & -\sin\phi & \cos\phi \end{bmatrix}, \tag{2}$$

$$R_y = \begin{bmatrix} \cos\psi & 0 & \sin\psi \\ 0 & 1 & 0 \\ -\sin\psi & 0 & \cos\psi \end{bmatrix}, \tag{3}$$

$$R_z = \begin{bmatrix} \cos\theta & \sin\theta & 0 \\ -\sin\theta & \cos\theta & 0 \\ 0 & 0 & 1 \end{bmatrix}. \tag{4}$$

If an IMU sensor is embedded in the cameras or if a vanishing point is detected in the images, the two orientation angles around x- and y-axis, i.e., ϕ and ψ, are known. Since R_x and R_y are given by (2) and (3), $R_y R_x x$ can be simply expressed by x. Then, we have

$$x'^{T}[t]_\times R_z x = 0. \tag{5}$$

Equation (5) represents the relative pose problem with two known orientation angles. The total DoF of (5) is reduced to $5 - 2 = 3$.

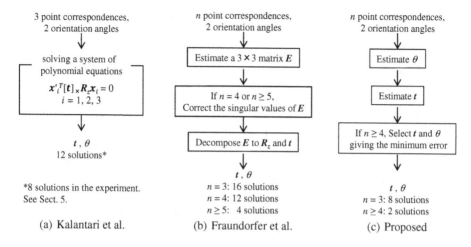

Fig. 2. Outlines of the conventional and proposed solutions.

Replacing $[t]_\times R_z$ by a 3×3 matrix E, (5) can be written in the linear form

$$x'^T E x = 0. \tag{6}$$

Here, $E_{1,1} = E_{2,2}$, $E_{1,2} = -E_{2,1}$ and $E_{3,3} = 0$. $E_{i,j}$ is the element of E at the i–th row and the j–th column.

E is called the essential matrix if and only if two of its singular values are nonzero and equal, and the third one is zero [13]. These constraints are expressed by

$$\det(E) = 0, \tag{7}$$

$$EE^T E - \frac{1}{2}\text{trace}(EE^T)E = 0_{3\times3}. \tag{8}$$

E has six parameters. However, E has only three DoFs due to the scale ambiguity and the above constraints [12].

Solving a nonlinear equation (5) and solving a linear equation (6) with the nonlinear constraints ((7) and (8)) are identical.

3   Previous Work

This section briefly describes the conventional solutions and points out their drawbacks. Their algorithm outlines are shown in Fig. 2(a, b).

3.1   Kalantari et al.'s Solution [11]

Kalantari et al. proposed an algorithm to obtain all unknowns in (5) by solving a system of multivariate polynomial equations.

First, the Weierstrass substitution is used to express $\cos\theta$ and $\sin\theta$ without the trigonometric functions: $\cos\theta = \frac{1-p^2}{1+p^2}$ and $\sin\theta = \frac{2p}{1+p^2}$, where $p = \tan\frac{\theta}{2}$. By substituting three point correspondences into (5) and by adding a new scale constraint $\|t\| = 1$, there are four polynomial equations in four unknowns $\{t_x, t_y, t_z, p\}$ of degree three. Kalantari et al. adopt a Gröbner basis method to solve the system of polynomial equations. The solutions are obtained by Gauss-Jordan elimination of 65×77 Macaulay matrix and eigenvalue decomposition of 12×12 Action matrix. Finally, at most 12 solutions are given from the eigenvectors.

Kalantari et al.'s 3-point algorithm is difficult to extend to the least squares case in which the degree of polynomial equations becomes higher and the size of matrices becomes a few hundred dimensions.

In the experiments in this paper, the size of the decomposed matrices and the number of the solutions are not same as those in Kalantari et al.'s original implementation. The details are described in Sect. 5.2.

3.2   Fraundorfer et al.'s Solution [12]

Fraundorfer et al. estimated the essential matrix in (6) instead of $\{t_x, t_y, t_z, p\}$. The most important contribution is to propose solutions to the least squares case.

Fraundorfer et al. proposed three algorithms for the cases of three, four and more than five point correspondences. The basic idea is very similar to the point correspondence based algorithms, i.e., Nistér's 5-point [3], Hartley's 7-point [9] and Hartley's 8-point [9] algorithm.

From a set of n point correspondences, (6) can be equivalently written as

$$M\,\mathrm{vec}(E) = 0_{n\times 1}, \tag{9}$$

where $M = \begin{bmatrix} x_1 \otimes x_1' & \cdots & x_n \otimes x_n' \end{bmatrix}^T$, $\mathrm{vec}(\ )$ denotes the vectorization of a matrix and $\otimes$ denotes the Kronecker product.

The solution of (9) is obtained by

$$E = \sum_{i=1}^{6-n} a_i V_i, \tag{10}$$

where V_i is the matrix corresponding to the generators of the right nullspace of the coefficient matrix M, and a_i is an unknown coefficient.

Estimating E is equivalent to calculate a_i. One of a_i can be set to one to reduce the number of unknowns due to the scale ambiguity of E. In the 3-point case, (7) and (8) are used to solve two unknowns. Similarly, (7) is used to solve one unknown in the 4-point case. For more than five point correspondences, the solution is obtained by taking the eigenvector corresponding to the smallest eigenvalue of $M^T M$.

An essential matrix can be decomposed to two R_zs and $\pm t$ [9,14]. Fraundorfer et al.'s 3-point, 4-point, and 5-point algorithms estimate at most four, three and one essential matrices, respectively. Therefore, they give at most 16, 12, and four solutions.

Fraundorfer et al.'s 3-point algorithm satisfies all the constraints. However, the 4-point algorithm considers only one constraint, and the 5-point algorithm ignores all constraints. For this reason, an estimated E of the 4-point and 5-point algorithms may not be an essential matrix. To correct the estimated E to an essential matrix, constraints are enforced by replacing the singular values of E so that two are nonzero and equal, and the third one is zero. The enforcement does not guarantee to optimize θ and t that minimize (6), but optimizes the minimum change of the Frobenius norm. The 4-point and the 5-point algorithm do not minimize the residual (6) under three DoFs. Therefore, they are not optimal solutions.

4   Proposed Solution

This section first describes the basic idea of the proposed solution in the minimal case, and then, explains how to extend the idea to the least squares case. The algorithm outline is shown in Fig. 2(c).

4.1   3-Point Algorithm for the Minimal Case

Equation (5) can be equivalently written as

$$v^T t = 0, \tag{11}$$

where $v = [x']_\times^T R_z x$.

Given three point correspondences, we have

$$At = 0_{3\times 1}, \tag{12}$$

where $A = [v_1, v_2, v_3]^T$ is a 3×3 matrix containing the unknown θ.

Since t must not be the trivial solution $t = 0_{3\times 1}$, (12) shows that A is singular and t is the nullspace of A. Consequently, θ is the solution of $\det(A) = 0$.

In the proposed 3-point algorithm, $\cos\theta$ and $\sin\theta$ are replaced by new unknowns c and s, respectively, instead of using the Weierstrass substitution. The reason is that the Weierstrass substitution changes the range of values from $-\pi \le \theta \le +\pi$ to $-\infty < p < +\infty$. This may cause computational instability. Furthermore, a symbolic fractional calculation complicates polynomial equations in the least squares case.

The unknowns c and s are obtained by solving the following system of polynomial equations:

$$\begin{cases} f_1(c, s) = \det(A) = 0, \\ g(c, s) = c^2 + s^2 - 1 = 0. \end{cases} \tag{13}$$

Equation (13) can be solved by the resultant based method, which is also known as the hidden variable method [15]. Let f_1 and g be polynomial equations of s and c be regarded as a constant, and the resultant $\mathrm{Res}(f_1, g, c) = 0$ is a fourth degree univariate polynomial in c. We obtain at most four solutions as the real roots of $\mathrm{Res}(f_1, g, c) = 0$.

As a result, θ is obtained by

$$\theta = \mathrm{atan2}(s, c). \tag{14}$$

Subsisting estimated θ into (12), t is obtained by the cross product of two arbitrary rows of A. The largest of these three cross products should be chosen for numerical stability [14].

If $v_i \times v_j$ is the largest, we obtain t up to scale,

$$t = \pm \frac{v_i \times v_j}{\|v_i \times v_j\|}. \tag{15}$$

The proposed 3-point algorithm gives at most eight possible combinations of four θs and $\pm t$.

4.2 4-Point Algorithm for the Least Squares Case

This section describes how to extend the proposed 3-point algorithm to the least squares case.

Given more than four point correspondences, the pose estimation problem is expressed by an optimization problem:

$$\underset{t, \theta}{\text{minimize}} \ \|Bt\|^2 \tag{16}$$

$$\text{subject to} \ \|t\| = 1$$

where $B = [v_1, \cdots, v_n]^T$ is an $n \times 3$ matrix containing the unknown θ, and $\|t\| = 1$ is a constraint to avoid the trivial solution $t = 0_{3 \times 1}$.

As known in Hartley's 8-point algorithm [9], the optimal t is the eigenvector corresponding to the smallest eigenvalue of $B^T B$, and the minimum error in the cost function $\|Bt\|^2$ is equal to the smallest eigenvalue of $B^T B$. The optimization problem (16) is essentially identical to the eigenvalue problem. However, the smallest eigenvalue of $B^T B$ represented by θ and imaginary numbers is difficult to compute directly.

To avoid the eigenvalue computation, this paper proposes a new cost function, $\det(B^T B)$. The determinant of a square matrix is equal to the product of all it's eigenvalues, and $B^T B$ is positive-semidefinite. Therefore, $\|Bt\|^2$ is expected to be minimized if $\det(B^T B)$ is minimized. The proposed 4-point algorithm minimizes $\det(B^T B)$ instead of $\|Bt\|^2$.

Similar to the proposed 3-point algorithm, θ is obtained by solving the following polynomial system of equations:

$$\begin{cases} f_2(c, s) = \dfrac{d}{d\theta} \det(B^T B) \Big|_{\substack{\cos \theta = c, \\ \sin \theta = s}} = 0, \\ g(c, s) = c^2 + s^2 - 1 = 0. \end{cases} \tag{17}$$

Here, $\frac{d}{d\theta}\det(\boldsymbol{B}^T\boldsymbol{B})\big|_{\substack{\cos\theta=c \\ \sin\theta=s}}$, denotes that $\cos\theta$ and $\sin\theta$ in $\frac{d}{d\theta}\det(\boldsymbol{B}^T\boldsymbol{B})$ are replaced by c and s, respectively.

The resultant $\text{Res}(f_2, g, c) = 0$ is an eighth degree univariate polynomial in c. We select the optimal θ from the real roots so that it minimizes $\det(\boldsymbol{B}^T\boldsymbol{B})$ or the smallest eigenvalue of $\boldsymbol{B}^T\boldsymbol{B}$.

Finally, we obtain the optimal $\boldsymbol{t}$ by taking the eigenvector corresponding to the smallest eigenvalue of $\boldsymbol{B}^T\boldsymbol{B}$. The proposed 4-point algorithm gives at most two possible combinations of one θ and $\pm\boldsymbol{t}$.

Moreover, the proposed 4-point algorithm includes the solutions of the proposed 3-point algorithm. For this reason, the proposed 4-point algorithm is a true extension of the 3-point algorithm. The proof is described in Appendix.

5 Experiments

This section evaluates the performance of the proposed solutions on synthetic data. The proposed solutions were compared with Kalantari et al.'s and Fraundorfer et al.'s solutions as well as Nistér's 5-point and Hartley's 8-point algorithms, which are standard methods for using only point correspondences. All program codes were written in MATLAB 2012b and implemented by the authors of this paper except for Nistér's 5-point algorithm[1]. Kukelova's automatic generator of Gröbner basis solvers [16][2] was used to implement the conventional 3-point algorithms. Kalantari et al.'s 3-point algorithm in the experiments computed 58×66 Macaulay matrix and 8×8 Action matrix due to the difference in the definition of the unknown orientation angle[3]. The simulations were performed on a windows 7 SP1 with a Core i7-3770 processor.

5.1 Synthetic Data

The robustness of the proposed solutions was evaluated under various image and angle noises on synthetic data.

3D points were generated randomly similar to Fraundorfer et al. [12] so that the 3D points have a depth of 50 % of the distance of the first camera to the scene. In the work of Fraundorfer et al. [12], two camera configurations are performed, i.e., sideway and forward motion with random rotation. To simulate a more realistic environment, random motion with random rotation was performed in these experiments. The baseline between the two cameras was 10 % of the distance to the scene.

Gaussian noise was added to two known orientation angles and the image points, which are projections of the 3D points onto the cameras. For an image noise test, the standard deviation of Gaussian noise was changed $0 \leq \sigma_{image} \leq 3$

---

[1] http://www.vis.uky.edu/~stewe/FIVEPOINT/

[2] http://cmp.felk.cvut.cz/minimal/automatic_generator.php

[3] The original derivation of Kalantari et al. [16] assumes that the unknown orientation angle is around y-axis, not z-axis as in this paper.

pixel for the image points and fixed $\sigma_{angle} = 0.5°$ for the angles. Similarly, for an angle noise test, the standard deviation of Gaussian noise was changed $0° \leq \sigma_{angle} \leq 3°$ for the angles and fixed $\sigma_{image} = 0.5$ pixel for the point correspondences.

Kalantari et al. and Fraundorfer et al. assume that the error in the two orientation angles measured by a low cost sensor is from 0.5° to at most 1.0°. However, information of the accuracy of almost all low cost sensors is not published. Some may have noise larger than 1.0°. Therefore, the error was assumed to be at most 3.0° in the experiments.

The estimation errors in θ and t were evaluated as follows:

$$Error(\theta_{est}, \theta_{true}) = \text{abs}(\theta_{est} - \theta_{true}), \tag{18}$$

$$Error(t_{est}, t_{true}) = \cos^{-1}\left(\frac{t_{est}^T t_{true}}{\|t_{est}\| \|t_{true}\|}\right), \tag{19}$$

where the subscript est and $true$ denote the estimated and the ground truth value, respectively. If an algorithm found multiple solutions, the one that had the minimum error was selected. The root mean square (RMS) errors in degrees are plotted over in 500 independent trials for each noise level in the result figures.

5.2 Estimation Error for the Minimal Case

The robustness of the proposed 3-point algorithm was evaluated in the minimal case and compared with the two conventional 3-point algorithms and Nistér's 5-point algorithm.

Figures 3 and 4 indicate that all the 3-point algorithms have almost the same performance. There is no difference between the DoFs of each algorithm. Thus, they solve the mathematically identical problems and estimate almost the same values. Nistér's algorithm is not influenced by the angle noise in Fig. 4 because it uses only point correspondences.

Nistér's algorithm is slightly better for estimating the rotation than the other methods. The difference is only approximately 1.0°. On the other hand, the 3-point algorithms estimate translation vectors much better than Nistér's algorithm. Hence, the 3-point algorithms are better to use if the two angles are known.

5.3 Estimation Error for the Least Squares Case

The robustness of the proposed 4-point algorithm was evaluated in the least squares case and compared with Fraundorfer et al.'s 5-point algorithm and Hartley's 8-point algorithm. The number of point correspondences was 100 in this experiment.

Figure 5 shows that the proposed algorithm is more stable than the others if the image noise is raised. From 0.4 to 1.0 pixel noises, the estimation errors in the algorithms of Fraundorfer et al. and Hartley increase considerably. There is

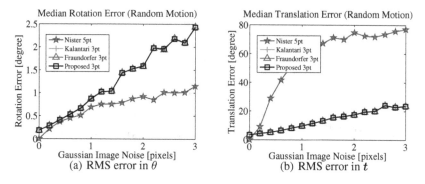

Fig. 3. Results of the minimal case with variable image noise ($0 \leq \sigma_{image} \leq 3$ pixel) and fixed angle noise ($\sigma_{angle} = 0.5°$).

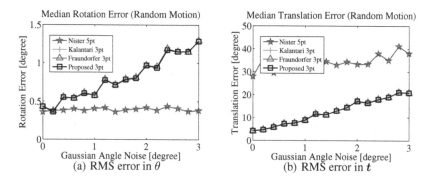

Fig. 4. Results of the minimal case with fixed image noise ($\sigma_{image} = 0.5$ pixel) and variable angle noise ($0° \leq \sigma_{angle} \leq 3°$).

no significant difference between them in a high level image noise. However, the proposed algorithm is robust in such cases.

Figure 6 shows that the proposed algorithm is more robust than that of Fraundorfer et al. in a practical scene. Their algorithm is much more sensitive to the angle noise and less accurate than Hartley's algorithm, which is not influenced by the angle noise, similarly to Nistér's algorithm. Fraundorfer et al.'s algorithm is effective for only less than 0.4° angle noise. On the other hand, the proposed algorithm is robust against to the angle noise up to 1.5°. This is 3 times as much as Fraundorfer et al.'s algorithm. Additionally, the estimation errors in the proposed algorithm rise gradually.

5.4   Estimation Error for the Number of Point Correspondences

The influence of changing the number of point correspondences was evaluated in the least squares case. The image and angle noise were fixed $\sigma_{image} = 0.5$ pixel

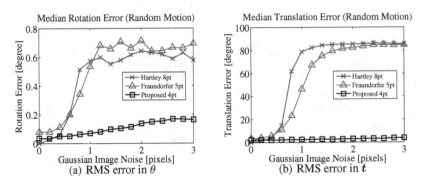

Fig. 5. Results of the least squares case with variable image noise ($0 \leq \sigma_{image} \leq 3$ pixel) and fixed angle noise ($\sigma_{angle} = 0.5°$).

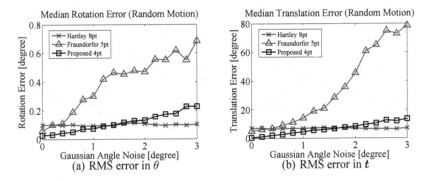

Fig. 6. Results of the least squares case with fixed image noise ($\sigma_{image} = 0.5$ pixel) and variable angle noise ($0° \leq \sigma_{angle} \leq 3°$).

and $\sigma_{angle} = 0.5°$, respectively. From four to 200 point correspondences were evaluated.

As shown in Fig. 7, the proposed algorithm outperforms the others regardless of the number of the point correspondences. It is notable that the proposed algorithm reaches the performance boundary at 60 point correspondences, whereas the conventional algorithms needs more than 100 point correspondences. This is very important for practical use since a few dozen point correspondences are generally obtained. Moreover, for more than 40 point correspondences, Fraundorfer et al.'s algorithm is worse than Hartley's algorithm, which uses only point correspondences. This result indicates that two known angles are not useful for Fraundorfer et al.'s algorithm in the case of many point correspondences.

5.5   Computation Time

The comparison of the computation time is summarized in Table 1. Note that the all computation times were measured in MATLAB 2012b.

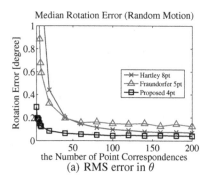
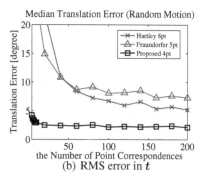

(a) RMS error in θ (b) RMS error in t

Fig. 7. Results of changing the number of point correspondences with $\sigma_{image} = 0.5$ pixel and $\sigma_{angle} = 0.5°$.

Table 1. Comparison of mean computation time [msec].

	The number of point correspondences						
	3	4	5	10	50	100	500
Kalantari et al.	75.64	n/a	n/a	n/a	n/a	n/a	n/a
Fraundorfer et al.	3.62	0.69	0.33	0.32	0.33	0.33	0.38
Proposed	0.38	0.41	0.40	0.40	0.41	0.41	0.48

The proposed 4-point algorithm is slightly slower than Fraundorfer et al.'s 5-point algorithm since the proposed algorithm solves an eighth degree polynomial by using roots command. The increase in the number of point correspondences seems to have no influence. According to the analysis of MATLAB profiler, most of the computation time was spent running svd command in Fraundorfer et al.'s 5-point algorithm and roots command and calculating the coefficients of the polynomial in the proposed 4-point algorithm. The increase in the number of point correspondences is not significant since matrix multiplication is well optimized in MATLAB. The conventional 3-point algorithms take much longer computation time to perform Gauss-Jordan elimination, rref command in MATLAB. However, Kalantari et al. [11] report that the total time of their C++ implementation is 0.002 ms on a laptop PC with a 1.6 GHz processor. Although they do not refer to the trade name of the CPU and the code optimization, they suggest that writing C++ improves the efficiency of the proposed algorithms dramatically. Generating point correspondences (point detection and matching), is one of the most time-consuming processes in practical 3D reconstruction. It takes more than 10 ms to detect points from a VGA image even if GPU implementation [17, 18]. For this reason, the computation time of the proposed solutions would be negligible.

6   Conclusions

This paper has proposed a robust least squares solution to the calibrated two-view geometry with two known orientation angles. Using the knowledge reduces the DoFs from five to three: one from a remaining angle and two from a translation vector. This paper had determined that the three parameters are obtained by solving a minimization problem of the smallest eigenvalue containing the unknown angle. The proposed solution minimizes a new simple cost function based on the matrix determinant in order to avoid the complicated eigenvalue computation. The estimated parameters are optimal since the cost function is minimized under three DoFs.

Experimental results for synthetic data showed that the robustness of the proposed solution is up to $1.5°$ angle noise, which is approximately three times that of a conventional solution. Moreover, 60 point correspondences, fewer than half those in conventional solutions, are sufficient to reach the performance boundary. The proposed solution is applicable for consumer IMU sensors to achieve highly accurate 3D reconstruction. Demonstrating in a practical scene is a future work.

Appendix

The proof of that the proposed 4-point algorithm including the 3-point algorithm is as follows.

Substituting three point correspondences into (17), we have

$$\frac{d}{d\theta}\det(\boldsymbol{B}^T\boldsymbol{B}) = \frac{d}{d\theta}\det(\boldsymbol{A}^T\boldsymbol{A})$$

$$= \frac{d}{d\theta}\det(\boldsymbol{A})^2 \tag{20}$$

$$= 2\det(\boldsymbol{A})\frac{d}{d\theta}\det(\boldsymbol{A}).$$

We can construct a system of polynomial equations as follows:

$$\begin{cases} f_3(c,s) = \det(\boldsymbol{A})\dfrac{d}{d\theta}\det(\boldsymbol{A})\Big|_{\substack{\cos\theta=c,\\ \sin\theta=s}} = 0, \\ g(c,s) = c^2 + s^2 - 1 = 0. \end{cases} \tag{21}$$

The solutions of $\mathrm{Res}(f_3, g, c) = 0$ include that of $\mathrm{Res}(f_1, g, c) = 0$.

References

1. Philip, J.: A non-iterative algorithm for determining all essential matrices corresponding to five point pairs. Photogram. Rec. **15**, 589–599 (1996)
2. Triggs, B.: Routines for relative pose of two calibrated cameras from 5 points. Technical Report, INRIA (2000)

3. Nistér, D.: An efficient solution to the five-point relative pose problem. In: Proceedings 2003 IEEE Computer Society Conference on Computer Vision and Pattern Recognition, vol. 2, II-195. IEEE (2003)
4. Stewénius, H., Engels, C., Nistér, D.: Recent developments on direct relative orientation. ISPRS J. Photogrammetry Remote Sens. **60**, 284–294 (2006)
5. Li, H., Hartley, R.: Five-point motion estimation made easy. In: 18th International Conference on Pattern Recognition, 2006, ICPR 2006, vol. 1, pp. 630–633. IEEE (2006)
6. Kukelova, Z., Bujnak, M., Pajdla, T.: Polynomial eigenvalue solutions to the 5-pt and 6-pt relative pose problems. BMVC **2008**, 2 (2008)
7. Kalantari, M., Jung, F., Guedon, J., Paparoditis, N.: The five points pose problem: A new and accurate solution adapted to any geometric configuration. In: Wada, T., Huang, F., Lin, S. (eds.) PSIVT 2009. LNCS, vol. 5414, pp. 215–226. Springer, Heidelberg (2009)
8. Pizarro, O., Eustice, R., Singh, H.: Relative pose estimation for instrumented, calibrated imaging platforms. In: Proceedings of Digital Image Computing Techniques and Applications, pp. 601–612, Sydney, Australia (2003)
9. Hartley, R.I., Zisserman, A.: Multiple View Geometry in Computer Vision, 2nd edn. Cambridge University Press, Cambridge (2004). ISBN: 0521540518
10. Fischler, M.A., Bolles, R.C.: Random sample consensus: a paradigm for model fitting with applications to image analysis and automated cartography. Commun. ACM **24**, 381–395 (1981)
11. Kalantari, M., Hashemi, A., Jung, F., Guédon, J.P.: A new solution to the relative orientation problem using only 3 points and the vertical direction. CoRR abs/0905.3964 (2009)
12. Fraundorfer, F., Tanskanen, P., Pollefeys, M.: A minimal case solution to the calibrated relative pose problem for the case of two known orientation angles. In: Daniilidis, K., Maragos, P., Paragios, N. (eds.) ECCV 2010, Part IV. LNCS, vol. 6314, pp. 269–282. Springer, Heidelberg (2010)
13. Faugeras, O.: Three-Dimensional Computer Vision: A Geometric Viewpoint. The MIT Press, Cambridge (1993)
14. Horn, B.K.P.: Recovering baseline and orientation from essential matrix. J. Optical Soc. Am. (1990)
15. Cox, D.A., Little, J.B., O'Shea, D.: Using Algebraic Geometry, 2nd edn. Springer, New York (2005)
16. Kukelova, Z., Bujnak, M., Pajdla, T.: Automatic Generator of Minimal Problem Solvers. In: Forsyth, D., Torr, P., Zisserman, A. (eds.) ECCV 2008, Part III. LNCS, vol. 5304, pp. 302–315. Springer, Heidelberg (2008)
17. Sinha, S.N., Frahm, J.M., Pollefeys, M., Genc, Y.: Gpu-based video feature tracking and matching. In: EDGE, Workshop on Edge Computing Using New Commodity Architectures, vol. 278, p. 4321 (2006)
18. Terriberry, T.B., French, L.M., Helmsen, J.: Gpu accelerating speeded-up robust features. In: Proceedings of 3DPVT '08 (2008)

Robust Iris Localisation in Challenging Scenarios

João C. Monteiro$^{(\boxtimes)}$, Ana F. Sequeira, Hélder P. Oliveira,
and Jaime S. Cardoso

INESC TEC and Faculdade de Engenharia, Universidade do Porto, Porto, Portugal
{joao.c.monteiro,ana.filipa.sequeira}@fe.up.pt,
{helder.p.oliveira,jaime.cardoso}@inescporto.pt

Abstract. The use of images acquired in unconstrained scenarios is giving rise to new challenges in the field of iris recognition. Many works in
literature reported excellent results in both iris segmentation and recognition but mostly with images acquired in controlled conditions. The
intention to broaden the field of application of iris recognition, such as
airport security or personal identification in mobile devices, is therefore
hindered by the inherent unconstrained nature under which images are
to be acquired. The proposed work focuses on mutual context information from iris centre and iris limbic and pupillary contours to perform
robust and accurate iris segmentation in noisy images. The developed
algorithm was tested on the MobBIO database with a promising 96 %
segmentation accuracy for the limbic contour.

Keywords: Biometrics · Iris segmentation · Unconstrained environment · Gradient flow · Shortest closed path

1 Introduction

In almost everyone's daily activities, personal identification plays an important
role. Biometrics represents a natural way of identification. Testing someone by
what this someone is, instead of relying on something he owns or knows seems
likely to be the way forward. The choice of a specific biometric trait is weighted
by a set of qualitative values that describe its overall quality: universality, uniqueness, collectability and permanence [11]. With all these variables in mind, the
iris presents itself as a leading candidate to become the standard biometric trait:
it is universal, the variability is huge which assures the uniqueness for each individual, apart from being an organ easily accessible and very difficult to modify.

Even though excellent rates of recognition are found in literature [6], these
results are associated with a set of acquisition conditions that constrain the
quality of the tested images. The majority of the developed iris recognition systems rely on near-infrared (NIR) imaging rather than visible light (VL). This
is due to the fact that fewer reflections from the cornea in NIR imaging result
in maximized signal-to-noise ratio (SNR) in the sensor, thus improving the contrast of iris images and the robustness of the system. NIR imaging, however,

© Springer-Verlag Berlin Heidelberg 2014
S. Battiato et al. (Eds.): VISIGRAPP 2013, CCIS 458, pp. 146–162, 2014.
DOI: 10.1007/978-3-662-44911-0_10

presents a series of hazards, as no instinctive response (such as blinking) is triggered in response to excessively strong illumination. Another typically imposed constraint to the user of an iris recognition system is the need to stop-and-stare at a close distance to the sensor (i.e. user collaboration). These factors create important limitations to the applicability of iris recognition algorithms in real-life conditions, such as military applications or bank account management. The development of iris recognition algorithms that are capable of encompassing such limitations has been gaining focus in recent years.

In this work we focus on *iris segmentation*, as proposed by Daugman in his 1993 pioneer work [8]. Iris segmentation consists on the detection of the two defining contours of the iris region: the *limbic contour* separates the iris from the sclera, and the *pupillary contour*, the iris from the pupil. The detection of these contours is the main goal of segmentation and an essential step in the development of high accuracy recognition systems.

We argue that iris segmentation can benefit from the simultaneous detection of the iris centre and iris external contour. When performed independently, both tasks are nontrivial since many other parts of the image may be falsely detected. However, the two tasks can benefit greatly from serving as context for each other. Central to our method to detect iris centre candidates is the use of gradient flow information with a specific gradient vector field template; the detection of the limbic contour relies on the search of strong closed contours around the centre candidates. Further context information can be used to localise the pupil region in the areas adjacent to the centroid of the segmented limbic contour.

This paper extends our initial work [18] in which a method for the detection of external iris contour was proposed. The main contributions of the present work are the detection and evaluation of the pupillary contour and the evaluation of the method in a new iris database [17].

2   Related Work

The original approach to the segmentation task was proposed by Daugman [8] and consisted in the maximisation of an integro-differential operator. In a different approach, Wildes [28] suggested a method involving edge detection followed by circular Hough transform (CHT). For years, several works in the iris biometrics field focused on Daugman's and Wilde's algorithms, presenting variations at many levels.

One example is the CHT-based method used for the segmentation step in Masek's algorithm [16]. Ma et al. [15] created a system that mixed both the CHT segmentation approach and the rubber sheet model normalization, introducing some concepts like pre-processing of iris images for specular reflection removal.

In the work of Abhyankar and Schuckers [1] segmentation starts with the transformation of the iris image into the wavelet domain. Enhancement of image contours is carried out by a process of thresholding and filtering low energy components of both high and low frequency components. The Canny edge detector is then applied to the enhanced image and CHT is used for the detection of both limbic and pupillary boundaries.

The integro-differential operator and the CHT are still widely used for segmenting iris images, offering good segmentation accuracy but also computational complexity. Radman et al. [22] addresses a simple solution for this problem by localizing the initial center of the pupil using a circular Gabor filter (CGF).

Circle or elliptic fitting methods appeared as a different approach. In the work of He et al. [9] an Adaboost-cascade iris detector is built to extract a rough position of the iris centre and then the centre and radius of the circular iris are localised by employing an elastic model named *"pulling and pushing"*. Roy et al. [24] consider the iris as a non-circular structure and use an elliptic fitting model to fit both the limbic and pupillary contours. Then they perfect it by a geometric active contour procedure based on an energy minimisation process. In the same line of work, the segmentation of the pupil and iris by fitting a rotated ellipse, after a sequence of procedures for compensating the detected noise, was proposed by Zuo and Schmid [29].

Since iris boundaries are often not circular or elliptical, curve fitting techniques can be valuable to approximate real iris contours [21]. To further improve segmentation performance, several methods attempted to use active contour models to accurately localise irregular iris boundaries [7,10,25,27]. The work of Lu and Lu [14] presented an illustrative example for both limbic and pupillary contour detection: first they used a deformable model to detect the pupillary contour, followed by the integro-differential operator to detect the limbic boundary. More recently, Pawar et al. [20] applied geodesic active contours to perform segmentation.

Considering less ideal iris images, the approach taken by Chen et al. [4] consisted in detecting the sclera region of the eye, thresholding and filtering the image to detect a rectangular region for iris localization. An edge map of the region of interest is then obtained with a horizontal Sobel operator, and a dynamic programming variation of the CHT algorithm was implemented to detect the limbic boundary. This method corrects the non-circularities of the off-angle iris and combines the intersection of circles obtained by the two CHT algorithms and a linear Hough transform to perform eyelid detection. In the work of Tan et al. [26], first, a rough position of the iris is extracted by performing a clustering-based scheme to distinguish between iris candidates and the remaining image. Then, the regions resulting from this iterative process are analysed for specific iris characteristics, such as roundness and relative position to other regions (for example, eyebrows could be distinguished from the iris as they are a dark region, horizontal, placed above the iris). The second step consists in iteratively finding the shortest path that maximizes the Daugman integro-differential operator so that the limbic and pupillary boundaries can be detected.

Gradient vector field based methods have appeared in literature such as in the work of Chen et al. [3]. In this work gradient flow around the iris center plays an important role in the segmentation of the limbic contour.

When analysing most of the methods cited in the literature, it is possible to detect some main drawbacks. In almost all of these methods, inner and outer boundaries, eyelashes and eyelids are detected in different steps, causing a considerable increase in processing time of the system. Usually, the inner and outer boundaries are detected by circle fitting techniques. This is a source of error, since the iris boundaries are not exactly circles and in noisy situations, the outer boundary of iris may not present sharp edges [2].

In some of the aforementioned algorithms, there are a lot of implicit or explicit assumptions about the acquisition process, which are no longer valid in unconstrained acquisition scenarios. Therefore, some of the promising results reported in the literature must be taken with caution and reassessed under these new, more challenging, conditions.

In recent years it has been recognized that the path forward, regarding iris recognition, is the development of algorithms that can work independently of subject collaboration and proper NIR illumination conditions, in order to achieve robust (i.e. accurate even with noisy images) and unconstrained (i.e. accurate for several sets of acquisition conditions: distance, movement, illumination) iris recognition and, in this way, become a real-world applicable method [23]. This paradigm shift led to the rise of new trends in the research of iris recognition, for example, exploring VL illumination instead of NIR.

3 Joint Detection of Iris Centre and Limbic Contour

Researchers are now paying more attention to the context to aid visual recognition processes. Context plays an important role in recognition by the human visual system, with many important visual recognition tasks critically relying on it.

The proposed work aimed to accomplish accurate iris segmentation by using simultaneously acquired information from two main sources: *iris centre* and *limbic contour*. Both sources contribute to discriminate between a series of iris segmentation candidates. Context information regarding typical iris characteristics in eye images, namely colour and shape, represented the basis of the developed algorithm. By using more than a single source of information, we aimed to lower the misdetection of areas likely to be wrongly segmented, such as eyebrows and glass frames.

3.1 Algorithm Overview

A simplification is adopted in relation to the main rationale outlined above. The simultaneous detection of the iris centre and limbic contour will be addressed by first over-detecting centre candidates, followed by a contour detection around each of them.

The centre candidates are estimated using a convergence index filter methodology [12]. Next, a window centred in each candidate is converted into the polar domain followed by shortest path algorithm to determine good closed paths around the centre. Using combined data from the centre and respective contour, the best pair centre/contour is selected. Finally, the pupillary segmentation is performed using a new polar image around the centroid of the detected limbic contour.

Typical iris images present two very distinct regions: a high intensity region corresponding to the eye and the skin, and the iris region, at least *partially circular* and *lower in intensity*. These two sources of knowledge can be presented separately but are intrinsically connected. The fact that the iris is a darker region against a brighter background translates into a specific divergent gradient orientation from its centre. At the same time the limbic contour (iris outer edge) will present a high gradient magnitude as well as a closed shape. The approach taken in this work was that of detecting pairs of iris centre and limbic contour candidates that maximise a quality factor weighted by the aforementioned combined knowledge. The segmentation of the pupillary contour is then performed in a limited region of interest, concentric with the previously segmented limbic contour.

3.2   Iris Centre Detection

Iris centre candidates are detected using a template matching algorithm based on gradient vector field orientation. Theoretically the gradient is a vector field that points in the direction of the greatest rate of increase of a scalar field. Considering an image as a scalar field, it is easy to perceive the gradient as a vector field that points from darker regions (of lower intensity) towards brighter regions (of higher intensity). Figure 1(b) depicts a simple example of gradient vector field orientation on a synthetic image.

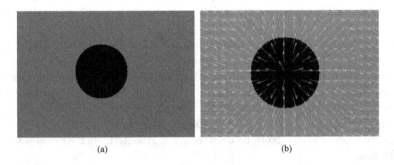

(a)   (b)

Fig. 1. Gradient orientation vector field in synthetic images. Notice how the vector field diverges from darker regions and converges to brighter regions.

The iris is surrounded by two distinct higher intensity regions: the sclera and the skin. With this in mind a divergent gradient orientation is expected from the center of the iris towards the aforementioned brighter regions, as observed in Fig. 2(b).

The centre candidates are, thus, detected by computing the cross-correlation, c_{corr}, between the gradient vector field orientation and the divergent template vector field depicted in Fig. 2(a). The c_{corr} values are calculated as:

$$c_{corr} = (f * g)[\mathbf{n}] \overset{def}{=} \sum_{\mathbf{m}} f^*[\mathbf{m}]g[\mathbf{n} + \mathbf{m}] \tag{1}$$

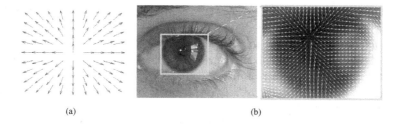

(a)   (b)

Fig. 2. The iris centre detection is based on two vector fields: (a) Template vector field and (b) Gradient orientation vector field.

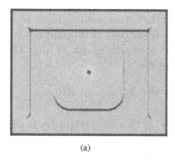

(a)

Fig. 3. Cross-correlation results on the synthetic image from Fig. 1(a) (Color figure online).

where f and g represent the gradient orientation vector field and the template vector field respectively. The resulting c_{corr} matrix can be graphically represented as exemplified in Fig. 3(a), where the values range from -1 to 1, with -1 being represented in blue and 1 in red. The centre candidates are detected as the N local maxima with the highest c_{corr} values.

3.3   Limbic Contour Detection

In the proposed method for limbic boundary detection we consider the image grid as a graph, with pixels as nodes and edges connecting neighbouring pixels. With this in mind the proposed algorithm defines a limbic contour candidate as the best closed contour around a given centre candidate.

The computation of this best contour is simplified by working in polar coordinates (relative to each iris centre candidate). In this domain a closed contour around a given point becomes a curve from the left side of the polar image ($\theta = 0°$) to the right side of the same image ($\theta = 360°$). With the aforementioned consideration of the image as a graph, computation of the best closed contour becomes computation of the shortest left-to-right path in polar domain. To better understand the proposed limbic contour detection algorithm, we start by introducing some graph concepts [19].

Graph Concepts. A *graph* $G = (V, A)$ is composed of two sets V and A. V is the set of nodes, and A the set of arcs (p, q), $p, q \in V$. The graph is *weighted* if a weight $w(p, q)$ is associated to each arc. The weight of each arc, $w(p, q)$, is a function of pixels values and pixels relative positions. A path from vertex (pixel) v_1 to vertex (pixel) v_n is a list of unique vertices $v_1, v_2, \ldots, v_n$, with v_i and v_{i+1} corresponding to neighbour pixels. The total cost of a path is the sum of each arc weight in the path $\sum_{i=2}^{n} w(v_{i-1}, v_i)$.

A path from a source vertex v to a target vertex u is said to be the *shortest path* if its total cost is minimum among all v-to-u paths. The distance between a source vertex v and a target vertex u on a graph, $d(v, u)$, is the total cost of the shortest path between v and u.

A path from a source vertex v to a sub-graph Ω is said to be the shortest path between v and Ω if its total cost is minimum among all v-to-$u \in \Omega$ paths. The distance from a node v to a sub-graph Ω, $d(v, \Omega)$, is the total cost of the shortest path between v and Ω:

$$d(v, \Omega) = \min_{u \in \Omega} d(v, u). \tag{2}$$

A path from a sub-graph Ω_1 to a sub-graph Ω_2 is said to be the shortest path between Ω_1 and Ω_2 if its total cost is minimum among all $v \in \Omega_1$-to-$u \in \Omega_2$ paths. The distance from a sub-graph Ω_1 to a sub-graph Ω_2, $d(\Omega_1, \Omega_2)$, is the total cost of the shortest path between Ω_1 and Ω_2:

$$d(\Omega_1, \Omega_2) = \min_{v \in \Omega_1, u \in \Omega_2} d(v, u). \tag{3}$$

Algorithm for Limbic Contour Detection. Intuitively, the limbic boundary appears as a closed contour in the image, enclosing the iris centre, and over

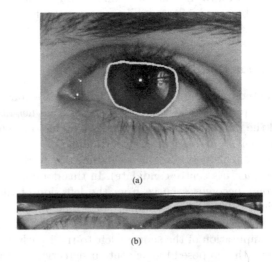

(a)

(b)

Fig. 4. (a) Original limbic contour in Cartesian coordinates; (b) corresponding left-to-right path in the polar domain.

pixels with a strong transition in the grey-level values. Assuming that paths through pixels with high directional derivative are preferred over paths through low directional derivative pixels, the limbic contour can then be found among the shortest closed paths enclosing the iris centre candidate.

A difficulty with searching for the shortest closed path enclosing a given point C is that small paths, collapsing in the point C, are naturally favoured. We overcome that difficulty by working on polar coordinates.

A circular window centred in each candidate is transformed to polar coordinates. A closed path in the original Cartesian coordinates (Fig. 4(a)) is transformed into a path from left to right margins in the window in polar coordinates, starting and ending in the same row of the transformed window (Fig. 4(b)).

Note that the main assumptions are (a) the candidate centre lies within the true limbic contour; (b) the limbic contour constitutes a closed path over pixels of strong directional derivative. The limbic contour is not necessarily circular and the candidate centre does not need to match the true iris centre for a correct contour detection.

Computation of the Shortest Closed Path. In spite of the efficiency of the computation of the shortest path between the whole left and right margins, or between two pre-defined points in the margins, or between one of the margins and a pre-defined point in the other margin, the search for the shortest path between the left and right margins with the constraint that the path should start and end in the same row seems to increase the complexity of the procedure. As typical, optimization with constraints is more difficult than without.

Had one been interested in the simple shortest path between the left and right margin and the computation would be very efficiently performed using dynamic programming. Assuming the simplifying assumption that the vertical paths do not zigzag back and forth, up and down, in the transformed image, the search may be restricted among connected paths containing one, and only one, pixel in each column between the two end-columns.

Formally, let I be an $N_1 \times N_2$ window (after polar coordinate transform) with N_1 columns and N_2 rows; define an admissible path to be

$$\mathbf{s} = \{(x, y(x))\}_{x=1}^{N_1} \text{ , s.t. } \forall x \ |y(x) - y(x-1)| \le 1,$$

where y is a mapping $y : [1, \cdots, N_1] \to [1, \cdots, N_2]$. That is, an admissible path is an 8-connected path of pixels in the image from left to right, containing one, and only one, pixel in each column of the image.

The first step is to traverse the image from the second column to the last column and compute the cumulative minimum cost C for each entry (i, j):

$$C(i, j) = \min \begin{cases} C(i-1, j-1) + w(p_{i-1,j-1}; p_{i,j}) \\ C(i-1, j) + w(p_{i-1,j}; p_{i,j}) \\ C(i-1, j+1) + w(p_{i-1,j+1}; p_{i,j}) \end{cases},$$

where $w(p_{i,j}; p_{l,m})$ represents the weight of the edge incident with pixels at positions (i, j) and (l, m). At the end of this process,

$$\min_{j \in \{1, \cdots, N_2\}} C(N_1, j)$$

indicates the end of the minimal connected path. Hence, in the second step, one backtrack from this minimum entry on C to find the optimal path.

Note that this procedure gives not only the shortest path between the left and right margins but also yields the shortest path between any point in the right margin and the whole left margin: for any point (N_1, j) in the right margin, $C(N_1, j)$ indicates the cost of the shortest path between (N_1, j) and the whole left margin, see Fig. 5. Finally, it should be clear how to change the initial conditions of the above procedure to yield the shortest path between two pre-defined points in the opposite margins.

Noting that if j and ℓ are two distinct points in the right margin, then the shortest paths between each of these points and the whole left margin do not intersect, it is trivial to conclude that there is at least one point m in the right margin for which the shortest path between m and the whole left margin starts also at row m. Note that the paths correspond to closed paths in the original window in Cartesian coordinates (not necessarily including the shortest one). Similarly, interchanging the role of the left and right margin, it is possible to obtain at least one point n in the left margin for which the shortest path to the whole right margin is closed. By computing all the paths from the left to the right margin (and vice-versa), a set of k closed contours is obtained for each centre candidate. The procedure is illustrated in Fig. 5.

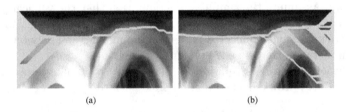

(a)   (b)

Fig. 5. Example of shortest path starting point detection. (a) shows all paths from the left margin to the right margin and (b) all the paths from the right margin to the left margin. As is easily deductable, at least one closed contour will result from this process.

Design of the Weight Function. The weight of an edge in the graph is a function of the values of the incident nodes (pixels). We start by computing the derivative in the radial direction (centred in the iris candidate position) in the original space, using a 3-point numerical differentiation, as defined in Eq. (4).

$$G_\theta(r) = \frac{I(r+h) - I(r-h)}{2h} \tag{4}$$

In the graph, to each edge incident with 4-neighbouring pixels correspond a weight determined by the derivative value of the two incident pixels, expressed as an exponential law, presented in Eq. (5).

$$f(g) = f_\ell + (f_h - f_\ell) \, \frac{\exp(\beta \, (255 - g)) - 1}{\exp(\beta \, 255) - 1} \tag{5}$$

with $f_\ell = 2, f_h = 32, \beta = 0.0208$ and g is the minimum of the derivative computed on the two incident pixels. For 8-neighbour pixels the weight was set to $\sqrt{2}$ times that value. The parameter β was experimentally tuned using a grid search method. The remaining parameters were manually optimised in some of our previous works [19].

3.4   Best Pair Centre/Contour

From the previously described steps a set of centre/contour candidate pairs (Cp) is built. An example of such candidate pairs is depicted in Fig. 6, where the yellow circles represent the centres and the purple curves the limbic contour candidates.

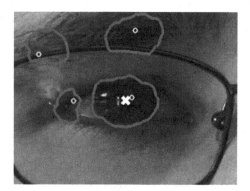

Fig. 6. Example of the centre/contour set of candidates. The centre candidates are represented by yellow circles, the detected contours by purple curves and the ground-truth iris centre by a white cross (Color figure online).

The joint decision for the centre and contour is taken to maximise the joint probability of the individual parts. In here, we assume that the joint probability is a monotonous function of the product of individual measures of quality, combined in an overall quality factor, Q. The discrimination between candidates is performed by choosing the pair with the highest Q. The quality factor is given by:

$$Q(Cp) = \frac{\mu(\Delta C) \cdot \rho_p}{|1 - S(C)|} \tag{6}$$

where $\mu(\Delta C)$ is the mean directional derivative alongside the contour, ρ_p is the cross-correlation value of the centre candidate, and S is the shape factor of the contour (with perimeter P and area A), given by:

$$S(C) = \frac{4\pi \cdot A}{P^2} \tag{7}$$

This way the best centre/contour pair, Cp_Q, is selected based on mutual information from both iris centre and limbic contour quality.

3.5   Pupillary Contour Detection

The detection of the pupillary contour was performed by taking into consideration the context knowledge concerning its relation with the limbic contour. Even though the iris and the pupil are not always exactly concentric structures [5], one can approximate the center of the pupil as the centroid of the previously segmented limbic contour. From this point the detection of the pupillary contour becomes a simple repetition of the methodology presented in the former sections. The only novel constraint to this new problem concerns the size of the structure of interest. As the pupil is a contractile structure, whose size is controlled by the lightning conditions of the acquisition environment, we set the range of possible pupil sizes as $[\frac{1}{4}, \frac{2}{3}]$ of the size of the iris [13]. We then proceed to compute the best closed path around the new centre considering only a limited region of interest in the polar domain.

4   Results

4.1   Tested Dataset

The proposed algorithm was tested on the MobBIO multimodal database [17], created in the scope of the 1st Biometric Recognition with Portable Devices Competition 2013, integrated in the ICIAR 2013 conference. The main goal of the competition was to compare different methodologies for biometric recognition using data acquired with portable devices. The referred database consists on data from three biometric modalities: face, iris and voice acquired from 105 individuals. Considering the iris modality of the MobBIO database, a total of 1640 images, half acquired from each eye, compose it. In the acquisition process we used an Asus Transformer Pad TF 300T, with Android version 4.1.1. The device has two cameras one frontal and one back camera. The camera we used was the back camera, version TF300T-000128, with 8 megapixel of resolution and autofocus. Regarding the iris images, a single image of both eyes was acquired and posteriorly cropped into two 200×300, one for each eye. All images were manually annotated for both the limbic and pupillary contours. Figure 7 depicts some examples of such images, where some of the most common noise factors that characterise this database, such as occlusions, reflections and illumination variations, can be easily discerned.

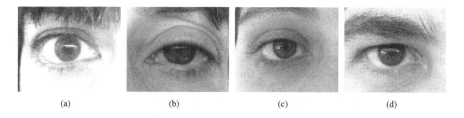

    (a)   (b)   (c)   (d)

Fig. 7. Example images from the MobBIO database.

The proposed algorithm was already tested on the UBIRIS.v2 iris image database [21] on our previous work [18]. Images in UBIRIS.v2 were captured under non-constrained conditions (at-a-distance, on-the-move and on the visible wavelength), with corresponding realistic noise factors.

4.2 Iris Centre Candidate Detection

The accuracy of the centre candidate detection step was computed as the minimum Euclidean distance between each center candidate and the manually annotated ground-truth centre. A mean distance of 5.04 ± 3.36 pixels was obtained for the tested dataset. Considering that the mean iris radius was 33.34 ± 6.90 pixels this result might seem not that promising. The observed deviations of the center candidates from the real iris center arise mainly from two causes: (a) the partial occlusion of the iris by the eyelids results in a deviation from an ideal circular shape and (b) the extent to which specular reflections contaminate the iris region causes the gradient flow to diverge towards those regions instead of the sclera.

However, given how the limbic contour detection algorithm is designed, there is no need to achieve perfect accuracy on the real iris centre with any of the detected candidates. As long as one of the candidates lies inside the iris/pupil region, the detection of a closed contour around it (not necessarily centred on it) is guaranteed. For the pupillary contour it is assumed that an accurate limbic contour detection was performed *a priori*, so that the new centroid lies inside the pupil, allowing the best closed contour detection as explained above.

4.3 Best Centre/Contour Pair Discrimination

The discriminative performance of the proposed quality factor, $Q(Cp)$, was analysed by computing the misdetection ratio, M_r. This value corresponds to the ratio between the number of images where the best centre/contour pair was not correctly discriminated and the total number of tested images. We have shown in our previous work [18] that mutual context information improves results obtained by singular sources of information. Working with the MobBIO dataset a M_r value of 0.88 % was obtained, confirming the powerful discriminatory ability of the designed quality factor.

4.4 Limbic Contour Segmentation Errors

To evaluate the segmentation accuracy of both the previously discriminated best limbic contour candidates and its respective pupillary contour, a series of metrics were computed. Table 1 summarises the most relevant results:

- Mean, median and maximum (Hausdorff) distance, in pixels, between the detected limbic contour and the manually annotated ground-truth;
- The accuracy of segmentation, which corresponds to the ratio of images where the mean deviation between the ground truth and the detected contour did not exceed 10 % of the radius of the iris;
- Mean percentage of false iris/pupil (FPR) and false non-iris/non-pupil (FNR) segmented pixels.

The first three measurements refer to point-to-point distances between the two referred contours and their respective ground-truths. Concerning solely the limbic contour, Fig. 8 presents the histogram describing the distribution of these three metrics for all tested images. The information presented in the histograms show that the segmentation errors are relatively low. The larger Hausdorff distances indicate, however, that contours tend to present a localized behaviour of higher deviation from the ground truth. This can be readily explained if the effect of eyelashes in the upper region of the eye is taken into account. As the eyelashes often present an higher contrast with the skin than the iris with the eyelashes, it is only safe to assume that a directional derivative weighted shortest path algorithm will tend to prefer the eyelash-skin boundary to the iris-eyelash boundary. Such effect can be more easily perceived through the visual analysis of the results presented in Fig. 9.

Table 1. Summary of the most relevant segmentation evaluation metrics.

Contour	Mean	Median	Hausdorff	Accuracy	FPR	FNR
Limbic	3.02 ± 1.55	2.08 ± 1.05	10.63 ± 5.46	0.96	0.0191	0.00325
Pupillary	3.90 ± 6.84	3.37 ± 6.86	8.47 ± 8.04	0.044	0.434	0.0085
	Pixels			$[0-1]$		

The obtained FPR and FNR value leads to some interesting conclusions. A 0.00325 FNR is an excellent indicator that very few iris pixels are classified as non-iris. This means that almost no useful recognition information is lost *a priori* due to faulty segmentation. The FPR also accounts for what was already referred in the discussion of the Hausdorff distance and observed in Fig. 9: the high contrast observed in the eyelash region causes a tendency of the closed paths to stick to the eyelash/skin boundary. This yields a strip of false iris pixels above the eye in the eyelash region that justifies the higher FPR values, in comparison with the FNR.

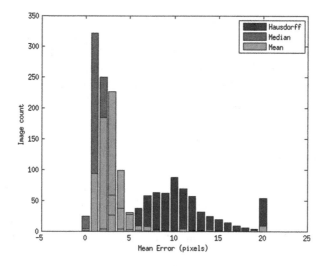

Fig. 8. Histogram of evaluation metric for the limbic contour detection.

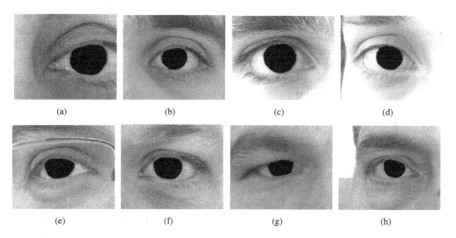

Fig. 9. Visual representation of the obtained limbic contour segmentation results. The true iris pixels are marked as black, while the false iris are marked red and the false non-iris green (Color figure online).

The analysis of the pupillary contour results corroborates some of the expectations regarding the difficulties of its segmentation in VW images. As stated on our previous work [18], the contrast between the pupil and the iris is extremely dependent on a set of hardly controllable factors (illumination, iris pigmentation, obstructions, etc.), thus creating a serious challenges as far as the development of robust segmentation algorithms is concerned. In the present work the obtained results seem to support the aforementioned claim. The 4.40 % segmentation accuracy and the 43.4 % false pupil rate results are good indicators of how difficult and non-trivial the process of pupillary segmentation is. One could argue that the obtained distance metrics in pixels are not very dissimilar to the values presented for the limbic contour. However, the considerably larger standard deviations, alongside the fact that the average pupil size is approximately one third of the average iris size dismiss such conclusions and only act as to further show how limited the proposed algorithm is, as far as pupil segmentation is concerned.

5   Conclusions

The use of mutual information from gradient orientation for centre detection and directional derivative magnitude for contour detection presented good results for future works. Using the extracted iris regions as inputs for a feature extraction and matching module is the obvious step to carry on after the segmentation algorithm.

However some improvements can be easily suggested to the proposed algorithm. First, improvements on the best centre/contour pair discrimination, so as to improve its robustness, by taking advantage of more powerful machine learning techniques, for example. So as to allow a fairer comparison with other state-of-the-art methods, a noise detection module is necessary. With this new module the number of points that could induce misleading results will be reduced, leading to improved recognition performance. When the noisy conditions of an image limit its usability for recognition tasks, further investigation into quality assessment metrics could improve the global recognition rates of the system. Finally, we argue that a recognition algorithm with no need of pupillary segmentation is probably the way forwarded in unconstrained acquisition settings. However, the same problem that concerns noise detection is applicable to pupil localisation: if the pixels corresponding to this region are not removed from the segmented iris mask, misleading information will be introduced in the recognition module, resulting in loss of accuracy. As accurate segmentation is rendered difficult by the intrinsic characteristics of the MobBIO images, estimating a probability of each pixel belonging to the pupil seems a more robust way of approaching the problem. Future works will certainly focus on these four points of interest.

Acknowledgements. The authors would like to thank Fundação para a Ciência e Tecnologia (FCT) - Portugal the financial support for the PhD grants with references SFRH/ BD/74263/2010 and SFRH/BD/87392/2012.

References

1. Abhyankar, A., Schuckers, S.: Iris quality assessment and bi-orthogonal wavelet based encoding for recognition. Pattern Recogn. **42**(9), 1878–1894 (2009)
2. Barzegar, N., Moin, M.: A new approach for iris localisation in iris recognition systems. In: Proceedings of the International Conference on Computer Systems and Applications, pp. 516–523 (2008)

3. Chen, R., Lin, X., Ding, T.: Iris segmentation for non-cooperative recognition systems. Image Process. **5**(5), 448–456 (2011)
4. Chen, Y., Adjouadi, M., Han, C., Wang, J., Barreto, A., Rishe, N., Andrian, J.: A highly accurate and computationally efficient approach for unconstrained iris segmentation. Image Vis. Comput. **28**(2), 261–269 (2010)
5. Daugman, J.: How iris recognition works. In: Proceedings of the International Conference on Image Processing. vol. 1, pp. I-33–I-36 (2002)
6. Daugman, J.: Probing the uniqueness and randomness of iriscodes: results from 200 billion iris pair comparisons. Proc. IEEE **94**(11), 1927–1935 (2006)
7. Daugman, J.: New methods in iris recognition. IEEE Trans. Syst. Man Cybern. B Cybern. **37**(5), 1167–1175 (2007)
8. Daugman, J.: High confidence visual recognition of persons by a test of statistical independence. IEEE Trans. Pattern Anal. Mach. Intell. **15**(11), 1148–1161 (1993)
9. He, Z., Tan, T., Sun, Z., Qiu, X.: Toward accurate and fast iris segmentation for iris biometrics. IEEE Trans. Pattern Anal. Mach. Intell. **31**(9), 1670–1684 (2009)
10. Houhou, N., Lemkaddem, A., Duay, V., Alla, A., Thiran, J.P.: Shape prior based on statistical map for active contour segmentation. In: 15th IEEE International Conference on Image Processing, pp. 2284–2287 (2008)
11. Jain, A., Hong, L., Pankanti, S.: Biometric identification. Commun. ACM **43**(2), 90–98 (2000)
12. Kobatake, H., Hashimoto, S.: Convergence index filter for vector fields. IEEE Trans. Image Process. **8**(8), 1029–1038 (1999)
13. Li, P., Liu, X., Xiao, L., Song, Q.: Robust and accurate iris segmentation in very noisy iris images. Image Vis. Comput. **28**(2), 246–253 (2010)
14. Lu, C., Lu, Z.: Local feature extraction for iris recognition with automatic scale selection. Image Vis. Comput. **26**(7), 935–940 (2008)
15. Ma, L., Tan, T., Wang, Y., Zhang, D.: Local intensity variation analysis for iris recognition. Pattern Recogn. **37**(6), 1287–1298 (2004)
16. Masek, L.: Recognition of human iris patterns for biometric identification. Towards non-cooperative biometric iris recognition. Ph.D. thesis (2003)
17. Monteiro, J.C., Oliveira, H.P., Rebelo, A., Sequeira, A.F.: MobBIO 2013: 1st Biometric Recognition with Portable Devices Competition (2013). http://paginas.fe.up.pt/~mobBIO2013/
18. Monteiro, J.C., Oliveira, H.P., Sequeira, A.F., Cardoso, J.S.: Robust iris segmentation under unconstrained settings. In: Proceedings of International Conference on Computer Vision Theory and Applications (VISAPP), pp. 180–190 (2013)
19. Oliveira, H., Cardoso, J., Magalhaes, A., Cardoso, M.: Simultaneous detection of prominent points on breast cancer conservative treatment images. In: Proceedings of the 19th IEEE International Conference on Image Processing. pp. 2841–2844 (2012)
20. Pawar, M., Lokande, S., Bapat, V.: Iris segmentation using geodesic active contour for improved texture extraction in recognition. Int. J. Comput. Appl. **47**(16), 448–456 (2012)
21. Proença, H., Filipe, S., Santos, R., Oliveira, J., Alexandre, L.A.: The ubiris.v2: a database of visible wavelength iris images captured on-the-move and at-a-distance. IEEE Trans. Pattern Anal. Mach. Intell. **32**(8), 1529–1535 (2010)
22. Radman, A., Jumari, K., Zainal, N.: Iris segmentation in visible wavelength environment. Proc. Eng. **41**, 743–748 (2012)
23. Ross, A.: Iris recognition: the path forward. Computer **43**(2), 30–35 (2010)

24. Roy, K., Bhattacharya, P., Suen, C., You, J.: Recognition of unideal iris images using region-based active contour model and game theory. In: 17th IEEE International Conference on Image Processing. pp. 1705–1708 (2010)
25. Shah, S., Ross, A.: Iris segmentation using geodesic active contours. IEEE Trans. Inf. Forensics Secur. **4**(4), 824–836 (2009)
26. Tan, T., He, Z., Sun, Z.: Efficient and robust segmentation of noisy iris images for non-cooperative iris recognition. Image Vis. Comput. **28**(2), 223–230 (2010)
27. Vatsa, M., Singh, R., Noore, A.: Improving iris recognition performance using segmentation, quality enhancement, match score fusion, and indexing. IEEE Trans. Syst. Man Cybern. B Cybern. **38**(4), 1021–1035 (2008)
28. Wildes, R.: Iris recognition: an emerging biometric technology. Proc. IEEE **85**(9), 1348–1363 (1997)
29. Zuo, J., Schmid, N.: On a methodology for robust segmentation of nonideal iris images. IEEE Trans. Syst. Man Cybern. B Cybern. **40**(3), 703–718 (2010)

Xtru3D: Single-View 3D Object Reconstruction from Color and Depth Data

Silvia Rodríguez-Jiménez$^{(\boxtimes)}$, Nicolas Burrus, and Mohamed Abderrahim

Department of Systems Engineering and Automation,
Carlos III University of Madrid, Leganés, Spain
{srjimene,nburrus,mohamed}@ing.uc3m.es

Abstract. 3D object reconstruction from single image has been a noticeable research trend in recent years. The most common method is to rely on symmetries of real-life objects, but these are hard to compute in practice. However, a large class of everyday objects, especially when manufactured, can be generated by extruding a 2D shape through an extrusion axis. This paper proposes to exploit this property to acquire 3D object models using a single RGB + Depth image, such as those provided by available low-cost range cameras. It estimates the hidden parts by exploiting the geometrical properties of everyday objects, and both depth and color information are combined to refine the model of the object of interest. Experimental results on a set of 12 common objects are shown to demonstrate not only the effectiveness and simplicity of our approach, but also its applicability for tasks such as robotic grasping.

Keywords: 3D reconstruction · Robotics · Vision · RGB-D · Kinect

1 Introduction

3D object reconstruction from a single viewpoint is an important topic in computer vision and in this work, the problem of recovering the 3D model of unknown objects lying on a table is addressed. This is of particular interest for applications that have to deal with new objects constantly, such as augmented reality or general-purpose robotic manipulation, which is the context of this paper (Fig. 1). On a real robotic platform, the robot will need to grasp and manipulate novel objects of which shape should be determined. With the availability of inexpensive RGB-Depth (RGB-D) cameras such as the Microsoft Kinect [1], dense color and depth information about the scene can be acquired in real-time with a good precision at short distances. Thus, a RGB-D image already contains a lot of information, but a single image only provides the geometry of the visible parts (Fig. 2). Due to self-occlusions, the hidden parts create empty gaps that have to be estimated using a priori knowledge.

The literature on object reconstruction from multiple views is large, but single view modeling has received a significant interest only recently, mostly motivated by robotic grasping applications. A first category of methods assumes that the

© Springer-Verlag Berlin Heidelberg 2014
S. Battiato et al. (Eds.): VISIGRAPP 2013, CCIS 458, pp. 163–178, 2014.
DOI: 10.1007/978-3-662-44911-0_11

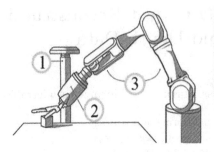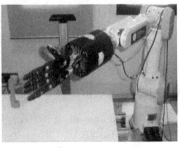

Fig. 1. Robotic platform which is the scenario of this paper: (1) The Kinect camera is located on the side, oriented to get a top view of the objects; (2) a 20-DoF, five-fingers anthropomorphic hand from Shadow; (3) a 7-DoF PA-10 arm.

objects to be modeled have a simple enough shape, and try to fit a predefined set of shape primitives [2] (spheres, cylinders, cones or boxes) or a combination of them [3]. This approach was made more general in other works such as [4] and [5] by using a database of objects with known shapes and a recognition module.

When an extensive database of object models is not available or practical, more generic a priori assumptions are required. The most common assumption is to rely on the symmetries of real-life objects [6]. The problem then becomes to find the nature of the symmetries in the partial point cloud. These are hard to estimate in practice because of the large search space and limited data, leading e.g. to limit the set of hypotheses to a vertical plane axis in a restricted range [7], or to focus on rotational symmetries [8].

Modeling 3D objects by symmetry is a common approach because many objects are symmetrical, but also, a large class of everyday objects can be generated by extruding a 2D shape along a particular path, be it a line segment (linear) or circle (rotational). The linear extrusion process is widely used by designers and engineers to generate 3D models from 2D sketch input (Fig. 3). This 2D shape is the extruded surface and their normals must be orthogonal to the extruded direction [9]. This approach is particularly adapted to the fast reconstruction of objects lying on a flat table, which is a common scenario in robotics, because the table plane normal provides a natural extrusion axis. For objects lying on a flat table, which is a common scenario in robotics, the table plane normal provides a natural extrusion axis. Thus, this paper proposes to leverage this property by reconstructing the hidden parts with an extrusion of the top view of the objects.

The contributions of this paper are three-fold. First, we propose a new technique to extrude an initial sparse point cloud output by a tabletop object detector. Second, we propose a refinement step that takes advantage of the complementarity of the depth and color images by carefully initializing a graph-cut based color segmentation with the depth data. Finally, a quantitative evaluation of the accuracy of the reconstructed meshes is performed on a set of 12 common use objects, showing that the effectiveness of our proposed method is

Fig. 2. Example of a point cloud from the Kinect camera. Left: view of the visible parts from everyday objects lying on a table. Right: same point cloud from top view, where empty gaps belong to occluded region and parts.

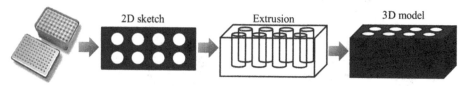

Fig. 3. Example of the extrusion process to generate a 3D model of a pipette tip box from 2D sketch.

comparable to the most recent approach using symmetries [7]. Some preliminary experiments for grasping applications are also conducted using the OpenRAVE simulator [10].

2   Global Overview

The presented approach achieves the acquisition of 3D models using a single RGB-D image integrating two main stages. In the following Sect. 3 the initial volume is computed and Sect. 4 shows its completion through color-based model refinement. This process includes several steps which are illustrated in Fig. 4.

In the first step, a table-top object detector identifies and extracts a cluster of 3D points belonging to the object. Then, the points from the top view of the object are considered as the extrusion profile, and they get extruded towards the table to fill a voxelized volume around the cluster of interest. Object concavities may get filled during the extrusion step, which we compensate by checking for the voxel consistency against the depth image.

Depth images output by low-cost RGB-D cameras are usually imprecise around the object borders, and frequently have holes due to reflections or other

Color and Depth Image

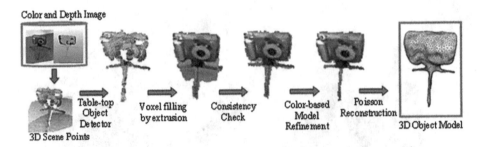

Fig. 4. Overview of our model acquisition process. The Kinect camera provides a depth and color image, which are used to obtain the initial volume. This stage includes three key points: table-top object detector, voxel filling by extrusion and consistency check. The computed model is the input of the color-based refinement model stage.

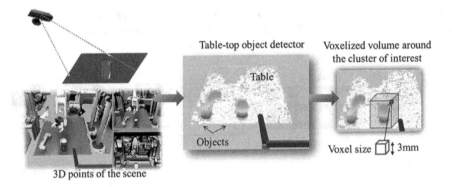

Fig. 5. Overview of the cluster extraction.

optical effects. Since the color image does not suffer from these issues, in the second step, we refine the object boundaries using color segmentation. The refined set of voxels is then given as an input to the final meshing algorithm.

3   Computation of the Initial Volume

3.1   Cluster Extraction

A table top object detector similar to [11] is run on the depth image. The dominant 3D plane is first fitted to the depth data using RANSAC, then points lying outside of a prism around the table plane are eliminated. Remaining points are then clustered using Euclidean distances with fixed thresholds. Clusters that are too small or do not touch the table are eliminated. The cluster of interest is then determined in a task-dependent way, e.g. by choosing the most central one (Fig. 5). To make the 3D processing faster and obtain a natural neighborhood between 3D points, a voxelized volume of fixed size is then initialized around the cluster, and the voxels corresponding to a cluster point are labeled

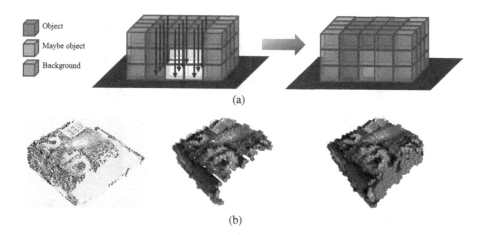

Fig. 6. Voxel filling by extrusion. (a) Overview of the proposed algorithm. (b) Left: raw point cloud of a box. Middle: voxelized mesh of the raw object cluster. Right: voxelized mesh after extrusion towards the table plane. Gray voxels correspond to unseen parts due to self-occlusions.

as "object". The voxel size is a user-defined parameter depending on the desired precision/speed tradeoff. All reconstructions shown in this paper are with 3 mm voxels.

3.2 Voxel Filling by Extrusion

The objective of this step is to "fill" the occluded parts by relying on the assumption that the object can be approximated by an extrusion process. Taking into account that the table plane normal provides the natural extrusion axis for most objects, it is not necessary to calculate the object axis to get the extrusion direction.

Instead, we consider the table plane normal as the extrusion direction of the top face of the object. The proposed algorithm is summarized in the following two points (Fig. 6 (a)):

1. For each voxel which is considered as "object", compute the line segment going from the voxel to the plane along the plane normal.
2. Label all voxels intersecting a line segment as "maybe object".

The result of this step is a rough estimation of the object volume. The model is then slightly smoothed by running a morphological closing to cope with the uncertainties around object borders in the depth image. The optimal structuring element size depends on the voxel size and the properties of the depth data. For voxels of 3 mm and a Kinect camera, we empirically found that a $3 \times 3 \times 3$ cube is a satisfying structuring element. An example of output is given in Fig. 6 (b).

Fig. 7. Consistency check to carve holes and concavities. Left: color image. Middle: colorized voxels after extrusion. Right: remaining voxels after consistency check. Holes and concavities that were wrongly filled by the extrusion algorithm are removed if they are visible.

3.3   Consistency Check

The extrusion step may fill regions of the object that correspond to holes or concavities. This can be corrected by checking the consistency of "maybe object" voxels against the depth image. This is done by reprojecting each voxel onto the depth image, and comparing the projected depth with the depth image.

If the difference is greater than a threshold δ_d, the voxel is labeled as "background". The threshold depends on the estimated accuracy of the depth sensor, and is set to 3 mm in all our experiments with the Kinect. The output of this process is illustrated in Fig. 7.

4   Color-Based Model Refinement

After the above steps, the obtained 3D object model may still have missing parts and irregularities due to missing or incorrect depth information in the RGB-D frame. Incorrect pixels in the depth image usually belong to object borders and areas of specular, transparent or reflective objects. Observing that the color image do not suffer from these issues, we propose to improve the quality of the model by first refining the object segmentation using the color image and then filling-in incorrect depth values using image inpainting.

4.1   Improvement of the Object Segmentation

There are many existing techniques for color-based segmentation, but this is still an open problem in the general case. However, when a good initialization is available, graph-based techniques [12] have proven very effective for foreground/background segmentation [13]. In particular, the GrabCut variant [14] combines graph cuts with Gaussian mixture models and is designed to take

Fig. 8. Snapshot of a refined object segmentation even when the foreground is similar to background. Left: color image, the object of interest is a storage jar on a color poster. Middle: initial segmentation. Pixels are marked as: unknown (black), object (white) and background (gray). Right: final object segmentation, after GrabCut. Pixels are marked as: object (white) and background (black).

advantage of a user provided mask. It is thus particularly adapted to the refinement of an initial segmentation. Recently, GrabCut has been extended in the work described in [15] to use depth information by combining the RGB and depth channels with a weighting factor. Instead of merging both information in a single energy, we propose to run GrabCut only on the color image, but using depth information for the initialization of an accurate mask. This approach takes a greater advantage of the complementarity of the techniques, since the depth image is misleading near the object borders, and the color information is not necessary and more sensitive to background clutter for the initial segmentation.

The initialization is thus taken from the initial model output by the algorithm of Sect. 3 using depth information only, re-projecting every 3D point from the volume onto the depth image. Then, pixels are labeled as object (foreground), background or unknown (if their projected depth is not consistent or they do not have depth information). Taking this initialization as a starting point, the mask is created. GrabCut can take four different initialization values according to pixels belong to foreground, background, most probably foreground or background. Pixels which have been considered as foreground and background will not be changed by the algorithm and thus ensure a good robustness to segmentation errors. To handle the uncertainty associated to edge pixels in the depth image, only pixels which are not on a boundary are marked using those definitive labels. The GrabCut algorithm on the color image is then run using the computed mask for one iteration.

Due to the accuracy of the initial mask, GrabCut performs well even if the object and the background have a similar color distribution or if the background is cluttered, as shown in Fig. 8.

4.2 Hole Filling Through Depth Inpainting

The obtained object segmentation is accurate but some pixels which have been classified as object after the color refinement do not have depth. Most of the

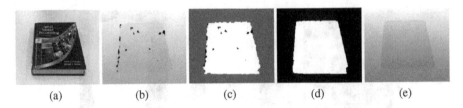

(a)   (b)   (c)   (d)   (e)

Fig. 9. 2D images results of the color-based model refinement using a book as illustrative example. Images from the Kinect camera: (a) color image and (b) depth image. (c) Initial segmentation re-projecting every 3D point from the volume of Sect. 3.3. Pixels are marked as: unknown (black), object (white) and background (gray). (d) Final object segmentation after GrabCut according to Sect. 4.1. Pixels are marked as: object (white) and background (black). (e) Depth image after hole filling through depth inpainting.

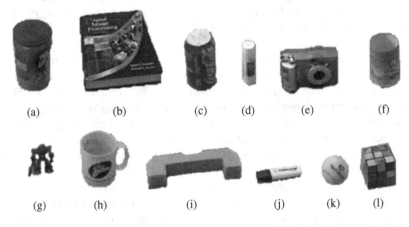

(a)   (b)   (c)   (d)   (e)   (f)

(g)   (h)   (i)   (j)   (k)   (l)

Fig. 10. The 12 real objects of the database: (a) baci, (b) book, (c) can, (d) glue, (e) camera, (f) pencil holder, (g) toy, (h) cup, (i) pink handle, (j) pen, (k) tennis ball, (l) Rubik's cube. For each object, at least 5 images have been acquired from the object in different orientations and places on the table.

hole filling methods use image interpolation or inpainting techniques to fill up the remaining holes using neighboring pixels. Recently, to improve the depth map output by Kinect, a cross-modal stereo vision approach has been presented in [16]. However, it does not benefit from a foreground/background segmentation. Furthermore, a hole-filling method using depth-based inpainting for 3D video was proposed in [17].

Following this, image inpainting is proposed in this work to fill missing depth values, but using the segmentation mask to fill pixels with only surrounding values of the same kind. Thus, object holes are filled only with depth information coming from the other "object" pixels and background holes are filled only with depth coming from surrounding "back-ground" values. The OpenCV implementation of Telea [18], a fast inpainting technique based on fast marching, is the used method. It takes as input the original depth image and an inpainting mask specifying the pixels to be filled. To fill the depth image, two masks are used depending on the pixel class:

1. Object: the target area to be filled corresponds to "object" pixels without depth value or with inconsistent depth values determined in Sect. 4.1. Pixels which belong to background are also marked as target area to prevent them from influencing the inpainting.
2. Background: the target area corresponds to pixels labeled as "background" without depth value. Similarly to the previous case, "object" pixels are also marked as target area.

Once the depth image has been refined and filled, the algorithm of Sect. 3.3 is run again. The improvement obtained after segmentation refinement and depth inpainting is shown in Fig. 9, filling pixels without depth information and border pixels whose depth was not correct. The final object model is obtained using Poisson surface reconstruction [19] on the voxelized point cloud to create a smooth mesh of the object.

5   Experiments

5.1   Evaluation of the Accuracy of the Reconstructed Mesh

The proposed algorithm has been tested on a set of 12 real objects with very different sizes and shapes, which are shown in Fig. 10. For each of the object, between 5 and 9 meshes have been acquired using our algorithm in the scenario showed in Fig. 1, where the objects lie off the table in different orientations and places. Therefore, the data set contains 72 reconstructed models which have been calculated from a single view of Kinect camera. For the evaluation, the geometric difference between reference and reconstructed meshes using our proposed algorithm has been calculated. The reference models have been acquired with a commercial laser scanner.

The processing time of the whole algorithm is currently less than 2 s on a 2 GHz computer for a point cloud with less than 30000 points, significantly improving computation time achieved in [7] with a similar number of points. Although this computation time is suitable for the current application, optimization is considered as future work.

A free 3D mesh processing software, MeshLab [20], has been used to compute the geometric difference between reference and reconstructed 3D models which should be well aligned in the same space. Iterated Closed Point (ICP) is used to align the meshes and the Hausdorff distance to measure the geometrical distance between them.

Figure 11 shows the mean and the standard deviation between reference and reconstructed meshes for all objects. The average error for all meshes is 3.87 mm and the standard deviation is 0.96 mm. Taking into account that the objects are similar to the set used in [7], our extrusion approach provides a similar effectiveness in comparison with earlier symmetry method and a significant improvement for large objects. With our method, the mean error is less than 5 mm in

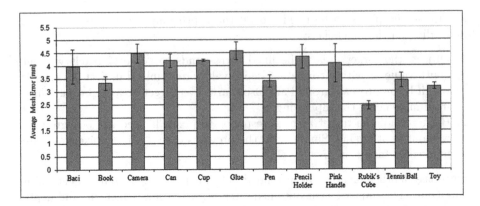

Fig. 11. Evaluation of the mean error and standard deviation between reference and reconstructed meshes for all objects of the database. The mean error is less than 5 mm in all objects, being the average error less than 4 mm.

all objects, independently of their size while in [7] the average error is less than 7 mm and 20 mm for bigger objects.

It is important to note that the experimental measurement gathered is statistically very rich in the sense that each object image was captured in different orientations and different locations on the table, as it is shown in Fig. 12. Such set takes into consideration most of the possible sources of errors, such as hiding different geometric details, reflections or other optical effects, which affect the obtained results and increase the error.

Figure 13 shows as, due to the position of the "pink handle" object, the error is lower when the visible parts provide enough information to approximate the geometry by an extrusion of its top-view (Case 2 and 3), but the error increases when the top-view is not very informative (Case 6).

Taking into account that the voxel size chosen in this work is 3 mm (Sect. 3.1) then it is fairly obvious that we cannot obtain reconstructions with errors less that the mentioned voxel value. This can be seen in the table of the average errors of the different objects, where only the Rubik's cube average error is 2.5 mm while the rest are above 3 mm. If more precision is required, we may scarify the speed and improve the accuracy of the reconstructed object models. This can be done if a particular task requires it.

5.2   Model Reconstruction Results

Figure 14 shows some meshes acquired using our algorithm for the tested set of 12 real objects. Figure 15 (a)–(c), shows objects for which a very good model could be obtained despite of a very sparse initial point cloud. The quality of the top view is essential for the approach, but it was made significantly more robust thanks to the segmentation and depth filling steps. Reconstruction is even possible in some cases where almost no information was present in the original

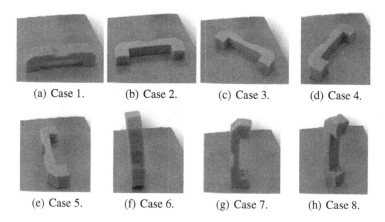

| (a) Case 1. | (b) Case 2. | (c) Case 3. | (d) Case 4. |

| (e) Case 5. | (f) Case 6. | (g) Case 7. | (h) Case 8. |

Fig. 12. The "pink handle" object in the 8 evaluated orientations on the table (Color figure online).

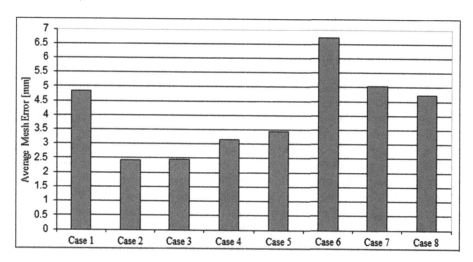

Fig. 13. Evaluation of the error for 8 evaluated orientations on the table for the "pink handle" object. Comparing to its reference model, the mean error is 4.09 mm and the standard deviation is 1.49 mm.

image. Figure 15 (d) and (e), gives examples of objects which have a geometry that cannot be roughly approximated by an extrusion of their top-view. Note that even if the obtained models are not very accurate, useful estimations for grasping are still obtained. Adding another camera with a different point of view would be enough to obtain a good model in these cases.

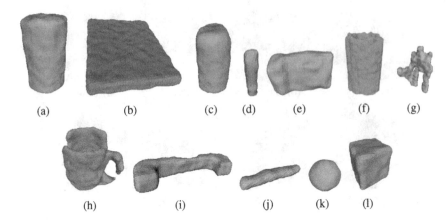

Fig. 14. Model reconstruction results of the 12 real objects of the database, shown in Fig. 10: (a) baci, (b) book, (c) can, (d) glue, (e) camera, (f) pencil holder, (g) toy, (h) cup, (i) pink handle, (j) pen, (k) tennis ball, (l) Rubik's cube.

5.3   Application to Grasping

Since grasping itself is not the main scope of this paper, the suitability of the acquired meshes for grasping has been tested on a single object as a representative way. Both planning and grasping experiments have been performed within OpenRAVE simulator [10]. It simulates grasps in many positions to determine a set of stable grasps for a given object, as illustrated in Fig. 16. Then it can be used for online path planning in a given scene, where the object is recognized and its pose estimated to perform the suitable grasp, which has been calculated off-line previously. Figure 17 shows the sequence of the trajectory in simulation and on the real robot of our scenario (Fig. 1), suggesting that the acquired mesh is suitable for grasping. A more exhaustive evaluation of grasping from a single viewpoint in simulation and on our robotic platform is considered as future work.

6   Discussion and Future Work

The method Xtru3D to reconstruct models of everyday man-made objects from a RGB-D camera single view has been proposed in this work. The precision of the method has been evaluated and validated by studying the difference between the reference and the reconstructed model for 12 real objects. The average error for all meshes is less than 4 mm and the standard deviation is less than 1 mm. Furthermore, compared to earlier methods, our approach provides 3D models with similar accuracy while improving run-times significantly. The improvement is even more significant, both in run-time and accuracy in the case of bigger objects.

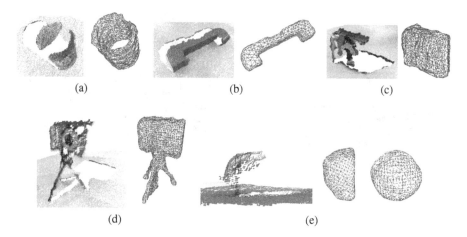

Fig. 15. Model reconstruction results of a (a) pencil holder, (b) a pink handle, (c) a camera, (d) a camera on a tripod and (e) a tennis ball. Left: initial point cloud. Right: final mesh using Poisson reconstruction ((e) side and front view).

Fig. 16. Five grasps of the grasp table generated by OpenRAVE for a pink handle whose mesh has been generated using the proposed algorithm.

The performed experiments run on different objects showed that the models are precise enough to be used for the computation of reliable grasping points in a robotic manipulation setup. Thus, the current system is an easy and effective approach but it has some limitations when objects have very thin structures, or with objects whose top-view is not very informative. However, thanks to the generality of the proposed algorithm, this could be compensated by adding more cameras as needed, applying the same technique on each view and finally merging the resulting voxels, similar to 2-stage extrusion [21]. Furthermore, symmetry and extrusion could complement one another, recently used by [22] determining the extruded shapes by the detection of planar reflection symmetries in the partial point cloud.

In order to handle a wider range of objects, future versions of the proposed methods are planned to account for rotational symmetries exploitation by adopting techniques of shape estimation such as those described [8]. Moreover, for manipulation applications, once the object is grasped, several approaches for model refinement have been considered: on the one hand, the integration of

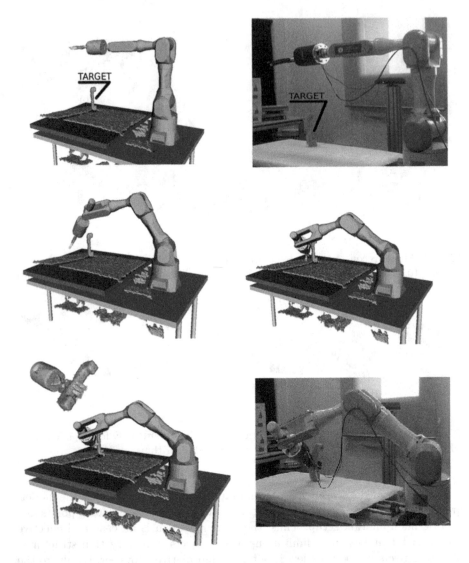

Fig. 17. Simulated and real sequence of the trajectory toward the selected grasping position, which has been calculated off-line previously. Both planning and grasping have been performed within OpenRAVE.

single view estimation with the incremental model refinements techniques of e.g. [23] and [24] would be interesting. On the other hand, focusing on recent advances on sensor fusion for manipulation of unknown objects, this model refinement could be developed fusing visual and tactile data [25]. Finally, future work will also integrate the proposed approach with an online grasp planner to enable fast online grasping and manipulation of unknown objects.

Acknowledgements. The research leading to these results has been funded by the HANDLE European project (FP7/2007–2013) under grant agreement ICT 231640-http://www.handle-project.eu.

References

1. Microsoft: Kinect for Xbox 360 (2010)
2. Kuehnle, J., Xue, Z., Stotz, M., Zoellner, J., Verl, A., Dillmann, R.: Grasping in depth maps of time-of-flight cameras. In: International Workshop on Robotic and Sensors Environments (ROSE), pp. 132–137 (2008)
3. Miller, A., Allen, P.: Graspit! a versatile simulator for robotic grasping. IEEE Robot. Autom. Mag. **11**, 110–122 (2004)
4. Sun, M., Kumar, S.S., Bradski, G., Savarese, S.: Toward automatic 3d generic object modeling from one single image. In: 3DIMPVT, Hangzhou, China (2011)
5. Thomas, A., Ferrari, V., Leibe, B., Tuytelaars, T., Van Gool, L.: Depth-from-recognition: inferring meta-data by cognitive feedback. In: 2007 IEEE 11th International Conference on Computer Vision. ICCV 2007, pp. 1–8. IEEE (2007)
6. Thrun, S., Wegbreit, B.: Shape from symmetry. In: 2005 Tenth IEEE International Conference on Computer Vision. ICCV 2005, vol. 2, pp. 1824–1831. IEEE (2005)
7. Bohg, J., Johnson-Roberson, M., León, B., Felip, J., Gratal, X., Bergstrom, N., Kragic, D., Morales, A.: Mind the gap-robotic grasping under incomplete observation. In: 2011 IEEE International Conference on Robotics and Automation (ICRA), pp. 686–693. IEEE (2011)
8. Marton, Z., Pangercic, D., Blodow, N., Kleinehellefort, J., Beetz, M.: General 3d modelling of novel objects from a single view. In: IEEE/RSJ International Conference on Intelligent Robots and Systems (IROS), pp. 3700–3705. IEEE (2010)
9. Benko, P., Martin, R.R., Varady, T.: Algorithms for reverse engineering boundary representation models. Comput. Aided Des. **33**, 839–851 (2001)
10. Diankov, R.: Automated construction of robotic manipulation programs. Ph.D. thesis, Carnegie Mellon University, Robotics Institute (2010)
11. Rusu, R., Bradski, G., Thibaux, R., Hsu, J.: Fast 3d recognition and pose using the viewpoint feature histogram. In: IEEE/RSJ International Conference on Intelligent Robots and Systems (IROS), pp. 2155–2162. IEEE (2010)
12. Boykov, Y., Jolly, M.P.: Interactive graph cuts for optimal boundary & region segmentation of objects in N-d images. In: Proceedings of Eighth IEEE International Conference on Computer Vision (ICCV), vol. 1, pp. 105–112 (2001)
13. Lombaert, H., Sun, Y., Grady, L., Xu, C.: A multilevel banded graph cuts method for fast image segmentation. In: IEEE International Conference on Computer Vision (ICCV), pp. 259–265 (2005)
14. Rother, C., Kolmogorov, V., Blake, A.: "GrabCut": interactive foreground extraction using iterated graph cuts. ACM Trans. Graph. **23**, 309–314 (2004)
15. Vaiapury, K., Aksay, A., Izquierdo, E.: GrabCutD: improved grabcut using depth information. In: Proceedings of the 2010 ACM Workshop on Surreal Media and Virtual Cloning. SMVC '10, New York, NY, USA, pp. 57–62. ACM (2010)
16. Chiu, W., Blanke, U., Fritz, M.: Improving the kinect by cross-modal stereo. In: 22nd British Machine Vision Conference (BMVC), Dundee, UK (2011)
17. Oh, K.J., Yea, S., Ho, Y.S.: Hole filling method using depth based in-painting for view synthesis in free viewpoint television and 3-d video. In: Picture Coding Symposium, 2009. PCS 2009, pp. 1–4 (2009)

18. Telea, A.: An image inpainting technique based on the fast marching method. J. Graph. GPU Game Tools **9**, 23–34 (2004)
19. Kazhdan, M., Bolitho, M., Hoppe, H.: Poisson surface reconstruction. In: Symposium on Geometry Processing, pp. 61–70 (2006)
20. MeshLab: Visual Computing Lab-ISTI-CNR (2011)
21. Shum, S., Lau, W., Yuen, M., Yu, K.: Solid reconstruction from orthographic views using 2-stage extrusion. Comput. Aided Des. **33**, 91–102 (2001)
22. Kroemer, O., Ben Amor, H., Ewerton, M., Peters, J.: Point cloud completion using symmetries and extrusions. In: Proceedings of the International Conference on Humanoid Robots (HUMANOIDS) (2012)
23. Krainin, M., Henry, P., Ren, X., Fox, D.: Manipulator and object tracking for in hand model acquisition. In: Proceedings of the Workshop on Best Practice in 3D Perception and Modeling for Mobile Manipulation at the International Conference on Robotics Automation (ICRA) (2010)
24. Krainin, M., Curless, B., Fox, D.: Autonomous generation of complete 3d object models using next best view manipulation planning. In: IEEE International Conference on Robotics and Automation (ICRA) (2011)
25. Bimbo, J., Rodríguez-Jiménez, S., Liu, H., Burrus, N., Seneviratne, I., Abderrahim, M., Althoefer, K.: Fusing visual and tactile sensing for manipulation of unknown objects. In: Proceedings of the ICRA 2013 Mobile Manipulation Workshop on Interactive Perception (2013)

Facial Landmark Localization and Feature Extraction for Therapeutic Face Exercise Classification

Cornelia Lanz[1]($\boxtimes$), Birant Sibel Olgay[1],
Joachim Denzler[2], and Horst-Michael Gross[1]

[1] Neuroinformatics and Cognitive Robotics Lab,
Ilmenau University of Technology, Ilmenau, Germany
cornelia.lanz@tu-ilmenau.de
[2] Computer Vision Group, Friedrich Schiller University Jena, Jena, Germany

Abstract. In this work, we examine landmark localization and feature extraction approaches for the unexplored topic of therapeutic facial exercise recognition. Our goal is to automatically discriminate nine therapeutic exercises that have been determined in cooperation with speech therapists. We use colour, 2.5D and 3D image data that was recorded using Microsoft's Kinect. Our features comprise statistical descriptors of the face surface curvature as well as characteristic profiles that are derived from face landmarks. For the nine facial exercises, we yield an average recognition accuracy of about 91 % in conjunction with manually labeled landmarks. Additionally, we introduce a combined method for automatic landmark localization and compare the results to landmark positions obtained from Active Appearance Model fitting as well as manual labeling. The combined localization method exhibits increased robustness in comparison to AAMs.

Keywords: Facial expressions · Curvature analysis · Point signatures · Line profiles · Therapeutic exercises

1 Introduction

Diseases like stroke or mechanical injury of the facial nerve can lead to a dysfunction of facial movements. These impairments of facial expressions and muscle control may have various consequences like eating difficulties and impaired face appearance, which can restrict daily life and can lead to social isolation. Similar to rehabilitation exercises that help to regain body functions, there are exercises for the recovery of facial expressions. Besides practising under supervision of a speech therapist, patients additionally have to conduct unattended exercises on their own. However, the incorrect conduction of exercises can impede the training success or even lead to further impairment. An accompanying training platform could enrich unsupervised training exercises by a feedback functionality [1].

© Springer-Verlag Berlin Heidelberg 2014
S. Battiato et al. (Eds.): VISIGRAPP 2013, CCIS 458, pp. 179–194, 2014.
DOI: 10.1007/978-3-662-44911-0_12

The design and implementation of such a training platform is a challenging and complex task that comprises several subtasks. In this work, we will focus on two subtasks – the automated facial landmark localization and the evaluation of features. However, in order to enable a better understanding of the context of our work, we also give a brief overview of the remaining subtasks. Figure 1(a) presents five of the involved subtasks, which will be discussed in the following.

Facial movements cause changes of the face surface, which can be captured by depth image sensors like Microsoft's Kinect[1] or Time-of-flight Cameras[2,3]. The extraction of *depth features* (see Fig. 1(a)) allows to examine the face surface, independently from skin colour and lighting conditions. Although there exist other systems that are capable of recording depth data with much higher depth resolution than the Kinect (e.g. [2]), we decided to use this sensor because of its moderate price. This makes our target application suitable for widespread use in low-cost training platforms. Furthermore, the Kinect allows to capture additional data channels such as intensity images in parallel to depth images. These might be helpful if depth information is not suitable to describe certain facial movements. For example, it can hardly be determined whether the eyes are closed by solely processing depth information. In a real-world scenario, where regions for feature extraction should be detected automatically, we additionally need a fully *automated facial landmark localization.*

The nine therapeutic face exercises that we focus on in this paper are rather static. The pace of the exercise conduction from neutral face to final state, e.g., both cheeks puffed, is not important. It is more relevant that the exercises final states are retained for a few seconds. Nevertheless, it is likely that additional information, obtained by examining the *dynamics* of an exercise instead of single *static* snapshots, may contain valuable information. Additionally, it is possible to reduce the amount of noise in the data by smoothing over time.

The *evaluation of the exercises*, which is essential for a feedback functionality, is a complex task. Besides the choice of appropriate technical tools, it is necessary to define in which cases an exercise is performed correctly and in which not. Additionally, it needs to be assessed how feedback should be communicated in order to be most beneficial for a patient.

Furthermore, it is necessary to collect a *database* of training and test images that contain the exercises performed by healthy people as well as the exercise conduction by people with dysfunction of facial expression abilities. In our experiments, nine therapeutic facial exercises are employed that had been defined in cooperation with speech therapists. In our studies, we only use training and test data recorded from exercises of healthy persons. We omit data recorded from persons with dysfunction of facial expressions, as we expect their ground-truth to be ill-defined. This is due to the circumstance, that incorrect conduction of an exercise may resemble other exercises, as shown in Fig. 1(b).

---

[1] http://www.xbox.com/en-US/kinect

[2] http://www.pmdtec.com/

[3] http://www.mesa-imaging.ch/

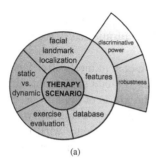

(a)   (b)

Fig. 1. (a) Different subtasks of the design and implementation of an automated therapeutic exercise platform. (b) Patient with facial paresis on his right side. Left image: The exercise *right cheek puffed* is conducted correctly because the bulge of the cheek is a passive process as reaction of a higher air pressure inside the mouth and a contraction of the buccinator on the left facial side. Right image: The exercise *left cheek puffed* is conducted incorrectly. The lack of contraction in the right buccinator leads to the bulge of the right cheek.

Since each of the above-mentioned subtasks covers diverse aspects, we focus on the landmark localization and the succeeding feature extraction for therapeutic exercise classification here. Our depth features are extracted from 2.5D images and 3D point clouds recorded by the Kinect Sensor. We refer to 2.5D images as 2D images that contain the object-to-camera distance instead of the object's intensity value. We analyse the facial surface by extraction of curvature information and surface profiles. Surface profiles comprise line profiles and point signatures. Line profiles are based on paths that connect two landmark points, whereas point signatures are based on radial paths around single landmark points.

We examine the features' *discriminative power* with respect to the classification of nine therapeutic exercises and their *robustness* regarding varying feature extraction regions. In the targeted real-time scenario, regions and points for feature extraction need to be determined automatically. We expected that this step leads to variations from manually located face regions and landmarks. Therefore, it is necessary that the features are robust against these deviations. Two different approaches for automated landmark localization have been tested: Active Appearance Models [3] and a combined approach that consists of learned spatial relations of the facial landmarks and tree-structured parts models.

2   Related Work

Automated recognition of therapeutic face exercises is a still relatively unexplored research field. In practice, there are already tools that support the patient with regard to exercising that is not supervised by a therapist. These tools comprise video tutorials (*LogoVid*[4]) or exercise diaries (*CoMuZu*[5]). However, at this moment there are no commercial solutions available that automatically recognize and evaluate a performed therapeutic exercise.

In [4] the benefit of facial exercises for the prevention of synkinesis after facial paresis is analyzed. Synkinesis is an involuntary associated facial movement such as eye closure during smiling. In order to determine the grade of synkinesis, [4] manually measure the eye opening width by using an image editing software. Reference [5] present a system for the diagnosis support of patients with facial paresis using 2D colour images. Therefore, they analyse facial asymmetries in the eyes, nose and mouth regions.

At present, there are no publications known to us that focus on the automated recognition of therapeutic facial exercises using depth information. Nevertheless, we can utilize approaches from works on face detection, as well as person and emotion recognition. Reference [6] use curvature of the surface of a 2.5D image to detect salient face features, like eyes and nose. A triplet consisting of a candidate nose and two candidate eyes is processed by a classifier that is trained to discriminate between faces and non-faces. Based on curvature information estimated on a 3D triangle mesh model, [7] classify 3D faces according to the emotional state that they represent.

Point signatures were developed by [8] as an approach for general 3D object recognition. Additionally, in [9] they present an enhanced point signature algorithm that is specialised on face recognition. Reference [10] extract point signatures in 2.5D images and Gabor filter responses in gray-level images and employ their combination for face recognition.

In this work, we follow the method proposed in [7] to create histograms of curvature types. We utilize the face recognition algorithm from [9] for the classification of our nine therapeutic exercises and supplement it with a similar approach that employs line profiles instead of radial profiles. In contrast to [7], where manually placed landmarks are used, we additionally evaluate our results with automatically located landmark positions.

3   Method

In the following, we briefly summarize the determination of surface curvature (Sect. 3.1) as far as it is necessary to understand the basic principles of our curvature feature types (Sect. 3.2). For detailed information, we refer to [11]. In Sects. 3.3 and 3.4 the extraction of line profiles and point signatures is presented. In the last section, we focus on the automation of the feature extraction process.

3.1   Curvature Analysis

Our aim is the classification of faces according to the therapeutic exercises a patient performs. Facial movement leads to a change of the face surface.

---

[4] http://www.comuzu.de

[5] http://www.logomedien.de/html/logovid7a.html

We analyse the surface by extracting curvature information from 2.5D range images and 3D point clouds. The parametric form of a surface in 3D is $s(u, v) = [x(u, v)\ y(u, v)\ z(u, v)]^T$, with u and v denoting the axes of the parameter plane (Fig. 2(a)). Based on this function, we can determine the first and the second fundamental forms, which uniquely characterize and quantify general smooth shapes. The elements of the first fundamental form $\mathbf{I}$ are:

$$\mathbf{I} = \begin{bmatrix} \mathbf{s_u} \cdot \mathbf{s_u} & \mathbf{s_u} \cdot \mathbf{s_v} \\ \mathbf{s_u} \cdot \mathbf{s_v} & \mathbf{s_v} \cdot \mathbf{s_v} \end{bmatrix}. \tag{1}$$

The subscripts denote partial differentiation. The elements of the second fundamental form $\mathbf{J}$ are:

$$\mathbf{J} = \begin{bmatrix} \mathbf{s_{uu}} \cdot \mathbf{n} & \mathbf{s_{uv}} \cdot \mathbf{n} \\ \mathbf{s_{uv}} \cdot \mathbf{n} & \mathbf{s_{vv}} \cdot \mathbf{n} \end{bmatrix}, \tag{2}$$

with $\mathbf{n}$ being the unit normal vector of the tangent plane in the point with parameters (u, v). Although both fundamental forms are a unique representation of the surface, combinations of both are more common for surface characterization, because they allow for an intuitive interpretation. Using $\mathbf{I}$ and $\mathbf{J}$, the shape operator matrix $\mathbf{W}$ can be computed by:

$$\mathbf{W} = \mathbf{I}^{-1} \cdot \mathbf{J}. \tag{3}$$

The mean curvature H gives information about the direction of the curvature (convex, concave) and is determined by:

$$H = \frac{1}{2} \, tr \, [\mathbf{W}], \tag{4}$$

with $tr\,[\mathbf{W}]$ being the trace of the shape operator $\mathbf{W}$. The Gaussian curvature K contains the information whether curvatures that are orthogonal to each other point in the same or in different directions (Fig. 2(b)). It is computed as follows:

$$K = det \, [\mathbf{W}]. \tag{5}$$

Opposed to the general parametric representation, the parametrization of a 2.5D range image takes a very simple form $s(u, v) = [u\ v\ z(u, v)]^T$. Because a 2.5D image is spanned by two axes that generate a discrete (pixel) grid, the derivation of s with respect to u and v is simplified and results in $\mathbf{s_u} = [1\ 0\ z_u]^T$ and $\mathbf{s_v} = [0\ 1\ z_v]^T$. Therefore, for the computation of H and K only the partial derivatives of z are relevant:

$$H = \frac{z_{uu} + z_{vv} + z_{uu}z_v^2 + z_{vv}z_u^2 - 2z_u z_v z_{uv}}{(1 + z_u^2 + z_v^2)^{\frac{3}{2}}}, \tag{6}$$

$$K = \frac{z_{uu}z_{vv} - z_{uv}^2}{(1 + z_u^2 + z_v^2)^2}. \tag{7}$$

3.2   Extraction of Curvature Information

Prior to feature extraction, we smooth the face surface using an average filter. We extract the mean and Gaussian curvature for each pixel, respectively 3D-point, in order to obtain information about the facial surface. This results in around 2×8000 to 2×13000 values per face, depending on the face-to-camera distance. In order to reduce the dimensionality of the feature space, we accumulate the curvature values in a histogram [7]. To maintain spatial information, we define four regions (A-D) from which histograms are extracted (Fig. 2(c)). Each histogram is weighted with the number of pixels of the region described by it. The selected cheek regions are axially symmetric, due to the fact that some of the therapeutic exercises are asymmetric and each face side contains valuable information. Two additional regions, in which high facial surface variation among all exercises is visible, were included into the feature extraction process. Further refinement of the regions was omitted in order to maintain a certain robustness in case of automatically determined regions.

The curvature type histogram feature is obtained by extraction of mean curvature H and Gaussian curvature K for every 2.5D pixel, respectively 3D point according to (4)–(7). In the next step, both values are combined to eight discrete curvature types as shown in Table 1 [6]. Subsequently, the discrete curvature types of each region are summarized with histograms. The concatenation

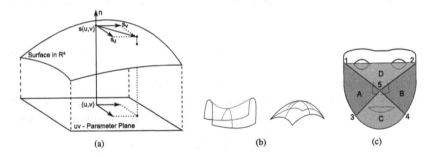

(a)   (b)   (c)

Fig. 2. (a) Surface in 3D with the corresponding parameter plane (image according to [11]). (b) Two surfaces with orthogonal maximum and minimum curvatures that point in different (left surface: hyperbolic convex) and in the same directions (right surface: elliptic convex). (c) Regions A-D are employed for curvature feature extraction. Region borders are derived from landmark points 1–5. The determination of the landmark points is explained in Sects. 3.5 and 4.1.

Table 1. Curvature type definition using mean and Gaussian curvature (H, K).

	$K < 0$	$K = 0$	$K > 0$
$H < 0$	Hyperbolic concave	Cylindric concave	Elliptic concave
$H = 0$	Hyperbolic symmetric	Planar	Impossible
$H > 0$	Hyperbolic convex	Cylindric convex	Elliptic convex

of these histograms forms the feature vectors that are subjected to the classification process. For each image, a 32 dimensional feature vector is extracted (8 curvature type histogram bins per each of the four regions).

3.3   Extraction of Line Profiles

Although curvatures are extracted from each pixel, their combination in a histogram blots out some of the local information. Line profiles, in comparison, contain highly localized information by describing paths along the face surface. Instead of using 2.5D images, line profiles are extracted from a point cloud in 3D. Each of the three dimensions is expressed in meter. For a 2.5D image, two dimensions are given in pixel units. However, the real world distance that is described by the difference of one pixel depends on the person-to-camera distance. The smaller the distance of an object to the camera is, the more pixels does this object cover on a 2.5D image. As a result, comparison of different line profiles is more difficult, when using 2.5D images.

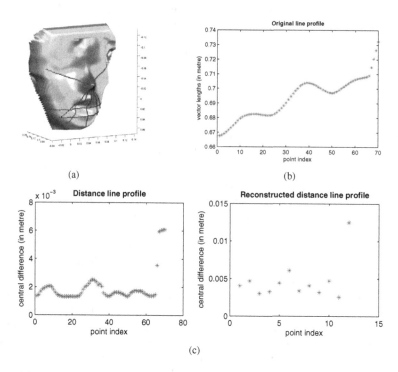

(a)   (b)

(c)

Fig. 3. (a) 3D face with marked paths of the nine line profiles. (b) Line profile from nose tip to the point of the chin for the exercise *A-shape*. The curve shows the length (in metre) of the position vector of each point p_n. The opening of the mouth, resulting in higher values, in the middle of the curve and the chin shape on the right are visible. (c) Left: Distance line profile. Right: The reconstructed line profile using the first 12 dct-coefficients.

In total, we extract nine line profiles from the 3D point cloud of the face. Every line profile connects two defined landmark points. Figure 3(a) shows the paths of the profile lines. Seven profiles start at the nose tip, connecting it in radial direction to silhouette points. Two line profiles are horizontally located and link two silhouette points.

The paths over the face consist of N equidistant points $p_n(x, y, z)$, with $n = 1...N$. Nearest-neighbour interpolation is employed in order to calculate missing points. The L2-norm of the position vectors of every 3D point p_n already creates a distinctive curve as can be seen in Fig. 3(b). However, in order to achieve invariance with respect to the viewpoint (i.e., translation and rotation operations of the facial point cloud), relatively coded central differences between the 3D points are calculated (left image of Fig. 3(c)).

The images show, that the curves consist of 70 samples. This value may vary because the size of the head (subject-specific) or the length of the curve (exercise-specific) may change. To get an identical size of the curve for every subject and every exercise and to reduce the amount of feature dimensions, we conduct a discrete cosine transform [12] on the curves and build our feature vector using the first 12 dct-coefficients. The right image of Fig. 3(c) shows, that the inverse discrete cosine transform with 12 coefficients yields a reasonable reconstruction of the original curve. We derived the line profiles from the point signature approach presented in the following section.

3.4   Extraction of Point Signatures

Similar to line profiles, point signatures are paths on a surface [8]. Instead of connecting two landmark points, the curve runs radially around a distinctive point p_0 of a 3D point cloud. As can be seen in Fig. 4(a), in our approach the point p_0 is located on the tip of the nose. In order to obtain the point signature, a sphere is centered into the point p_0 of the 3D point cloud. The intersection of the sphere with the facial points forms a curve Q in the three-dimensional space (Fig. 4(b)). The depth information of these intersection points, combined with the value of the sphere radius, contains characteristic and unique information about the depth value distribution in the surrounding area of the point p_0. However, taking the absolute depth values of this intersection points is not reasonable (as already discussed for the line profiles in Sect. 3.3) because they are not independent with respect to translation and rotation of the head. As a result, we create a reference curve Q' that can be employed to calculate relative depth information. To obtain this curve, we fit a plane P through the set of intersection points. The plane is determined with regression analysis by a singular value decomposition that gives the surface normal of the plane. The plane is now shifted along its normal vector into the point p_0. This results in a new plane called P' (Fig. 4(c)).

In the next step, the curve Q is projected onto P' building a new curve Q'. Now the curve Q' is sampled around the approximated surface normal at p_0 with a rotation angle of 15 degrees. For each sampled point in Q' the distance to its corresponding point in Q is collected. The starting position for the distance

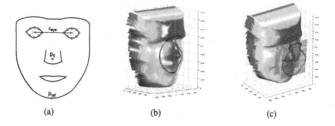

Fig. 4. (a) Landmark points and line segments that are employed for the extraction of point signatures. (b) Intersection curve Q of the sphere with the 3D point cloud. (c) The planes P (red) and P' (magenta). The projected curve Q' is marked on P' (Color figure online).

sampling needs to be equal between the different images to obtain curves that are comparable. Therefore, we define a starting position, which is determined by a reference point p_{ref}. The reference point is located on the chin as marked in Fig. 4(a). The sphere radius length has to be determined such that the arising path does not protrude beyond the surface of the face and no background points are sampled. The length of the radius is computed from the eye distance d_{eye}, multiplied by a factor f. The eye distance is estimated from the distance between the mean positions of each eye that are obtained by the landmark positions of each eye (Fig. 4(a)). We use the following values for the empirically determined factor f to extract five different point signatures that cover varying areas of the face: 0.4, 0.5, 0.7, 0.8 and 1.0.

Sampling of the radial curve with a fixed interval of 15 degrees generates 24 values per point signature. The more point signatures are extracted, the more precisely the surface of the face can be described. However, a high amount of point signatures leads to a high-dimensional feature space. Again, we reduce the dimension of the feature vector to twelve values by applying discrete cosine transform on each point signature as shown in Sect. 3.3.

3.5   Automation of the Feature Extraction Process

The features presented above have in common that distinct facial areas need to be determined for extraction. Manual determination of these landmarks and regions is not feasible in a real-world application. Thus, they have to be detected automatically, which may lead to less accurate localizations. In this work, we compare two different approaches for landmark localization: Active Appearance Models and a tree-structured parts model algorithm that is combined with a 3D spatial relations model.

AAMs are mainly applied in the field of facial expression recognition on 2D gray-value images ([3,13]). On the basis of several training images a combined mean texture and shape model is derived. The fitting of this mean model to a new and unknown face is improved by determination of a coarse initialization position using the Viola and Jones face detector [14]. In the next step the AAM adapts itself to the new face by minimizing the error between the model intensities and the image intensities. The parameters that describe the fitted model are usually subjected to classification of facial expressions. In contrast to this, the AAM can be used for the mere detection of landmarks without further consideration of the model parameters [15]. In this paper, we focus on the application of AAMs for the detection of the 58 landmarks only (Fig. 5(b)).

Tree-structured parts models are an approach for face detection, pose estimation and landmark localization [16]. In total 68 landmarks are located in this approach. The number of landmarks on the face silhouette is similar to the number of silhouette landmarks detected by the AAM approach. However, tests showed that the placement of landmarks in the center of the face, e.g., in the nose or eye region, is too imprecise for the targeted scenario. Therefore, only the information of the silhouette landmark positions is kept.

A spatial relations model and surface curvature are computed in a parallel process in order to localize the landmarks in the upper, rigid face half (Fig. 5(a)). The spatial relations model comprises a smaller subset of landmarks, which was derived from the landmarks and regions that are necessary for feature extraction. The idea of the spatial relations model is based on the fact that distances and angles between the landmarks of a face lie in a constrained range. The model is computed from training data and centered in the nose tip of a face (Fig. 5(c)). In total, 14 position vectors show the direction and absolute value to 14 landmarks (Fig. 5(d)). Additionally, for each landmark the maximum deviation of the training data from the mean position is computed. As a result, a spherical search space can be constructed around each position vector tip by using the maximum deviation distance as radius. In order to be able to fit the model to a new image with unknown landmark localizations, the nose tip and the nose ridge vector must be detected (Fig. 5(e)). This can be done via curvature analysis and Support Vector Machine (SVM) classification because of the distinctive surface of the nose. The 3D mean model is then translated and rotated so that the model reference vector and the nose ridge vector are congruent. Possible landmark candidates lie in each of the 14 spherical search spaces that are centered at the tip of a vector. Now, the previously computed curvature information can additionally be used as input for 14 single SVMs in order to further reduce the landmark candidate number. For each of the 14 landmarks a separate SVM is trained. In the end, for each landmark a centroid of the remaining candidates is computed and defined as the new landmark position.

In contrast to the rigid upper face half, the lower one has a more dynamic surface appearance. As a result, mean and Gaussian curvature are not appropriate for landmark localization in this area. In the last step, upper face half landmarks from the spatial relations model and lower face half landmarks from the tree-structured parts model are fused to one landmark set. Thus, at present, both processes are parallel and independent from each other. Our future goal is to combine the results of both approaches for complementary verification and error minimization.

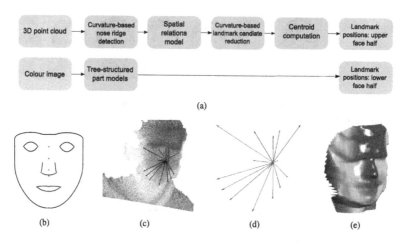

Fig. 5. (a) Process of landmark localization. (b) The 58 landmark positions of the Active Appearance Model. (c) Spatial relations model fitted on a face. (d) 3D spatial relations model. (e) Face with nose ridge vector (red) (Color figure online).

The AAM and the tree-structured parts model are fitted on the 2D intensity images. Subsequently, we need to transform these landmark positions to positions in depth images. Therefore, intrinsic and extrinsic camera parameters were determined by camera calibration [17]. They can be employed to align the 2.5D images with their corresponding intensity images. As a result, corresponding points have the same position in the images of both channels, and the labeled landmark positions can be accordingly transferred. Additionally, these camera parameters can be used to transform the points of the 2.5D image to a discrete 3D point cloud [17].

4   Experiments

In the first section of the experimental part, we focus on the dataset and the exercises that are used for our experiments. The evaluation of the features discriminative power with respect to the classification of therapeutic exercises is presented in Sect. 4.2. Results from experiments that test the robustness of the features related to variations of region borders are given in the last section.

4.1   Exercises and Dataset

In cooperation with speech therapists, we selected a set of nine therapeutic face exercises by certain criterions. The exercises should train the lips, the cheeks, and the tongue and should be beneficial for various types of facial muscle dysfunctions, e.g. paresis of muscles or muscle imbalance. Furthermore, the selected exercises should be easy to practice and should build a set of sub-exercises that can be combined to more complex dynamic exercise units, e.g. by alternating

Fig. 6. Exercises that have been selected in cooperation with speech therapists (l. to r.): pursed lips, taut lips, A-shape, I-shape, cheek poking (right/ left side), cheeks puffed (both/ right/ left side(s)). For better visualization colour images are shown.

between them. The exercises have to be performed in an exaggerated manner, to enable a maximum training effect, and have to be retained for around two or three seconds. The speed of the performance is not important. Although some of these are vocal exercises, it is not necessary to vocalize a continuous sound while performing the shape. Images that visualize the exercise conduction are shown in Fig. 6.

Due to the lack of a public database that shows the performance of therapeutic exercises, we recorded a dataset, which contains eleven persons, who conducted the nine exercises. For each exercise, there are around seven images, showing different states of exercise conduction. This amounts to a total size of 696 images in the dataset. Some parts of the scene, which was captured by the Kinect may be shadowed, if they are seen by the depth camera but are not illuminated by the infrared projector. This leads to invalid values in the 2.5D image [18]. These values were removed by replacing them with the mean depth values of adjacent valid neighbour pixels. For every depth image, there exists a corresponding colour image that has been recorded with maximum time difference of 16 ms. The colour images have been labeled manually with 58 landmark points that were used for the training of the AAM (Fig. 5(b)), or for the feature extraction from depth data. The transferability of landmark positions between the 2.5D image and the colour image was already explained in Sect. 3.5.

4.2 Evaluation of the Discriminative Power

The following section gives an overview of the classification results. Since we wanted to evaluate the basic suitability of the described features for the task of classifying therapeutic exercises, we extracted the features from regions obtained via manually labeled landmarks, thus excluding other influences like deviating region borders. We evaluated each feature group individually and in combination. Training and classification was performed by applying SVMs of the LIBSVM package [19]. We tested linear SVM and a Radial Basis Function kernel. Optimal values for the penalty parameter C and the kernel parameter γ were obtained by a grid search on the training set [20]. In order to avoid overfitting to the training set, we employed a 5-fold cross-validation during parameter optimization. In combination with the amount of data (696 images, 232 feature dimensions), the linear SVM led to the best results because it avoided overfitting. The dataset was split up into training and test set using the leave-one-out cross-validation.

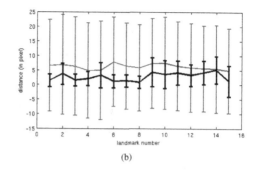

(a)   (b)

Fig. 7. (a) The 15 landmarks that are relevant for feature extraction. (b) The plot shows the mean values and standard deviations for the distances (in pixel units) between the manually labeled landmark positions and the positions localized by AAMs (red) and by the combined approach (black). Six pixel correspond to about 0.95 cm (Color figure online).

Additionally, all images of the person present in the test images were excluded from the training set. This approach is consistent with the mentioned application scenario in which the images of the test person will not be part of the training data. Linear discriminant analysis (LDA) was used prior to the linear SVM classification in order to reduce the feature dimensions from 232 to 8. LDA is a linear transformation of the feature space that maximizes the between-class separability and minimizes the within-class variability [21]. We obtained an average recognition accuracy over the nine classes of 90.89 %. Detailed results for the single features are given in Fig. 8.

4.3   Evaluation of the Automated Landmark Localization

As mentioned before, in a real-world scenario regions and landmark points for feature extraction have to be detected automatically. Therefore it is crucial, to employ a robust landmark localization. Although AAMs usually comprise 58 landmarks, in this section we constrain our evaluation to the landmarks that are relevant for our succeeding feature extraction (Fig. 7(a)). Figure 7(b) shows the mean pixel distances and standard deviations between the manually labeled landmarks and the two automated localization approaches. The AAMs are visualized in red and the combined parts and spatial relations model approach is visualized in black. The localization using the combined approach led to smaller deviations than using AAMs. A deviation of six pixels corresponds to about 0.95 cm. Additionally, it can be seen that the landmarks in the upper rigid half of the face were more robustly detected than the landmarks in the lower face half. Better localization resulted from the more distinctive and invariant surface shape in these landmark areas. Furthermore, images were labeled manually on 2D colour images. The landmarks with the smallest deviations are landmarks that are easier to label in the colour image because of distinctive visual properties, e.g., the darker inner eye corners or the edge between cheek and nose wing.

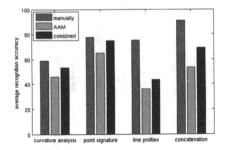

Fig. 8. The bar plot shows the average recognition rates (in %) for each of the three feature groups. As expected, feature extraction from manually determined regions and landmarks led to better results than the extraction from automatically determined areas using AAMs and combined models.

4.4 Evaluation of Feature Extraction from Automatically Determined Regions

In this section, we evaluate the robustness of our different features types with respect to varying region borders and landmark positions. Figure 8 shows the results for each of the three feature types for manually and automatically localized landmarks. For manual determination of the landmark positions, curvature analysis is weaker than point signatures and line profiles with respect to the discrimination of nine therapeutic exercises. This result occured because curvature information for several pixels is combined into histograms, and therefore, averaged over larger regions. However, curvature analysis achieved better results for automatically detected landmarks than the line profiles because it covers a larger region. Thus, small deviations of the silhouette landmarks have less influence on the regions used for feature extraction, especially if a landmark is incorrectly localized outside the face region.

As shown in Sect. 4.3, the combined approach led to more robust landmark localization than the AAMs. As expected, this resulted in better average recognition rates for each of the feature types. By concatenating the different feature types a rate of 90.89 % correct exercise classification was obtained if manual labeling is used and 69.14 % if the combined localization approach is used.

5   Summary and Discussion

In this paper, we presented several aspects that are necessary for the design and implementation of an automated training platform for patients with facial muscle dysfuctions. We introduced nine therapeutic exercises, which - in cooperation with speech language therapists - were determined as beneficial for the planned application scenario. Additionally, the automated classification of these exercises was evaluated. The presented approach employs 2.5D depth images and 3D point clouds and is based on three different feature types: curvature analysis, point signatures, and line profiles. The features were evaluated with respect to their discriminative power for exercise classification. Additionally, we examined their robustness regarding varying locations of feature extraction. This is relevant for all applications, planned for practical use, where a manual detection of landmarks is not feasible.

Curvature analysis, in the form we have implemented it, is rather global compared to point signatures and line profiles and showed a relatively robust performance. However, with suitable landmark localizations point signatures and line profiles outperform curvature analysis. We used two approaches for automated landmark detection: Active Appearance Models and tree-structured parts models. The latter lead to the best results. Line profiles showed only weak contribution to the classification process, if the landmark positions are detected automatically. Nevertheless, the results based on manually defined regions are promising.

Acknowledgements. We would like to thank the m&i Fachklinik Bad Liebenstein (in particular Prof. Dr. med. Gustav Pfeiffer, Eva Schillikowski) and Logopädische Praxis Irina Stangenberger, who supported our work by giving valuable insights into rehabilitation and speech-language therapy requirements and praxis. This work is partially funded by the TMBWK ProExzellenz initiative, Graduate School on Image Processing and Image Interpretation.

References

1. Lanz, C., Denzler, J., Gross, H.M.: Facial movement dysfunctions: conceptual design of a therapy-accompanying training system. In: Wichert, R., Klausing, H. (eds.) Ambient Assisted Living - Advanced Technologies and Societal Change. Springer, Heidelberg (2013)
2. Grosse, M., Schaffer, M., Harendt, B., Kowarschik, R.: Fast data acquisition for three-dimensional shape measurement using fixed-pattern projection and temporal coding. Opt. Eng. **50**, 100503 (2011)
3. Cootes, T., Edwards, G., Taylor, C.: Active appearance models. IEEE Trans. Pattern Anal. Mach. Intell. **23**, 681–685 (2001)
4. Nakamura, K., Toda, N., Sakamaki, K., Kashima, K., Takeda, N.: Biofeedback rehabilitation for prevention of synkinesis after facial palsy. Otolaryngol. Head Neck Surg. **128**, 539–543 (2003)
5. Gebhard, A., Paulus, D., Suchy, B., Wolf, S.: A system for diagnosis support of patients with facialis paresis. KI **3/2000**, 40–42 (2000)
6. Colombo, A., Cusano, C., Schettini, R.: 3d face detection using curvature analysis. Pattern Recogn. **39**, 444–455 (2006)
7. Wang, J., Yin, L., Wei, X., Sun, Y.: 3d facial expression recognition based on primitive surface feature distribution. In: International Conference on Computer Vision and Pattern Recognition, vol. 2, pp. 1399–1406 (2006)
8. Chua, C.S., Jarvis, R.: Point signature: a new representation for 3d object recognition. Int. J. Comput. Vis. **25**, 63–85 (1997)
9. Chua, C.S., Han, F., Ho, Y.K.: 3d human face recognition using point signature. In: Proceedings of the 4th International Automatic Face and Gesture Recognition Conference, pp. 233–238 (2000)

10. Wang, Y., Chua, C.S., Ho, Y.K.: Facial feature detection and face recognition from 2d and 3d images. Pattern Recogn. Lett. **23**, 1191–1202 (2002)
11. Besl, P., Jain, R.: Invariant surface characteristics for 3d object recognition in range images. Comput. Vis. Graph. Image Process. **33**, 33–80 (1986)
12. Salomon, D.: Data Compression: The Complete Reference. Springer, New York (2004)
13. Martin, C., Werner, U., Gross, H.M.: A real-time facial expression recognition system based on active appearance models using gray images and edge images. In: International Conference on Automatic Face and Gesture Recognition (2008)
14. Viola, P., Jones, M.: Robust real-time face detection. Int. J. Comput. Vis. **57**, 137–154 (2004)
15. Haase, D., Denzler, J.: Anatomical landmark tracking for the analysis of animal locomotion in x-ray videos using active appearance models. In: Heyden, A., Kahl, F. (eds.) SCIA 2011. LNCS, vol. 6688, pp. 604–615. Springer, Heidelberg (2011)
16. Zhu, X., Ramanan, D.: Face detection, pose estimation and landmark localization in the wild. In: International Conference for Computer Vision and Pattern Recognition, pp. 2879–2886 (2012)
17. Hartley, R., Zisserman, A.: Multiple View Geometry in Computer Vision. Cambridge University Press, Cambridge (2000)
18. Khoshelham, K.: Accuracy analysis of kinect depth data. In: ISPRS Workshop Laser Scanning, vol. 38 (2011)
19. Chang, C.C., Lin, C.J.: LIBSVM: a library for support vector machines. ACM Trans. Intell. Syst. Technol. **2**, 27:1–27:27 (2011). http://www.csie.ntu.edu.tw/~cjlin/libsvm
20. Hsu, C., Chang, C., Lin, C.: A practical guide to support vector classification. TR available at http://www.csie.ntu.edu.tw/~cjlin/papers/guide/guide.pdf (2009)
21. Webb, A., Copsey, K., Cawley, G.: Statistical Pattern Recognition. Wiley, New York (2011)

A Curious Vision System for Autonomous and Cumulative Object Learning

Pramod Chandrashekhariah$^{(\boxtimes)}$, Gabriele Spina, and Jochen Triesch

Frankfurt Institute for Advanced Studies (FIAS),
Johann Wolfgang Goethe University, Frankfurt am Main, Germany
{pramod,spina,triesch}@fias.uni-frankfurt.de

Abstract. We introduce a fully autonomous active vision system that explores its environment and learns visual representations of objects in the scene. The system design is motivated by the fact that infants learn internal representations of the world without much human assistance. Inspired by this, we build a curiosity driven system that is drawn towards locations in the scene that provide the highest potential for learning. In particular, the attention on a stimulus in the scene is related to the improvement in its internal model. This makes the system learn dynamic changes of object appearance in a cumulative fashion. We also introduce a self-correction mechanism in the system that rectifies situations where several distinct models have been learned for the same object or a single model has been learned for adjacent objects. We demonstrate through experiments that the curiosity-driven learning leads to a higher learning speed and improved accuracy.

Keywords: Active vision · Unsupervised learning · Autonomous vision system · Vision for robotics · Humanoid robot · Icub · Object recognition · Visual attention · Stereo vision · Intrinsic motivation

1 Introduction

One of the hallmarks of biological organisms is their ability to learn about their environment in a completely autonomous fashion. Future generations of robots assisting humans in their homes should similarly be able to autonomously acquire models of their working environment and any objects in it. While computer vision has made much progress in developing object recognition systems that can deal with many object classes, these systems need to be trained with supervised learning techniques, where a large number of hand-labeled training examples is required. Only recently, researchers have started addressing how a robot can learn to recognize objects in a largely autonomous fashion, *e.g.*, [1], how learning can be made fully online [2,3] and how the need for a human teacher can be minimized [4]. To this end, current attention systems of robots [5] have to be extended such that they support an efficient autonomous learning process.

© Springer-Verlag Berlin Heidelberg 2014
S. Battiato et al. (Eds.): VISIGRAPP 2013, CCIS 458, pp. 195–211, 2014.
DOI: 10.1007/978-3-662-44911-0_13

The central inspiration of our approach is the concept of intrinsic motivation [6–8]. Children learn and build internal representations of the world without much external assistance. Instead, they are intrinsically motivated to explore and play and thereby acquire knowledge and competence. In short, they are curious. It has been proposed that infants' interest in a stimulus may be related to their current learning progress, *i.e.*, the improvement of an internal model of the stimulus [9]. We adopt the same idea to build a "curious" vision system whose attention is drawn towards those locations and objects in the scene that provide the highest potential for learning. Specifically, our system pays attention to salient image regions likely to contain objects, it continues looking at objects and updating their models as long as it can learn something new about them, it avoids looking at objects whose models are already accurate, and it avoids searching for objects in locations that have been visited recently. We show that our system learns more efficiently than alternative versions whose attention is not coupled to their learning progress.

2   Object Learning

Our system is implemented on the iCub robot head [10]. Its basic mode of operation is as follows. An attention mechanism generates eye movements to different locations. Any object present at the current location is segmented and tracked while learning proceeds. If the object is unfamiliar then a new object model is created. If the object is already familiar, then its model is updated if necessary. Learning proceeds for as long as the model can be improved. Then a new focus of attention is selected. Figure 1 shows the system architecture, which is explained in detail in the following sections.

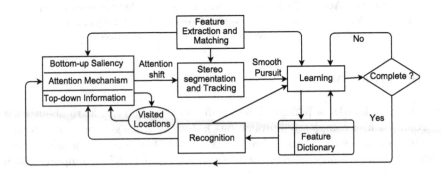

Fig. 1. System architecture.

We describe objects as spatial arrangements of local image features, an approach that is robust to occlusions, local deformations, variation in illumination conditions, and background clutter, *e.g.*, [11]. To this end, image features are extracted at interest points detected with the Harris corner detector [12]. We use Gabor wavelet features, which have the shape of plane waves restricted by a

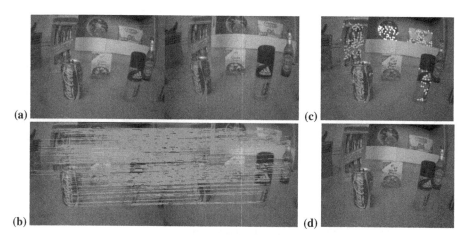

Fig. 2. Several objects are placed in front of the robot that analyzes the scene using its cameras (a). Harris corner points are detected and matched across left and right image using Gabor-jets (b). A low resolution saliency map is used to select the most salient interest points in the scene. Interest points on left image are clustered based on their location and stereo disparity (c). Spurious clusters with less than 3 features are removed. Attention shifts to the most salient object that is segmented out from the scene (d).

Gaussian envelope function. At each interest point we extract a 40-dimensional feature vector, which we refer to as a Gabor-jet, resulting from filtering the image with Gabor wavelets of 5 scales and 8 orientations, *e.g.*, [13]. The choice of the features is motivated by the fact that they have a similar shapes as the receptive fields of simple cells found in the primary visual cortex of mammals [14].

2.1   Stereo Segmentation and Tracking of the Object

To segment a potential object at the center of gaze from the background, we make use of stereo information. We find correspondences between interest points detected in the left and right image by exhaustively comparing Gabor-jets extracted at the interest points from left and right image, see Fig. 2a,b. Each interest point in the left image is associated with the best matching interest point in the right image if the similarity S between the two jets (we use the normalized inner product) is above a preset threshold (0.95 in our current implementation). We then cluster the matched interest points from the left image (that is used for learning) into different groups according to their image location and disparity (Fig. 2c). We use a greedy clustering scheme that starts with a single interest point and adds new ones if their x-position, y-position, and disparity are all within 5 pixels of any existing cluster member. Figure 2d shows how the object at the center of gaze is properly segmented from other objects which are at a similar depth but different spatial location or at a close-by spatial location but different depth.

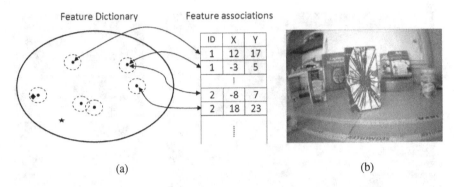

Feature Dictionary   Feature associations

ID	X	Y
1	12	17
1	-3	5
⋮		
2	-8	7
2	18	23
⋮		

(a)   (b)

Fig. 3. (a) Feature dictionary. • : Cluster centers (dotted lines indicate the boundaries). ⋆ : Input for which new cluster is created. ◇ : Input for which no new cluster is created. (b) An example showing distance vectors on an object.

After segmentation the cameras are moved to bring the object to the center of view and keep it there — in case the object is moving — by a tracking scheme. To this end, the mean location of foreground features is calculated, then this location is tracked with both eyes using a model-free tracking scheme called Democratic Integration (DI) [15]. DI is a multi-cue tracking system that provides a fast and robust way of tracking unknown objects in a changing environment. Once the object is at the center of gaze, model learning starts.

2.2   Learning Object Models

Once an object has been segmented and fixated, its novelty or familiarity is determined by the recognition system described in Sect. 2.4. If the object is already familiar, the recognition module provides the unique identity of the object, *i.e.*, an object index that was assigned when the object was first encountered. Otherwise a new object index is assigned.

Object learning involves the generation of a model that has a set of associations between the Gabor wavelet features and the object index [16]. An association is made between a feature and an object index if they occur together during learning and it is labeled with the distance vector between the location of the feature and the center of the object, *i.e.*, the point on the object on which gaze is centered (see Fig. 3b).

2.3   Feature Dictionary

Object learning is carried out in an on-line fashion. There are no separate training and testing/recognition phases. As the system starts learning, the models for all the objects are learnt incrementally using a shared feature dictionary accumulating information about objects and the associated feature vectors. We use a single-pass clustering scheme that updates the feature dictionary for every input feature vector. Let $\mathcal{C}$ be the set of clusters and n be the number of clusters in the feature dictionary. Once the system starts learning it adds features from the objects in the scene. Each input feature vector $\mathcal{J}$ has an associated object index k and the distance vector (x, y) to the object center measured in pixels.

In the beginning, when the dictionary is empty, a cluster is created and it will be represented by the input vector. Subsequently, when the number of clusters grows, the algorithm decides to either assign a feature to an existing cluster (without altering its representation) if the similarity value S is higher than a threshold θ (equal to 0.95) (see $\diamond$ in Fig. 3a) or make it a new cluster otherwise ($\star$ in Fig. 3a). During each update, object index and distance vector are associated to the same cluster. When a feature matches an existing cluster, a possible duplicate association of this cluster to the current object is avoided. If the object index is the same and if the feature locations are within a euclidean distance of 5.0 pixels the association is neglected. The algorithm can be summarized as follows:

Algorithm 1. Online learning of feature dictionary.

Initialize $n \leftarrow 0$, $\theta \leftarrow 0.95$.
loop
    Provide new feature vector $\mathcal{J}$ and distance vector (x, y).
    Obtain object index k from recognition (new or existing)
    Calculate $i_{win} = \arg\max_i S(\mathcal{J}, \mathcal{C}_i)$
    if $S(\mathcal{J}, \mathcal{C}_{i_{win}}) < \theta$ **then**
        $n \leftarrow n + 1$, $\mathcal{C}_n \leftarrow \mathcal{J}$
        Store association of $\mathcal{C}_n$ with object k at (x, y)
    else
        if $\mathcal{C}_{i_{win}}$ not associated with object k at (x, y) **then**
            Store association of $\mathcal{C}_{i_{win}}$ with object k at (x, y)
        end if
    end if
end loop

2.4 Recognition

In our work recognition is an integral part of the learning process. When the robot looks at an object the features on the segmented portion are sent to the recognition module and compared with the features in the dictionary. We use a generalized Hough transform [17] with a two dimensional parameter space for recognition. Each feature votes in the space of all object identities and possible centroid locations based on their consistencies with the learned feature associations. Features with a similarity value higher than 0.95 will cast one vote each for the object identities that they match in the feature dictionary. Votes having information about object's identity as well as object's location are then aggregated in discretized bins in Hough space. We use bins of size 5×5 pixels in our work. If the number of votes in a bin favoring a particular object index is greater than a predefined threshold (10 in this implementation) we declare the object as being present at the corresponding location. However, if there are different bins voting for the same object at different locations in the scene due to possible false feature matching, the location with the maximum number of votes is marked as the expected location. In the end, the recognition module returns a set of locations corresponding to those objects in the model whose voting support was sufficient.

3 Attention Mechanism

Our attention mechanism controls what the robot will look at, for how long it will keep looking at it, and where it should avoid looking. We embody curiosity in the attention mechanism by introducing the following ways of guiding attention to where learning progress is likely.

3.1 Bottom-Up Saliency at Interest Points

We have adapted a bottom-up saliency model developed by Itti et al. [18]. In this model the conspicuity of each image location in terms of its color, intensity, orientation, motion, etc. is encoded in a so-called saliency map. We make use of stereo information to select the most salient point in the scene. Images from both eyes are processed to obtain left and right saliency maps. Since objects are represented as features extracted at interest points, our attention mechanism only considers points in the saliency map that are associated with a pair of interest points matched between left and right image (all other points are neglected). In this way we restrict attention to locations of potential objects that the system could learn about. The saliency values for the matched interest points are computed using a 2-dimensional gaussian centered on them, with $\sigma = 1.5$ and a cutoff value of 0.05. This has the effect of bringing out clusters of high salience more than just isolated pixels of high salience.

When there are no other variations in the visual characteristics of the scene it is very likely that the attention mechanism continues to select the same location as the most salient point. To avoid this we temporarily inhibit the saliency map around the current winner location by subtracting a Gaussian kernel at the current winner location. This allows the system to shift attention to the next most salient location. To avoid constant switching between the two most salient locations, we also use a top-down inhibition of already learned objects below.

3.2 Attention Based on Learning Progress

It has been argued that infants' interest in a stimulus is related to their learning progress, *i.e.*, the improvement of an internal model of the stimulus [9]. We mimic this idea in the following way. When the robot looks at an object, it detects whether the object is familiar or not. If the object is new it creates a new object model making new associations in the shared feature dictionary. If the object is known, the model is updated by acquiring new features from the

Fig. 4. The IM system updates the model of the object finding new features on it while it is rotated by a human operator. Red dots represent features found on the object when the model is first created, purple dots represent new features found on the object during the model update, green dots represent shared features that have previously been associated with this object but found at a different location on the object (Color figure online).

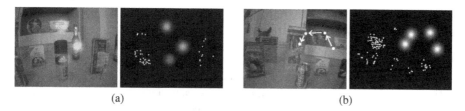

(a)   (b)

Fig. 5. (a) Top-down rejection of familiar objects: When objects become familiar to the robot they will be inhibited for further selection by removing the corresponding interest points. Color blobs indicate recognized objects whose interest points have been removed. (b) Top-down rejection of visited locations: The robot inhibits recently visited locations (white blobs).

object. The attention remains focused on the object until the learning progress becomes too small. As a side effect, the robot continues learning about an object when a human interferes by rotating or moving it, exposing different views with unknown features (Fig. 4).

3.3   Top-Down Rejection of Familiar Objects

The third mechanism to focus attention on locations where learning progress is likely makes use of the system's increasing ability to recognize familiar objects. A purely saliency-based attention mechanism may select the same object again and again during exploration, even if the scope for further learning progress has become very small. Therefore, once there are no more new features found on certain objects, our system inhibits their locations in the saliency map wherever they are recognized (Fig. 5a). To this end, the models of these objects are used to detect them in every frame using the recognition module. The interest points on the saliency map that are in the vicinity of the object detections are removed from being considered for the winner location.

3.4 Top-Down Rejection of Recently Visited Locations

We have incorporated an inhibition-of-return mechanism that prevents the robot from looking back to locations that it has recently visited. To this end, the absolute 3D coordinates of the visited locations are saved in the memory and they are mapped onto the pixel coordinates on images from the cameras in their current positions to know the locations for inhibition. In our experiments, a list of the 5 most recently visited locations is maintained and close-by interest points are inhibited for the next gaze shift (Fig. 5b). In order to ease exploration of regions beyond the current field of view, we have also added a mechanism to occasionally turn the head in a new direction. To this end, the space of possible head directions is parcellated into 4 quadrants. Whenever the robot has visited ten locations in one quadrant it shifts to the opposite quadrant.

4 Self-correction Mechanism

We introduce a self-correction mechanism in the system that discovers if there are any inaccuracies in the object representations in the dictionary and tries to rectify them. Ignoring the problems caused by variations in illumination conditions and object deformations, the inaccuracies can primarily arise because of two reasons: (1) The representation for an object is incomplete or (2) The representation of an object has incorporated portions of other objects in the scene. This can lead to the following problems, respectively

1. When the object is seen at different instants of time during the learning process in different poses, there will be duplications of the object in the dictionary with different models for different poses.
2. When two objects in the scene are overlapping or in contact with each other during learning, then there will be a single object model assigned to both objects.

We address these issues using the techniques described in the next sections.

4.1 Merging Technique

An object may change its pose while it is in focus or otherwise. When an object is changing its pose while it is in focus it is easy to incorporate the changes into the object model using the approach described in Sect. 3.2. However, this is not possible when the object changes its pose when the focus of the robot was on other objects in the scene. This makes the system learn duplicate identities which will continue to exist in the dictionary even after revealing previously learned poses at a later time. To understand this, let us consider the example shown in Fig. 6. The figure shows a scenario wherein the robot had seen one side

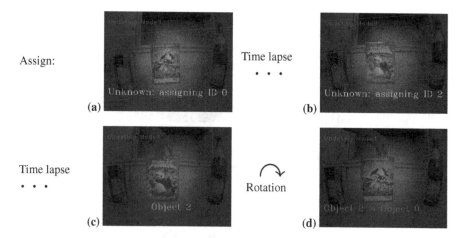

Fig. 6. Merging technique illustrated: (a) One side of the object assigned ID 0 at the first instant. (b) Other side of the object assigned ID 2 at the second instant. (c) Object is identified as ID 2. (d) After rotation, the recognition module identifies that the object has two data base entries and merges them.

of the object and assigned the identity number (ID) 0 (Fig. 6a). Later it only saw the other side of the same object and assigned ID 2 (Fig. 6b). Later the robot sees the object again and identifies it as object 2 (Fig. 6c) the user slowly rotates and reveals the other side of the object which is also updated into the representation for object 2 in the dictionary. We now have two identities for the same object only one of which will be updated based on the initial appearance match. We avoid this by identifying such an event using recognition module (see Sect. 2.4) that is always running in the background. While the object is being updated the recognition module identifies that there is another ID for the object that is currently being updated (Fig. 6d). This indicates that there are duplicate IDs for this object in the model data base. We hence merge the IDs as well as their corresponding feature associations in the dictionary into one. This technique also helps to merge duplicate identities caused by variations in illumination conditions and object deformations.

4.2 Splitting Technique

When two objects are seen together in the scene that are in contact with each other, the system learns a single representation for them since it doesn't know about the distinction of the appearances of the objects in the real world (see example in Fig. 7). In the future, when one of these two objects appears in the scene on its own the system would recognize it with the same object ID. This is akin to the situations wherein only a part of the object or one particular pose of the object is visible while the system is still able to recognize the object (see Sect. 2.4). Hence, in the case of two objects, the error goes unnoticed unless it is explicitly discovered. We again use the recognition module for identifying such

Assign:

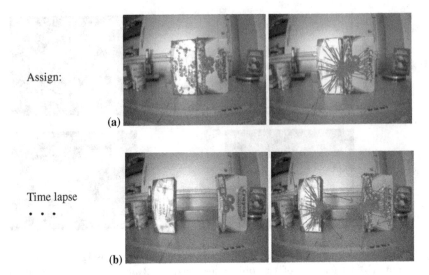

(a)

Time lapse

. . .

(b)

Fig. 7. (a) Splitting technique illustrated: (a) Two objects that were kept together are learned with a single object ID. The corresponding features and their distance vectors vote for a single object centroid location in the scene. (b) When these two objects are separated in the scene, the features now vote for centroid locations that are concentrated at two different locations in the scene, indicating that the object model should be split into two.

an event in order to rectify the identities in the dictionary. Figure 7a shows feature locations on the combined object and their corresponding distance vectors with respect to the object centroid. When these two objects are separated and kept apart in the scene the features vote for the centroid of the object that are concentrated at two different locations in the scene (Fig. 7b). This gives rise to two recognitions (see Sect. 2.4). This is an indication that there were two objects encapsulated with a single identity. We then split the corresponding features in the dictionary into two groups based on the votes and associate them with two different object IDs.

5   Experiments and Results

The system described above incorporates several mechanisms to make it intrinsically motivated to seek out new information or, simply put, to make it curious. To evaluate the benefits of this curiosity, we test the performance of the system by incorporating one or more of the attention mechanisms in a staged manner. We will label the full system including all mechanisms as the IM (intrinsic motivation) system. Note that these tests are performed without the two self-correction mechanisms of merging and splitting of object models.

5.1   Experimental Setup

The model is implemented on an iCub robot head [10] (Fig. 8). It has two pan-tilt-vergence eyes mounted in the head supported by a yaw-pitch-twist neck. It has 6 degrees of freedom (3 for the neck and 3 for the cameras). Images are acquired from the iCub cameras at 27 fps with resolution of 320×240 pixels. Experiments are performed placing iCub in a cluttered environment with various objects in the scene that are placed at different depths with partial occlusions. The background comprises walls, doors and book shelves. Figure 8 shows the objects, which have different sizes and shapes.

5.2   Evaluation Method

To evaluate the system, we let the robot autonomously explore its environment for 5 min and then test its performance using previously recorded and manually segmented ground truth images. During ground truthing we manually control the robot to look at each object present in the scene. The robot will extract features on the objects, that are manually segmented, until it does not find any new feature. This period was observed to be less than 10 frames on an average for static objects, but more for rotating/moving objects (see below). Once all the features are collected on all the objects, they are tested with the model generated by the system at the end of the learning process. To evaluate the performance of the system we consider the following parameters: Number of objects learnt, number of visits on an object (to test the exploration efficiency), accuracy of the object models (in terms of repeated object identities, missed/wrong detections, recognition rate), and time taken for learning the objects. Since the object identities depend on the order in which objects are learnt, we programmed the systems to store representative images of the object together with the self-assigned object ID (Fig. 11). These images are displayed while testing and allow a visual verification of the correctness of the recognition.

Fig. 8. Experimental setup and objects used in the experiments. Black frames indicate the objects used in the dynamic object scenario.

5.3 Two Experimental Scenarios

In the following we describe two testing scenarios using static and dynamically changing scenes.

In the first scenario, objects are static and iCub has to actively explore the scene and learn about the objects. We set a time span of 5 min during which iCub learns as many objects as possible. We place 12 objects in the scene allowing partial occlusions. Object locations are varied from one experiment to another.

In the second scenario we tested the ability of the system to update the model of an object with new features (Fig. 4). We used only 3 objects that are rotated by a human to dynamically change the objects' appearance while iCub learns about them. The learned object models are evaluated with separate test images showing the objects in four different poses.

5.4 Results

In this section we illustrate the performance of our system in a staged manner. We have employed bottom-up saliency in all the experimental scenarios. We will demonstrate a further improvement in attention and learning mechanism by using top-down information and learning progress parameters on top of this.

We will first illustrate the effect of top-down information on the system's performance in the static object scenario. Figure 9 compares the system's performance with and without top-down information. We report average values over 10 experiments carried out with different objects, locations, and lighting conditions. Error bars represent maximum and minimum values. Figure 9a shows the number of objects learnt by the system in 5 min that were validated by ground truth. Figure 9b shows the number of revisits of objects during exploration. In the absence of top-down information the system visits some objects repeatedly although little new information is available there. Similarly, Fig. 9c shows the

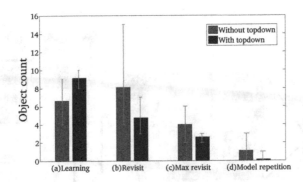

Fig. 9. Comparison of system performance with and without top-down information in the static object scenario. (a) Total number of objects learnt. (b) Total number of revisits of objects. (c) Maximum number of object revisits. (d) Number of objects whose models were duplicated

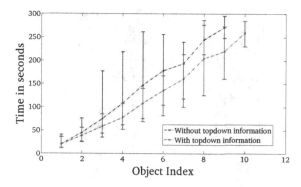

Fig. 10. Comparison of the system with and without topdown attention in terms of the time taken by the system to learn the first n object models.

maximum number of revisits across all objects. Figure 9d shows the number of objects whose models were incorrectly duplicated, *i.e.*, the system did not recognize the object when visiting it at a later time and created a second object model for the same object. Figure 10 shows the comparison in terms of time taken by the system to learn the first n objects. Across all measures, the system using top-down information is superior to the one without. One can expect a higher performance on a robot that has higher visual range and resolution covering more objects in the scene.

Our system looks at an object for as long as it finds something new to learn about. To evaluate the benefit of this feature we compare the full system (IM) to a version that only looks at an object for a fixed duration (equal to 3 s which was observed to be sufficient for learning an arbitrary object) before shifting gaze (No IM). Table 1 compares the recognition accuracies of both versions in the static object scenario. Recognition accuracy is defined as the percentage of features of the object model matched with ground truth. We observe that the recognition accuracy is higher for the IM case, even though the objects are static. This is somewhat surprising since for static objects a single frame should be sufficient to learn an accurate model. We suspect that the advantage of the IM system in this setting is due to subtle variations in lighting and camera noise that slightly alter object appearance from frame to frame.

The advantage of the full IM system becomes much clearer in the rotating object scenario. For this experiment we used the three objects marked by black rectangles in Fig. 8. The objects are rotated by a human operator as the robot learns about them (see Fig. 4). It is observed that the full IM system avoids duplicate representations for the same object. Figure 12 shows feature to object associations after learning. The features corresponding to an object model are collected and their distance vectors are marked from the center of the object. Figure 12a shows that for the IM case the features are densely populated covering most of the parts of the object. As our object models are pose invariant what is depicted in the picture is the aggregation of feature vectors from all poses that

Fig. 11. Static scene.

Table 1. Recognition accuracy.

Object	No IM	IM
Coca cola	50.00 %	64.28 %
Book	29.6 %	56.0 %
CD cover	–	–
Tool kit	100 %	100 %
Cookie box	66.66 %	84.37 %
Crayon box	89.7 %	85.29 %
Beer bottle	71.15 %	82.69 %
Deo body spray	46.15 %	73.01 %
Tea box	26.56 %	70.31 %
Sugar box	84.0 %	81.91 %
water bottle	43.18 %	61.36 %
paper box	–	80.55 %

are captured in the model. Figure 12b shows that for the other case there are duplicate models for the same object in the feature dictionary as the system in this case fails to realize that an object seen sometime later exhibiting different pose is the same object hence learning a new object model with new identity. The features are also not dense enough to identify the objects with high reliability. This is evident from Table 2 that lists the number of associated features in the feature dictionary for every object and the corresponding models. As shown in Table 3, the full IM system also has superior recognition accuracy. Recognition accuracy is defined as the percentage of features of the object model matched with ground truth. Four different poses of every object are shown to the system to see how well it can recognize. We observe that the recognition accuracy is substantially higher for the IM case.

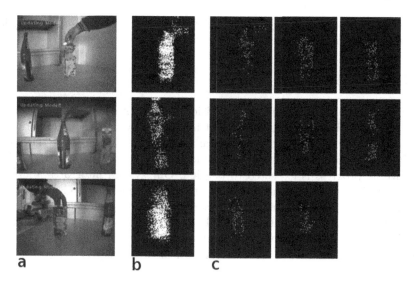

Fig. 12. Features belonging to the model for the learnt object are marked at locations given by distance vectors from the object center that were saved in the feature dictionary. (a) Objects during their learning progress. (b) For IM: Features cover the object densely and the object model is not duplicated. (c) For No IM: Features are sparse and there are duplications of object representations in the feature dictionary.

Table 2. Representation in feature dictionary.

Pose	Milk packet		Water bottle		Tea box	
	No IM	IM	No IM	IM	No IM	IM
Pose 1	57 %	100 %	19 %	53 %	–	100 %
Pose 2	–	96 %	32 %	57 %	28 %	100 %
Pose 3	21 %	100 %	–	–	–	100 %
Pose 4	31 %	68 %	–	–	–	100 %

Table 3. Recognition accuracy (rotation case).

	Milk packet		Water bottle		Tea box	
	No IM	IM	No IM	IM	No IM	IM
Model 1	63	1511	27	535	55	1601
Model 2	82	–	35	–	44	–
Model 3	69	–	65	–	–	–

The system performance recorded as a video can be viewed at: http://fias. uni-frankfurt.de/neuro/triesch/videos/icub/learning/

6   Conclusions

We have presented a "curious" robot vision system that autonomously learns about objects in its environment without human intervention. Our experiments comparing this curious system to several alternatives demonstrate the higher learning speed and accuracy achieved by focusing attention on locations where the learning progress is expected to be high. Our system integrates a sizeable number of visual competences including attention, stereoscopic vision, segmentation, tracking, model learning, and recognition. While each component leaves room for further improvement, the overall system represents a useful step towards building autonomous robots that cumulatively learn better models of their environment driven by nothing but their own curiosity.

Acknowledgements. This work was supported by the BMBF Project "Bernstein Fokus: Neurotechnologie Frankfurt, FKZ 01GQ0840" and by the "IM-CLeVeR - Intrinsically Motivated Cumulative Learning Versatile Robots" project, FP7-ICT-IP-231722. We thank Richard Veale, Indiana University for providing the code on saliency.

References

1. Kim, H., Murphy-Chutorian, E., Triesch, J.: Semi-autonomous learning of objects. In: Conference on Computer Vision and Pattern Recognition Workshop, CVPRW '06, p. 145 (2006)
2. Wersing, H., Kirstein, S., Gtting, M., Brandl, H., Dunn, M., Mikhailova, I., Goerick, C., Steil, J., Ritter, H., Krner, E.: Online learning of objects in a biologically motivated visual architecture. Int. J. Neural Syst. **17**(4), 219–230 (2007)
3. Figueira, D., Lopes, M., Ventura, R., Ruesch, J.: From pixels to objects: enabling a spatial model for humanoid social robots. In: IEEE International Conference on Robotics and Automation, ICRA 2009, pp. 3049–3054 (2009)
4. Gatsoulis, Y., Burbridge, C., McGinnity, T.: Online unsupervised cumulative learning for life-long robot operation. In: 2011 IEEE International Conference on Robotics and Biomimetics (ROBIO), pp. 2486–2490 (2011)
5. Begum, M., Karray, F.: Visual attention for robotic cognition: a survey. IEEE Trans. Auton. Ment. Dev. **3**(1), 92–105 (2011)
6. Baranes, A., Oudeyer, P.-Y.: R-iac: robust intrinsically motivated exploration and active learning. IEEE Trans. Auton. Ment. Dev. **1**(3), 155–169 (2009)
7. Schmidhuber, J.: Formal theory of creativity, fun, and intrinsic motivation (1990–2010). IEEE Trans. Auton. Ment. Dev. **2**(3), 230–247 (2010)
8. Baldassarre, G.: What are intrinsic motivations? a biological perspective. In: 2011 IEEE International Conference on Development and Learning (ICDL), vol. 2, pp. 1–8 (2011)
9. Wang, Q., Chandrashekhariah, P., Spina, G.: Familiarity-to-novelty shift driven by learning: a conceptual and computational model. In: 2011 IEEE International Conference on Development and Learning (ICDL), vol. 2, pp. 1–6 (2011)

10. Metta, G., Sandini, G., Vernon, D., Natale, L., Nori, F.: The icub humanoid robot: an open platform for research in embodied cognition. In: Proceedings of the 8th Workshop on Performance Metrics for Intelligent Systems, PerMIS '08, pp. 50–56. ACM, New York (2008)
11. Agarwal, S., Roth, D.: Learning a sparse representation for object detection. In: Heyden, A., Sparr, G., Nielsen, M., Johansen, P. (eds.) ECCV 2002. LNCS, vol. 2353, pp. 113–127. Springer, Heidelberg (2002)
12. Harris, C., Stephens, M.: A combined corner and edge detector. In: Proceedings of Fourth Alvey Vision Conference, pp. 147–151 (1988)
13. Wiskott, L., Fellous, J.-M., Kuiger, N., von der Malsburg, C.: Face recognition by elastic bunch graph matching. IEEE Trans. Pattern Anal. Mach. Intell. **19**(7), 775–779 (1997)
14. Jones, J., Palmer, L.: An evaluation of the two-dimensional Gabor filter model of simple receptive fields in cat striate cortex. J. Neurophysiol. **58**(6), 1233–1258 (1987)
15. Triesch, J., Triesch, J., von der Malsburg, C.: Democratic integration: self-organized integration of adaptive cues. Neural Comput. **13**, 2049–2074 (2001)
16. Murphy-Chutorian, E., Triesch, J.: Shared features for scalable appearance-based object recognition. In: Seventh IEEE Workshops on Application of Computer Vision, WACV/MOTIONS '05 Volume 1, vol. 1, pp. 16–21 (2005)
17. Ballard, D.H.: Generalizing the hough transform to detect arbitrary shapes. In: Fischler, M.A., Firschein, O. (eds.) Readings in Computer Vision: Issues, Problems, Principles, and Paradigms, pp. 714–725. Morgan Kaufmann Publishers Inc., San Francisco (1987)
18. Itti, L., Koch, C.: Computational modelling of visual attention. Nat. Rev. Neurosci. **2**(3), 194–203 (2001)

Single Camera Hand Pose Estimation from Bottom-Up and Top-Down Processes

Davide Periquito[✉], Jacinto C. Nascimento, Alexandre Bernardino,
and João Sequeira

Instituto de Sistemas e Robótica, Instituto Superior Técnico, Lisboa, Portugal
davide.periquito@ist.utl.pt

Abstract. In this paper we present a methodology for hand pose estimation from a single image, combining bottom-up and top-down processes. A fast bottom-up algorithm generates, from coarse visual cues, hypotheses about the possible locations and postures of hands in the images. The best ranked hypotheses are then analysed by a precise, but slower, top-down process. The complementary nature of bottom-up and top-down processes in terms of computational speed and precision permits the design of pose estimation algorithms with desirable characteristics, taking into account constraints in the available computational resources. We analyse the trade-off between precision and speed in a series of simulations and qualitatively illustrate the performance of the method with real imagery.

Keywords: Pose estimation · Geometric moments · Hammoude metric · Simulation

1 Introduction

There has been a considerable effort in Human-Computer Interface (HCI) research to create user friendly interaction systems by directly employing the communication and manipulation skills of humans. Adopting such direct sensing in HCI, will permit the deployment of a large spectrum of applications in more complex and sophisticated computing environments such as virtual environments or augmented reality systems. A great focus has been put in the use of hands for interaction devices. The human hand is the most effective interaction tool due to its dexterous functionality in communication and manipulation. A wide range of interaction styles can be reported in the literature. For instance, hand gestures both in static and dynamic settings to build control interfaces [1–3], multimodal user interfaces [4], object manipulation interfaces [5,6] or surgical manipulations [7]. However, to be useful in practice, the interfaces listed

This work was supported by the European Commission project POETICON++ (FP7-ICT- 288382) and the Portuguese FCT projects [PEst-OE/EEI/LA0009/2011] and VISTA (PTDC/ EIA-EIA/105062/2008).

© Springer-Verlag Berlin Heidelberg 2014
S. Battiato et al. (Eds.): VISIGRAPP 2013, CCIS 458, pp. 212–227, 2014.
DOI: 10.1007/978-3-662-44911-0_14

above need to achieve real-time functionality and precise motion measurement of human hand [8]. Furthermore, they should deal with some challenges among which we highlight: (i) automatic initialisation; (ii) accuracy for long sequences; (iii) independence regarding the activity; (iv) robustness to drift and occlusions; (vi) computational efficiency; (vii) ability to tackle the high dimensionality of the problem (i.e. Degrees of Freedom (DOF)); and (viii) ability to operate with mobile cameras and in uncontrolled environments.

The focus of this paper is the hand pose estimation from a single camera using a pre-trained set of rigid poses. In this context, the hand can be seen as an interaction device with large complexity, with over than 27 degrees-of-freedom (DOF), forming a very effective and general purpose interactive tool for HCI [9]. To achieve this goal we propose a principled way of combining two different sources of information collaborating for the efficient estimation of human hand pose in digital images, herein denoted as *bottom-up* and *top-down*. The *bottom-up* process computes very fast descriptors of the hand pose that, despite their low precision, pre-filter the image information to reduce the computation of the more precise, but slower *top-down* process.

The idea of combining bottom-up and top-down approaches has been successfully exploited in other applications. For instance, in [10], two different methods are used to build models for person detection. First a bottom-up approach searches for body part candidates in the image, which are then clustered to find and identify assemblies of parts that might be people. Simultaneously, a top-down approach is used to find people by projecting the previous assembled parts in the image plane. Other approaches are applied in the context of medical imaging, where the two above mechanisms are combined via online self-retraining [12] and co-training [13] to achieve robustness in the segmentation of the left ventricle from ultrasound images. The combination of bottom-up and top-down processes is crucial for the efficiency and reliability of detection and tracking algorithms. In one hand, the amount of image information to process is huge and thus requires top-down constraints given by models. However, matching the models to the image must be guided by bottom-up processes for efficiency. We evaluate our method with real imagery and study the trade-off between the bottom-up and top-down processes in a series of simulations.

Our paper is organised as follows. Section 2 describes related work. In Sect. 3 we describe the method's architecture, which is divided in to the following major components: (i) the machine learning part (offline) and (ii) the matching strategy between the observed image and the generated hypotheses (online). In Sect. 4 some experiments concerning realistic scenarios are presented. Finally, Sect. 5 presents the conclusions of the paper and provides directions for further research work.

2   Related Work

Two main classes of approaches for hand pose estimation are usually considered depending on the adopted representation for the hand. Considering only part of the hand (i.e. palm, fingers or fingertips) we are facing a *partial* pose estimation. However, if one considers the entire model of the hand, a *full* DOF of the hand model pose must be estimated [11]. The former approach basically comprises hand localisation and feature extraction along with gesture classification. It is demonstrated that when the hand undergoes a rigid motion, the pose can be estimated using only the palm position and the fingertip locations [14,15]. However, these approaches do not account for any other kinematics, besides the ones that are targeted to a specific and dedicated task. This suggests temporal approaches able to extend and generalise the kinematics of the hand leading to a full reconstruction of the hand motion. This usually comprises (i) a feature extraction stage (that contributes for the state update) and (ii) an initialisation/prediction model (containing the hand motion) to feed the tracker. The tracking can be based on a local search where the *single hypothesis* is viewed as the best estimate and is considered corresponding to a best fit based on some optimisation criteria. See for instance [16] where the optimisation is based on the error in joint links and fingertips, or using silhouette based error measures [17] minimised trough Nelder Mead Simplex. The Nelder Mead technique has also been used in [18], in which *reflect*, *expand* and *contract* are defined as the transformations to perform the Nelder Mead search in each iteration.

Kalman filtering is suited for the above mentioned single hypothesis tracking, since it provides the best estimate under the Gaussian assumption (e.g. [19]). However, Kalman filter as a recursive linear estimator, is a special case applying only to Gaussian densities. For more general settings, i.e. uncontrolled scenarios with occlusions, hand motion, substantial clutter or lighting changes, single hypothesis tracking performance is jeopardised, not allowing for robustness over long sequences. Thus, *multiple hypotheses* should be maintained throughout the tracking process. There is considerable amount of approaches in this direction, basically following three distinct paths such as particle filtering (PF) [20,21], tree based filter [22,23], or Bayesian networks [24].

Other class of approaches are known as *single frame* pose estimation. This is a more recent technique in which the pose estimation is achieved without making any assumptions on time coherence. This makes the problem more difficult to solve. One of the benefits of this kind of approach is that, it can lead to building algorithms for automatic initialisation or re-initialisation in tracking-based systems. Another motivation for this approach is the rapid motion of the hand and fingers. Images of consecutive frames can be very different, making time coherence assumptions useless. Relevant approaches in this topic have been proposed for object detection [25,26], image database indexing [27,28] or 2D-3D mappings [29,30].

In the field of human body pose estimation, two classes of estimators are possible to identify: top-down and bottom-up [37]. Top-down approaches consist in matching a projection of the human body model with the observed image, while in Bottom-up approaches individual body parts are found and then assembled into a human body image. Sometimes these approaches can also be considered as instances of model-based (or generative) and model-free (or discriminative) approaches, respectively [37]. An example of a top-down approach is [32]. The estimation process consists is computing the pose parameters that minimises the error between observation and the projection of the human body model. In order to achieve fast and efficient solutions, a local search is performed in the neighbourhood of an initial pose estimation. In fact, the main shortcoming presented in top-down approaches is the requirement of initial pose estimates which sometimes demand for manual initialization. Other issues are the computational effort of rendering the human body model and the calculation of the distance between the rendered model and the image observation. Top-down approaches also present some problems with (self)occlusions because the errors may be propagated through body parts. An inaccurate estimation for the head part, for example, may cause significant orientation errors of lower body parts. To cope with some of these issues other techniques were used, i.e. by applying gradient descent on the cost function [34].

Bottom-up based approaches, instead, do not attempt to obtain, from the beginning, a complete and precise description of the pose. They are typically used to find coarse or partial descriptors of the object to detect, that are latter refined by a *Top-down* model imposing a more detailed level of representation. These models have been applied successfully to the problem of full human body estimation because they can limit the search space of the *Top-down* processes and allow for automatic initialisation of trackers. For instance, in the human body pose estimation problem, a *bottom-up* process detects body parts and then uses them to assemble a full human body. The main problems associated with the bottom-up process are normally the quantity of detected false positives due to the coarse level of representation. Another drawback is the need of part detectors for most body parts since missing information is likely to result in less accurate pose estimation. In [31], the first step is to find a person in the image, so body parts are learned by the trackers and a possible assembly is found by applying RANdom SAmple Consensus (RANSAC). Heuristics are used to remove unlikely poses, and a prior pose determines the likelihood function of the assembly.

Given the limitations of individual bottom-up and top-down approaches, a greater attention was devoted to their combination. According to [33] a hierarchical classification is possible in order to achieve better performance for initial positioning of a full human body posture estimation problem. This way, they first build the torso and head and then the rest of the limbs of the model. More recent works [35,36], have proposed various directions by combining particle filtering algorithms for tracking human body parts, and model-free approaches. It is demonstrated that the combination of bottom-up and top-down principles can lead to a better performance [36,38]. The computational cost to render the human body model can be drastically reduced when using bottom-up approaches to generate a small number of hypotheses, to be then tested with the top-down models. Furthermore, bottom-up false positives can be removed by projecting them into the image and using the top-down model to confirm if the produced hypotheses are correct. Other ways are possible to achieve such combination. For instance, in [39] the integration is performed by using the correspondence between interest points (texture) in the set, and tracking with optical flow estimation along with contours, using the Kalman Filter (KF). In [38] both approaches are also integrated, in order to address the problem of tracking multiple limbs of the human body. In the bottom-up part the detection is made by a rectangular contour template, which identifies possible body

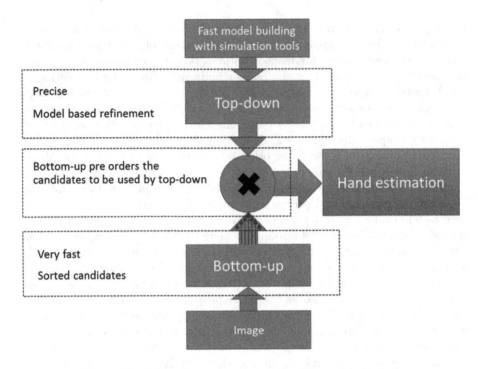

Fig. 1. Algorithm schematic: an overview (see text in Sect. 3).

limb hypotheses, whereas the top-down approach looks for possibilities to assemble the human body model with the detected rectangles. The model is built taking into consideration the constrain that limbs keep certain poses between each other. Other example is [40] where a mixed approach is applied for 2D tracking. The bottom-up layer is achieved by implementing the Adaboost Algorithm for object detection (in this case hockey players) and to deal with new instances in the image. On the Top-down method a "mixture particle filter" (MPF) is applied in order to track multiple players. Therefore the Adaboost is trained to detect players and combined with the MPF to construct their distribution.

The work presented herein situates in the context of single frame pose estimation fusing top-down and bottom-up methods. The algorithm presented has two main advantages: (i) the bottom-up provides an efficient reduction over the training set, having a significant impact on the computational cost, and (ii) the use of the top-down process provides an improved estimation accuracy. Fusing these two methods we can achieve faster performance and reliable estimation, in both synthetic and real environments.

3   Algorithm

In this paper we combine bottom-up and top-down processes for the detection of specific gestures and pose estimation of a human hand. We will illustrate the process and perform experiments with a pointing gesture. The top-down process is encoded in templates of the hand silhouettes computed offline. For each hand gesture that we intend to detect, a database of silhouettes is created on a dense discretisation of the orientation space. Then, at runtime, we will search for the best match between the data stored in the database and the actual image information. Because exhaustive template matching of all possible pose hypotheses is computationally expensive, a bottom-up process performs a fast moment-based filtering of colour blobs in the image that are likely to contain hands on certain poses. The candidates are then ranked by quality so that the top-down process, performing a more detailed matching operation, can concentrate its resources on the most promising ones (Fig. 1). Through this process we intend to achieve both a fast computation, promoted by the bottom-up process, and a good precision of the estimates achieved by the top-down process. The steps of the approach are next described in detail.

3.1   General Approach

This section describes the procedure of the proposed framework. The creation of the top-down models comprise a training stage with the following steps:

1. Computation of the necessary quaternions to generate training hand pose hypotheses images. A total of 23900 quaternions are used.
2. The quaternions are then used to generate hand pose hypothesis in the Open-RAVE simulator [41] with an existing humanoid 3D model. Subsequently, 23900 images are produced corresponding to hand pose hypotheses, from those a total of 23500 images are used for algorithm training.
3. The images are segmented (*i.e.* the silhouettes or contours are obtained) and corrected in perspective to simulate frontal views.
4. The geometric moments of the contours are computed.
5. The silhouettes are stored in a database, together with both the binary masks and the geometric moments. Also, the ground truth poses (*i.e.* quaternions) are stored.

The previous items are fulfilled an in offline fashion. Afterwards, the online test step performs the matching between the acquired hand silhouette (*i.e.* a test image) and the pre-trained database of canonical pose hypotheses described above. In run-time, each acquired image silhouette is also pre-processed as in the training stage (*i.e.* through the colour segmentation process, perspective correction and binarisation). Then, the geometric moments of the newly acquired mask are used to rank the pose hypotheses in descending order of match quality. The best ranked hypotheses constitute the output of the bottom-up stage of the algorithm and are passed to the top-down stage. The top-down procedure then computes a more precise match using Hammoude metric also known as the Jaccard distance [43].

3.2   Training Images Generation

To generate hypotheses on OpenRAVE we place a virtual camera on the simulated model looking at a 3D realistic human hand model. By moving the camera

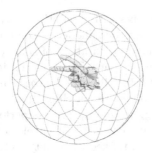

Fig. 2. Illustration of the virtual sphere sampling for acquiring the training set. The center of each hexagon corresponds to different camera positions.

Fig. 3. Some image samples generated with the OpenRAVE simulator.

around at a constant distance to the hand we create a virtual sphere sampling (see Fig. 2 for an illustration). To represent the orientation of the camera we use quaternions. Uniform samples (see Fig. 3) of the orientation sphere are generated by drawing quaternions from a Gaussian distribution. For each sample a difference of 5° (degrees) is guaranteed in the generation process. Finally a virtual image of the hand, taken from this orientation and pointing towards the hand, is acquired and stored in the model database (see Fig. 4 first and second steps).

3.3   Segmentation and Localization

One of the most important steps in the algorithm is the hand segmentation. To accomplish this, we use the HSV colour space, which allows better luminosity invariance. For the image segmentation, a Histogram Backprojection algorithm is used [44], resulting in the likelihood of each pixel belonging to the hand. Basically, this algorithm assumes that a colour histogram is known *a priori*, describing the probability of occurrence of colours in human hands. This histogram can be learned from a set of training data contains patches of the

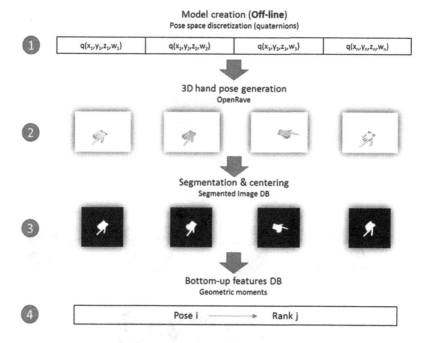

Fig. 4. Proposed algorithm, offline phase.

human skin. The algorithm then tries to localise, in the image domain, the region of the object being looked for. A salience map is created, i.e. a probability map for the presence of the object for each and every pixel on the image. After the filtering process the result is a segmented hand, though with some noise. To clean up the image we make some image morphological processing, by filling the holes inside the hand and removing out spurious objects. Subsequently, we obtain a binary image with a segmented hand. This method is applied in the offline and online phases of the algorithms in an identical fashion.

For better matching with the training samples, the hand centroid (x_0, y_0) is placed in the centre of the image, though this centring procedure induces an additional rotation of the hand that must be taken into account. One can interpret this effect as if a virtual camera is rotated in pan and tilt angles so as to centre the object in its field of view. The homography that corresponds to this rotation is given by [36]:

$$x_1 = \frac{c_t s_p + c_p x_0 - s_t s_p.y_0}{c_t c_p - s_p x_0 - s_t c_p y_0}, \quad y_1 = \frac{s_t + c_t y_0}{c_t c_p - s_p x_0 - s_t c_p y_0} \quad (1)$$

where c_p, s_p, c_t, s_t stand for $\cos(p)$, $\sin(p)$, $\cos(t)$, $\sin(t)$, respectively, (x_1, y_1) represent the pixels after the rotation, p and t are the equivalent pan-tilt camera angles that centre the point (x_0, y_0) in the camera frame:

$$p = arctan(x_1), \quad t = arctan(y_1 c_p) \quad (2)$$

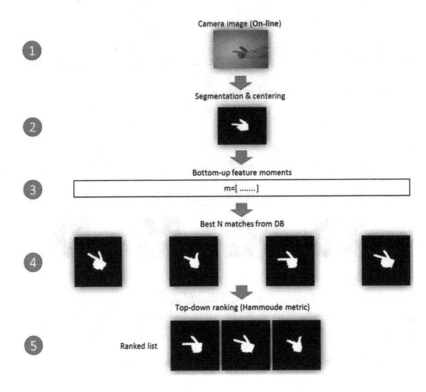

Fig. 5. Proposed algorithm, online phase.

The application of homography (2) introduces some perspective errors but the approximation is still acceptable. This process is applied during the third step of the offline phase (Fig. 4) and the second step of the online phase (Fig. 5). Since we are working in a 2D image plane the Z coordinate can be interpreted as an area normalisation factor that will be used in the matching metrics.

3.4 Pose Estimation

In order to obtain a faster algorithm, we try to pre-compute in the offline stage all the information needed in the estimation (online) stage. This is accomplished by storing the hand masks and their geometric moments for all the images in the training set. The geometric moments will be used for bottom-up ranking of pose hypotheses, whereas the full masks will be used in the top-down process through the application of the Hammoude metric.

Geometric Moments and Their Match. To obtain fast descriptors of hand characteristics, posture and shape, we use geometric moments. These are made invariant to position and scale by centring and normalising by area:

$$u_{pq} = \frac{\sum_x \sum_y (x - x_0)^p (y - y_0)^q I(x, y)}{M_{00}^{1 + \frac{p+q}{2}}} \tag{3}$$

where u_{pq} stands for the moment of order $p + q$, M_{00} for hand area and $I(x, y)$ for image pixel. According to our studies, it is essential to keep the moments of order higher than 4th, since the higher the order the more discriminative characteristics we get. In contrast, lower orders describe the hand position and area, which we want to be invariant. The computation of image moments and their normalization constitutes the last step of the offline phase (Fig. 4) and the thirs step of the online phase illustrated in Fig. 5.

To get the matching distance between trained and observed images, a Mahalanobis-like distance is used:

$$d = \sum_{p,q} \frac{(\tilde{n}_{pq} - n_{pq}^i)^2}{var(n_{pq})} \tag{4}$$

$\tilde{n}_{pq}$ is the moment calculated in an observed image, n_{pq}^i the moment trained in the train set hypotheses and $var(n_{pq})$ is the variance of the moment in the training set. By minimising the function we have the most likely hypothesis. This is used in the fourth step of the online phase diagram in Fig. 5.

Hammoude Metric. To evaluate with higher precision the match between the observed silhouettes and the ones in the database, we use the Hammoude metric [42,43] that is defined as follows:

$$d_{HMD}(y_1, y_2) = \frac{\#((R_{y_1} \cup R_{y_2}) \setminus (R_{y_1} \cap R_{y_2}))}{\#(R_{y_1} \cup R_{y_2})} \tag{5}$$

where R_{y_1} represents the image region delimited by the contour y_1 (similarly for R_{y_2}), $\sharp$ denotes the number of pixels within the region by the expression in parenthesis, and\denotes the minus operation between the sets. We then convert this value to a likelihood, $p(y_1|y_2)$, by:

$$p(y_1|y_2) = 1 - d_{HMD}(y_1, y_2) \tag{6}$$

This constitutes the last step of the online phase diagram in Fig. 5.

4   Results

In this section, we experimentally validate the performance of the top-down/bottom-up architecture for the hand pose estimation of a pointing gesture. We first access the performance of each component individually. Then we experimentally illustrate the performance of the overall system.

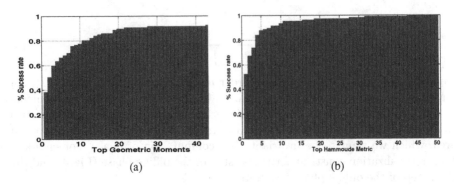

Fig. 6. Cumulative matching characteristic for (a) geometric moments and (b) Hammoude metric.

4.1   Top-Down *vs* Bottom-up

We start by illustrating the performance of the bottom-up component. To do so, we use a previously generated training set (23500 frames), and use a given test hand pose image. We compute the geometric moments (see Eq. (3)) for that observed image and rank accordingly (see Eq. (4)). We repeat this procedure for all images in the test set (*i.e.* 400 frames). Figure 6(a) shows the cumulative rank of the geometric moments in which the bars represent the probability of hitting the correct hypotheses (*i.e.* hand poses). From this example, we see that the accuracy to first choose the correct hypothesis is 38 % (left most bar in the histogram). The accuracy of 90 % is reached for the top 23 matched hypothesis.

To compare the obtained results with the top-down component, we follow the same procedure (*i.e.* building the rank of the database for each test image). Figure 6(b) shows the achieved results for the cumulative ranks. The performance accuracy is now 52 % for the first choice. Also, it is illustrated that a faster convergence is achieved, where only 10 hypotheses suffice for achieving 90 % accuracy. This allows us to conclude that the top-down mechanism definitively improves the quality of the detection with respect to the bottom-up method alone.

4.2   Pose Estimation

To assess the performance of the full hand pose estimation process, we first study how can we select the proper number of candidates provided by the bottom-up process. We have experimented numbers of candidates in the set $R = \{1, 10, 100, 1000, 10000, 23500\}$. Say that we vary the number of hypotheses in the range R. We then assess the performance of the hand pose estimation by using the top-down approach over that number of candidates.

The error metric used is the orientation error defined as:

$$\varepsilon = 2 \arccos(p \cdot q) \tag{7}$$

where $p \cdot q$ stands for the inner product between two quaternions. The error in Eq. (7) is computed between the ground truth hand pose of the test image and the angle of the training image with maximum likelihood, as computed by the top-down process. Finally, the average of the orientation errors ε_{AV} is taken to assess the overall performance on the test set.

Table 1 (left) shows the average of the orientation error ε_{AV} (in degrees) and the time to compute the pose estimation, and Table 1 (right) shows the relation between the number of hypotheses used and the mean and standard deviation of the orientation error.

Table 1. Left: Mean and standard deviation (in parenthesis of the cell) order statistics of the orientation error ε_{AV} (in degrees) and time spent ((s)-seconds, (ms)-milliseconds) for the hand pose estimation. The experiment is repeated for the top candidates moments defined in the range R. Right: Relation between the number of hypotheses and the estimation error.

# Cand. Mom	Time	$\varepsilon_{AV}(°)$
1	25.2 (0) (ms)	17.8 (34.6)
10	4.21 (0.06) (s)	7.34 (15.4)
100	5.99 (0.98) (s)	5.86 (3.06)
1000	11.90 (2.74) (s)	5.77 (3.00)
10000	69.07 (5.33) (s)	5.77 (3.00)
23500	122 (8.11) (s)	6.06 (3.50)

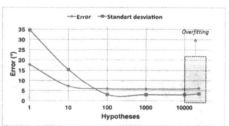

As we can see, the time spent has a significant impact when the number of top samples grows. For online applications this is of paramount importance, where the time should be as low as possible[1]. Notice that, the orientation error regarding the ground truth is remarkably under 8 %, being the best value achieved for 1000 candidate moments. However, the error value achieved for 100 frames is quite similar, thus being possible to use less than 1000 frames. This allows us to conclude that the geometric moments are, indeed, an important filtering step to reduce the number of hypotheses to be tested in the top-down stage, to about 4 % of the training set. Moreover, the integration of top-down provides higher accuracy (as already detailed in Sect. 4.1) where a small orientation error is obtained. Recall that, (see Sect. 3.2) a discretization of 5° is used, meaning that the top-down procedure exhibits remarkable accuracy.

From Table 1 (left) we observe that the error at the bottom line grows at high number of candidates. The reason is that, due to the great number of possibilities available, many are ambiguous, resulting in very small differences for classification. This leads to an effect similar to over-fitting.

---

[1] The time results shown in Table 1 (left) were obtained in a non-optimised Matlab code. This could be drastically reduced using a C++ base programming or by optimising the algorithm in order to take advantage of GPU and/or by using multi-core computation.

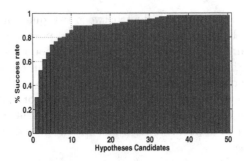

Fig. 7. Cumulative matching characteristic using top 1000 candidate hypotheses.

Fig. 8. Six snapshots of the sequence (top) poses recovered by the algorithm (bottom).

Figure 7 shows the cumulative rank when combining the bottom-up and top-down procedures. It can be seen that an accuracy of 90 % is promptly reached using about 10 candidates.

As a final experiment we evaluated several sequences in real settings. The goal is to recover the pose of a real human hand using the model learned with the OpenRAVE. We present the results of a sequence containing 50 frames. Figure 8 shows some snapshots of the sequence as well as the recovered poses. We may notice some small differences between the shape of the hand (see 1st and 3rd rows of Fig. 8) and the corresponding poses (2nd and 4th rows). This happens due to the CAD model used in the generation process with OpenRAVE (see illustrations in Fig. 3) that is a slightly different from the human hand.

We should stress that the presence of shadows and poor illumination in real settings can jeopardise the silhouette recovery, leading to an incorrect ranking of hypotheses and misleading pose recovery. Although the segmentation used in our scenario suffices for a correct estimation, this is an issue to take into consideration for other environments.

5   Conclusions

In this paper we propose a 3D hand posture estimation framework. The architecture combines bottom-up and top-down approaches, providing an efficient tool for hand orientation detection. The algorithm presented is twofold. First, the bottom-up process allows for an efficient reduction of candidates over the training set, having a significant impact on computational time. Second, the use of the top-down process provides an improved estimation accuracy. Fusing these two methods we can achieve faster performance and reliable estimation, in both synthetic and real environments. We conclude that this method generates a good hypothesis estimator which is crucial for a fully automatic initialisation of tracking algorithms. In future work we will focus on the integration of this proposed methodology in a full tracking framework (e.g. a particle filter architecture) and the addition of new hand postures for more general applications.

References

1. Turk, M.: Gesture recognition. In: Stanney, K.M. (ed.) Handbook of Virtual Environments: Design, Implementation, and Applications, pp. 223–238. Lawrence Erlbaum Associates, Mahwah (2002)
2. Lenman, S., Bretzner, L., Thuresson, B.: Using marking menus to develop command sets for computer vision based hand gesture interfaces. In: 2nd Nordic Conference on Human- Computer Interaction, pp. 239–242. ACM Press (2002)
3. Nielsen, M., Storring, M., Moeslund, T.B., Granum, E.: A procedure for developing intuitive and ergonomic gesture interfaces for HCI. In: 5th International Gesture Workshop, pp. 409–420 (2003)
4. Quek, F., McNeill, D., Bryll, R., Duncan, S., Ma, X.-F., Kirbas, C., McCullough, K.E., Ansari, R.: Multimodal human discourse: gesture and speech. ACM Trans. Comput.-Hum. Interact. 9(3), 171–193 (2002)
5. Bowman, D.: Principles for the design of performance-oriented interaction techniques. In: Stanney, K.M. (ed.) Handbook of Virtual Environments: Design, Implementation, and Applications, pp. 201–207. Lawrence Erlbaum Associates, Mahwah (2002)

6. Buchmann, V., Violich, S., Billinghurst, M., Cockburn, A.: FingARtips: gesture based direct manipulation in augmented reality. In: 2nd International Conference on Computer Graphics and Interactive Techniques in Australasia and South East Asia, pp. 212–221. ACM Press (2004)

7. Liu, A., Tendick, F., Cleary, K., Kaufmann, C.: A survey of surgical simulation: applications, technology, and education. Presence: Teleoper. Virtual Environ. **12**(6), 599–614 (2003)

8. Erol, A., Bebis, G., Nicolescu, M., Boyle, R.D., Twombly, X.: A review on vision-based full DOF hand motion estimation. In: CVPR (2005)

9. Rehg, J.M., Kanade, T.: Visual tracking of high DOF articulated structures: an application to human hand tracking. In: Eklundh, J.-O. (ed.) ECCV 1994. LNCS, vol. 801, pp. 35–46. Springer, Heidelberg (1994)

10. Ramanan, D., Forsyth, D.A., Zisserman, A.: Tracking people by learning their appearance. IEEE Trans. PAMI **29**(1), 65–81 (2007)

11. Erol, A., Bebis, G., Nicolescu, M., Boyle, R.D., Twombly, X.: Vision-based hand pose estimation: a review. CVIU **108**, 52–73 (2007)

12. Carneiro, G., Nascimento, J.C.: Incremental on-line semi-supervised learning for segmenting the left ventricle of the heart from ultrasound data. In: ICCV (2013)

13. Carneiro, G., Nascimento, J.C.: The use of incremental co-training to reduce the training set size in pattern recognition methods: application to left ventricle segmentation in ultrasound. In: CVPR (2012)

14. O'Hagan, R.G., Zelinsky, A., Rougeaux, S.: Visual gesture interfaces for virtual environments. Interact. Comput. **14**, 231–250 (2002)

15. Sato, Y., Saito, M., Koik, H.: Real-time input of 3D pose and gestures of a user's hand and its applications for HCI. In: Proceedings of the Virtual Reality 2001 Conference (VR'01), p. 79 (2001)

16. Rehg, J., Kanade, T.: Digiteyes: vision-based hand tracking for human-computer interaction. In: Workshop on Motion of Non- Rigid and Articulated Bodies, pp. 16–24 (1994)

17. Ouhaddi, H., Horain, P.: 3D hand gesture tracking by model registration. In: International Workshop on Synthetic-Natural Hybrid Coding and Three Dimensional Imaging (1999)

18. Lin, J.Y., Wu, Y., Huang, T.S.: 3D model-based hand tracking using stochastic direct search method. In: 6th IEEE International Conference on Automatic Face and Gesture Recognition, p. 693 (2004)

19. Stenger, B., Mendonca, P.R.S., Cipolla, R.: Model-based 3D tracking of an articulated hand. In: CVPR (2001)

20. Lin, J., Wu, Y., Huang, T.S.: Capturing human hand motion in image sequences. In: Workshop on Motion and Video, Computing, pp. 99–104 (2002)

21. Bray, M., Koller-Meier, E., Gool, L.V.: Smart particle filtering for 3D hand tracking. In: 6th IEEE International Conference on Automatic Face and Gesture Recognition, pp. 675–680 (2004)

22. Stenger, B., Thayananthan, A., Torr, P.H.S., Cipolla, R.: Filtering using a tree-based estimator. In: ICCV, pp. 1063–1070 (2003)

23. Thayananthan, A., Stenger, B., Torr, P.H.S., Cipolla, R.: Learning a kinematic prior for tree-based filtering. BMVC **2**, 589–598 (2003)

24. Sudderth, E.B., Mandel, M.I., Freeman, W.T., Willsky, A.S.: Visual hand tracking using nonparametric belief propagation. In: IEEE CVPR Workshop on Generative Model Based Vision, p. 189 (2004)

25. Tomasi, C., Petrov, S., Sastry, A.: 3D tracking = classification + interpolation. ICCB **2**, 1441–1448 (2003)

26. Stenger, B., Thayananthan, A., Tor, P.H.S., Cipolla, R.: Hand Pose estimation using hierarchical detection. In: Sebe, N., Lew, M., Huang, T.S. (eds.) ECCV/HCI 2004. LNCS, vol. 3058, pp. 105–116. Springer, Heidelberg (2004)
27. Athitsos, V., Sclaroff, S.: Estimating 3D hand pose from a cluttered image. In: CVPR, vol. 2, pp. 432–439 (2003)
28. Zhou, H., Huang, T.: Okapi-chamfer matching for articulated object recognition. In: ICCV,pp. 1026–1033 (2005)
29. Rosales, R., Athitsos, V., Sigal, L., Sclaroff, S.: 3D Hand pose reconstruction using specialized mappings. In: ICCV, vol. 1, pp. 378–385 (2001)
30. Rosales, R., Sclaroff, S.: Algorithms for inference in specialized maps for recovering 3D hand Pose. In: 5th IEEE International Conference on Automatic Face and Gesture Recognition, p. 0143 (2002)
31. Micilotta, A.S., Ong, E.-J., Bowden, R.: Real-time upper body detection and 3D Pose estimation in monoscopic images. In: Leonardis, A., Bischof, H., Pinz, A. (eds.) ECCV 2006. LNCS, vol. 3953, pp. 139–150. Springer, Heidelberg (2006)
32. Gavrila, D.M.: The visual analysis of human movement: a survey. CVIU **73**, 82–98 (1999)
33. Gavrila, D.M., Davis, L.S.: Tracking of humans in action: a 3-D model-based approach. In: Proceedings of the ARPA Image Understanding, Workshop (1996)
34. Delamarre, Q., Faugeras, O.: 3D articulated models and multi-view tracking with physical forces. CVIU **81**(3), 328–357 (2001)
35. Borenstein, E., Ullman, S.: Combined top-down/bottom-up segmentation. IEEE Trans. PAMI **30**(12), 4–18 (2008)
36. Brandao, M., Bernardino, A., Santos-Victor, J.: Image driven generation of pose hypotheses for 3D model-based tracking. In: 12th IAPR Conference on Machine Vision Applications (2011)
37. Poppe, R.: Vision-based human motion analysis: an overview. CVIU **108**, 1–17 (2007)
38. Ramanan, D., Forsyth, D.A., Zisserman, A.: Tracking people by learning their appearance. IEEE Trans. PAMI **29**(1), 65–81 (2007)
39. Kyrki, V.: Integration of model-based and model-free cues for visual object tracking in 3cd. In: International Conference on Robotics and Automation, pp. 1554–1560 (2005)
40. Okuma, K., Taleghani, A., de Freitas, N., Little, J.J., Lowe, D.G.: A boosted particle filter: multitarget detection and tracking. In: Pajdla, T., Matas, J.G. (eds.) ECCV 2004. LNCS, vol. 3021, pp. 28–39. Springer, Heidelberg (2004)
41. Diankov, R.: Openrave: a planning architecture for autonomous robotics. Technical report. Robotics Institute, Pittsburgh, PA (2008)
42. Nascimento, J.C., Marques, J.S.: Robust shape tracking with multiple models in ultrasound images. IEEE Trans. Image process. **17**(3), 392–406 (2008)
43. Hammoude, A.: Computer-assited endocardial border identification from a sequence of two-dimensional echocardiographic images. Ph.D. thesis. University Washington (1988)
44. Swain, M.J., Ballard, D.H.: Color Indexing. IJCV **7**(1), 11–32 (1991)

Shape from Motion Blur Caused by Random Camera Rotations Imitating Fixational Eye Movements

Norio Tagawa$^{(\boxtimes)}$

Graduate School of System Design, Tokyo Metropolitan University,
6-6 Asahigaoka, Hino-shi, Tokyo, Japan
`tagawa@sd.tmu.ac.jp`

Abstract. Small involuntary vibrations of the human eyeball called "fixational eye movements" play a role in image analysis, such as for contrast enhancement and edge detection. This mechanism can be interpreted as stochastic resonance by biological processes, in particular, by neuron dynamics. We propose two algorithms that use the motion blur caused by many small random camera motions to recover the depth from a camera to a target object. The first is a two-step recovery method that detects the motion blur of an image and then analyzes it to determine the depth. The second method directly recovers the depth without explicitly detecting the motion blur, and it is expected to be highly accurate. From the view point of a computational optimality, in this study we evaluate the performance of the second method called direct method through numerical simulations using artificial images.

Keywords: Shape from motion blur · Random camera rotation · Fixational eye movements · Stochastic resonance

1   Introduction

Vibration noise is a serious concern for hand-held cameras, for vision systems mounted on mobile platforms, such as planes, cars, or mobile robots, and, of course, for biological vision systems. Traditionally, computer vision researchers have considered camera vibration to be a mere nuisance and have developed various mechanical stabilizations [1] and filtering techniques [2] to eliminate the jittering caused by the vibration. In contrast, new devices that take advantage of the vibrational noise generated by mobile platforms, the dynamic retina (DR) [3] and the resonant retina (RR) [4], have been proposed for contrast enhancement and edge detection, respectively. The mechanism of these devices can be interpreted as stochastic resonance (SR) [4]. SR can be viewed as a noise-induced enhancement of the response of a nonlinear system to a weak input signal; these systems include bistable devices [5] and threshold detectors [6], and SR naturally appears in many processes of neural dynamics [7].

© Springer-Verlag Berlin Heidelberg 2014
S. Battiato et al. (Eds.): VISIGRAPP 2013, CCIS 458, pp. 228–243, 2014.
DOI: 10.1007/978-3-662-44911-0_15

As an example of vibration noise, we focus on the small vibrations of a human eyeball; these vibrations occur when we gaze at an object and are called "fixational eye movements." It has been reported that these vibrations may serve not only as an intrinsic function to preserve photosensitivity, but they may also assist with image analysis, which can be considered to be a realization of a biological SR phenomenon [8]. Although DR and RR offer massive parallelism and simplicity, we proposed a depth recovery method that uses random camera rotations [9], which hints at having the potential of fixational eye movements, i.e., depth perception. This method [9] employs a differential scheme based on the gradient method for "shape from motion" [10–12]. Fixational eye movements are classified into three types: microsaccade, drift, and tremor, as shown in Fig. 1. To reduce the linear approximation error in the gradient method, this method uses the camera rotations to imitate tremor, which is the smallest of the three types. However, if the texture in an image is fine relative to the size of the image motion, the method suffers from an aliasing problem; namely, there is a large error in the spatiotemporal differentials of the image intensity used in the gradient method. In this study, in order to avoid the above mentioned aliasing problem, we propose a new scheme based on an integral form and using the same camera rotations adopted by the previous method [9]. Small random rotations of a camera during exposure can generate two-dimensional motion blur in the images. The degree of the blur is a function of the pixel position due to the perspective projection, and it also depends on the depth value corresponding to each pixel. Therefore, the depth map can be recovered by analyzing the motion blur.

Several depth recovery methods using motion blur have already been proposed, but those use blurring caused by definite and simple camera motions. For example, one uses blur caused by a translational camera motion [13], and another uses blur caused by an unconstrained camera motion composed of translation and rotation [14]. The depth recovery performance of those methods may depend on the direction of a texture in the images, i.e., if the texture has stripes that are parallel to the image motion, there is little blur and accurate depth recovery is difficult. The random camera rotations used in this study are effective for arbitrary textures. Although in controlled studies we can use complicated but deterministic motions, random camera rotations are easier to implement in actual systems, since there is no need to control a camera with precision.

We use the above-mentioned motion-blurred image and an unblurred reference image. The three-dimensional rotations of the camera were modeled as Gaussian random variables. With this approach, we can construct two kinds of methods. The first is the "two-step method" in which the motion blur is first detected as a space-variant point-spread function, and the depth map is computed analytically from the blur distribution. The other method, called the "direct method", estimates the depth map directly without explicit detection of the motion blur. Although the latter method requires an iterative numerical search, the accuracy of the recovered depth map can be expected to be high by computational optimality. Therefore, in this article, after introducing the

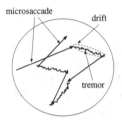

Fig. 1. Fixational eye movements are classified as microsaccade, drift, or tremor.

two methods, we consider the direct method and confirm its performance. It is expected that the performance of the proposed scheme depends on the degree of the motion blur. For the same point-spread function, i.e., the fixed deviation of the random camera rotations, a finer texture allows for the more accurate observation of the blur. To confirm this property quantitatively, we carry out numerical experiments using artificial images.

2   Motion Blur Caused by Random Camera Rotations

2.1   Camera Motions Imitating Tremor

We use a perspective projection system as our camera-imaging model. A camera is fixed with an (X, Y, Z) coordinate system; the center of the lens center, corresponding to a viewpoint, is at the origin O, and the optical axis is along the Z-axis. By taking the focal length as the geometrical unit, without loss of generality, we can set the projection plane, i.e., the image plane, at $Z = 1$. The point $(X, Y, Z)^{\top}$ on an object is projected to an image point $\boldsymbol{x} \equiv (x, y, 1)^{\top} = (X/Z, Y/Z, 1)^{\top}$.

We will briefly explain the model for imitating the tremor component of fixational eye movements, that was proposed in our previous study [9]. Analogous to a human eyeball, we can set the camera's rotation center at the back of the lens center with Z_0 along the optical axis, and we will assume that there is no explicit translational motion of the camera. This rotation can also be represented with the same components of the rotational vector $\boldsymbol{r} = (r_X, r_Y, r_Z)^{\top}$, using the origin as the center of rotation. On the other hand, this difference between the origin and the rotation center implicitly causes a translational vector $\boldsymbol{u} = (u_X, u_Y, u_Z)^{\top}$, and it is formulated as follows:

$$\begin{bmatrix} u_X \\ u_Y \\ u_Z \end{bmatrix} = \begin{bmatrix} r_X \\ r_Y \\ r_Z \end{bmatrix} \times \begin{bmatrix} 0 \\ 0 \\ Z_0 \end{bmatrix} = Z_0 \begin{bmatrix} r_Y \\ -r_X \\ 0 \end{bmatrix}. \tag{1}$$

Generally, translational motion is needed to recover depth, and our method can cause this implicitly by simply rotating the camera. This system can be easily controlled because there are no explicit translations. This means that, in general, it is simple to develop and control the system. Additionally, with this

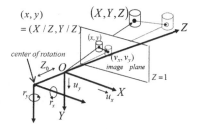

Fig. 2. Coordinate system and camera motion model used in this study.

system, Z_0 can be simply known beforehand, and hence an absolute depth can be recovered; note that a general camera motion enables us to obtain only the relative depth. The coordinate system and the camera motion model used in this study are shown in Fig. 2.

From Eq. 1, we know that r_Z causes no translation. Therefore, we set $r_Z = 0$ and define $r = (r_X, r_Y, 0)^\top$ as a rotational vector, similar to an eyeball. In this study, to simplify the motion model, $r(t)$ is treated as a stochastic white process, in which t indicates time and $r(t)$ is measured absolutely from the value at a reference time, i.e., $r(t)$ is not defined here as the relative value between successive frames. We ignore the temporal correlation of the tremor, which forms the drift, and we assume that the fluctuation of $r(t)$ at each time step obeys a two-dimensional Gaussian distribution with mean 0 and variance σ_r^2 for each component, where σ_r^2 is assumed to be known:

$$p(r(t)|\sigma_r^2) = \frac{1}{(\sqrt{2\pi}\sigma_r)^2} \exp\left\{-\frac{r(t)^\top r(t)}{2\sigma_r^2}\right\}. \tag{2}$$

In the above description, to simplify the theoretical analysis, we define r as a rotational velocity. In the actual system, we have no choice but to use a differential rotation, but for small values of the rotation angle, Eq. 1 and the other equations below hold approximately.

2.2   Relation Between Motion Blur and Depth

We can measure randomly fluctuating images with the proposed camera motion model. The previous method that used this camera motion model adopted a strategy based on differentials, i.e., the temporal differentials of many image pairs were considered to be measurements, and the optical flow field was implicitly analyzed [9]. Because of the aliasing problem, this differential-based method cannot deal with images that have fine texture details; thus, in this study, we focus on an integral-formed method that analyzes the image accumulated from measurements with small random rotations.

With sufficient exposure time, the accumulated image, i.e., the motion-blurred image, $f_m(x)$ can be modeled as a convolution of an unblurred reference image $f_0(x)$ with a two-dimensional point-spread function $g_x(\cdot)$ as follows:

$$f_m(\boldsymbol{x}) = \int_{\mathcal{R}} g_{\boldsymbol{x}}(\boldsymbol{x}') f_0(\boldsymbol{x} - \boldsymbol{x}') d\boldsymbol{x}' + n(\boldsymbol{x}), \tag{3}$$

where $n(\boldsymbol{x})$ is the noise, $\mathcal{R}$ is a local support region of $g_{\boldsymbol{x}}(\cdot)$ around $\boldsymbol{x}$, and $\int g_{\boldsymbol{x}}(\boldsymbol{x}') d\boldsymbol{x}' = 1$ holds. It is expected that the degree of the motion blur in $f_m(\boldsymbol{x})$ depends on the local depth value and is reflected in the degree of the spread of $g_{\boldsymbol{x}}(\cdot)$. In the following, we examine the relation between $g_{\boldsymbol{x}}(\cdot)$ and the depth value.

The optical flow $\boldsymbol{v} = (v_x, v_y, 0)^\top \equiv d\boldsymbol{x}/dt$ caused by a camera motion can be generally formulated using the inverse depth $d(\boldsymbol{x}) = 1/Z(\boldsymbol{x})$, as follows:

$$\boldsymbol{v} = -\left(I - \boldsymbol{x}\boldsymbol{k}^\top\right)\left(\boldsymbol{r} \times \boldsymbol{x} + d(\boldsymbol{x})\boldsymbol{u}\right). \tag{4}$$

Hence, using Eq. 1, the optical flow caused by our camera model can be written as

$$\boldsymbol{v} = -\left(I - \boldsymbol{x}\boldsymbol{k}^\top\right)\left(\boldsymbol{r} \times \boldsymbol{x}\right) - Z_0 d(\boldsymbol{x})\left(\boldsymbol{r} \times \boldsymbol{k}\right), \tag{5}$$

where I indicates a 3×3 unit matrix and $\boldsymbol{k}$ is the unit vector that indicates the optical axis, i.e., $\boldsymbol{k} = (0, 0, 1)^\top$. The component representation is

$$v_x = xy r_X - (1 + x^2) r_Y - Z_0 r_Y d, \tag{6}$$

$$v_y = (1 + y^2) r_X - xy r_Y + Z_0 r_X d. \tag{7}$$

In addition, from Eq. 2, $\boldsymbol{v}$ can be considered as a two-dimensional Gaussian random variable with mean $\boldsymbol{0}$ and the variance-covariance matrix

$$\begin{aligned}
V[\boldsymbol{v}] &= \sigma_r^2 \left\{\left(I - \boldsymbol{x}\boldsymbol{k}^\top\right)\left(I - \boldsymbol{k}\boldsymbol{x}^\top\right)\right\}^2 + 2\sigma_r^2 Z_0 d(\boldsymbol{x})\left(I - \boldsymbol{x}\boldsymbol{k}^\top\right)\left(I - \boldsymbol{k}\boldsymbol{x}^\top\right) \\
&\quad + \sigma_r^2 Z_0^2 d(\boldsymbol{x})^2 \left(I - \boldsymbol{k}\boldsymbol{k}^\top\right) \\
&= \sigma_r^2 \begin{bmatrix} x^2 y^2 + (1 + x^2 + Z_0 d)^2 & 2xy(1 + \frac{x^2+y^2}{2} + Z_0 d) \\ 2xy(1 + \frac{x^2+y^2}{2} + Z_0 d) & x^2 y^2 + (1 + y^2 + Z_0 d)^2 \end{bmatrix}.
\end{aligned} \tag{8}$$

From the above discussion, we see the intensity at each pixel is combined with that of neighboring pixels, and the optical flow defined by Eq. 5 can be approximated by the relative displacement from the neighboring pixels per unit time. Therefore, it is clear that $g_{\boldsymbol{x}}(\cdot)$ can be modeled approximately by a two-dimensional Gaussian distribution that has the same variance-covariance matrix as in Eq. 8. Hence, the motion blur caused by our camera model depends on the depth map, and Eq. 3 can be used as an observation equation that includes the unknown variable $d(\boldsymbol{x})$. Hereafter, we will use the notation $g_{\boldsymbol{x}}(\cdot; d)$ to clarify that the blur is a function of depth.

3   Algorithms for Depth Recovery

3.1   Principle of Proposed Algorithms

The blurring distribution is detected in an image domain, not in a frequency domain. The processing schemes can be classified as a one-step method and a two-step method. In the one-step method, the unknown value set $\{d_i\}_{i=1,\cdots,N}$ (N indicates the number of pixels in the image) is determined with the full set of constraints. The point-spread functions $\{g_{\boldsymbol{x}}(\cdot; d)\}$, each of which has a Gaussian form and has the variance-covariance matrix formulated by Eq. 8, have to be determined simultaneously for each pixel in the image. As a result, $\{d_i\}$ is optimal. However, this method is not an analytical method and requires iterative computations.

On the other hand, in the two-step method, the variance-covariance matrix of the Gaussian distribution is first detected at each pixel, with no use of the constraint in Eq. 8. After that, $\{d_i\}$ is determined from the variance-covariance matrices using the constraint in Eq. 8. This method analytically computes $\{d_i\}$, which simplifies the computations. However, it is not optimal, and this can be seen by relaxing the Gaussian constraint and estimating the variance-covariance matrix as a simple statistic, which further reduces the computational cost.

In the following, these two methods will be briefly explained.

3.2   Two-Step Method

In the first step, the Gaussian property is ignored, and hence, $w_{\boldsymbol{x}}(\cdot)$ instead of $g_{\boldsymbol{x}}(\cdot; d)$ is used as the point-spread function. The local support of $w_{\boldsymbol{x}}(\cdot)$ is defined as a square discrete region with $P \times P$ pixels, and, using a dictionary order, the P^2-dimensional vector $\boldsymbol{w}_i$ is introduced as a discrete representation of $w_{\boldsymbol{x}}(\cdot)$, where i indicates the pixel index. Additionally, the discrete representations of the local image intensity of $f_0(\boldsymbol{x})$ and $f_m(\boldsymbol{x})$ are defined as $\boldsymbol{f}_0^i$ and $\boldsymbol{f}_m^i$, respectively. These are also P^2-dimensional vectors that consist of local intensity values around the pixel i. Using $\boldsymbol{f}_0^i$, the $P^2 \times P^2$ matrix $\boldsymbol{F}^i$ is defined as follows:

$$\boldsymbol{F}^i = \begin{bmatrix} \boldsymbol{f}_0^{i+1} & \boldsymbol{f}_0^{i+2} & \cdots & \boldsymbol{f}_0^{i+P^2} \end{bmatrix}. \tag{9}$$

By ignoring the constraint $\sum_k \boldsymbol{w}_{i(k)} = 1$, which generally holds for the components of the point-spread function $\boldsymbol{w}_{i(k)}$, an objective function for each pixel i can be defined as follows:

$$J_i(\boldsymbol{w}_i) = \left(\boldsymbol{F}^{i^\top} \boldsymbol{w}_i - \boldsymbol{f}_m^i \right)^\top \left(\boldsymbol{F}^{i^\top} \boldsymbol{w}_i - \boldsymbol{f}_m^i \right). \tag{10}$$

By differentiating $J_i(\boldsymbol{w}_i)$ with respect to $\boldsymbol{w}_i$ and setting it to zero, the following solution can be derived:

$$\hat{\boldsymbol{w}}_i = \left(\boldsymbol{F}^i \boldsymbol{F}^{i^\top} \right)^{-1} \boldsymbol{F}^i \boldsymbol{f}_m^i. \tag{11}$$

In the next step, we estimate the variance-covariance matrix of $\hat{\boldsymbol{w}}_i$ by regarding it as a probabilistic density and determine $\{d_i\}$ from the estimated variance-covariance matrix using the relation in Eq. 8. Each component can be simply estimated as follows:

$$\hat{\boldsymbol{V}}_{i(1,1)} = \sum_{k=1}^{P^2} x(k)^2 \hat{\boldsymbol{w}}_{i(k)}, \tag{12}$$

$$\hat{V}_{i(1,2)} = V_{i(2,1)} = \sum_{k=1}^{P^2} x(k)y(k)\hat{w}_{i(k)}, \tag{13}$$

$$\hat{V}_{i(2,2)} = \sum_{k=1}^{P^2} y(k)^2 \hat{w}_{i(k)}, \tag{14}$$

where $(x(k), y(k))$ indicates the two-dimensional coordinate values corresponding to the pixel k, with the center of the local support at $(0,0)$.

From Eq. 8 and the estimates computed by Eqs. 12, 13, and 14, equations with respect to each d_i can be derived as follows:

$$1 + x_i^2 + Z_0 d_i = \sqrt{\frac{\hat{V}_{i(1,1)}}{\sigma_r^2} - x_i^2 y_i^2} \equiv \alpha_i, \tag{15}$$

$$1 + \frac{x_i^2 + y_i^2}{2} + Z_0 d_i = \frac{\hat{V}_{i(1,2)}}{2x_i y_i \sigma_r^2} \equiv \beta_i, \tag{16}$$

$$1 + y_i^2 + Z_0 d_i = \sqrt{\frac{\hat{V}_{i(2,2)}}{\sigma_r^2} - x_i^2 y_i^2} \equiv \gamma_i. \tag{17}$$

Using the minimum mean-square criterion, d_i is estimated as

$$\hat{d}_i = \frac{1}{Z_0} \left(w_\alpha \alpha_i + w_\beta \beta_i + w_\gamma \gamma_i - (w_\alpha + \frac{w_\beta}{2})x_i^2 - (w_\gamma + \frac{w_\beta}{2})y_i^2 - 1 \right), \tag{18}$$

where w_α, w_β, and w_γ are the weights corresponding to Eqs. 15, 16, and 17, respectively, and $w_\alpha + w_\beta + w_\gamma = 1$ holds. In particular, if $w_\alpha = w_\beta = w_\gamma = 1/3$, Eq. 18 becomes

$$\hat{d}_i = \frac{1}{Z_0} \left(\frac{\alpha_i + \beta_i + \gamma_i}{3} - \frac{x_i^2 + y_i^2}{2} - 1 \right). \tag{19}$$

Using the Taylor series expansion of the right-hand side of Eq. 15 through the first-order term, $\sum_k w_{i(k)} = 1$, the error component can be formulated as $\delta V_{i(1,1)}/(2\sqrt{V_{i(1,1)}\sigma_r^2 - x_i^2 y_i^2 \sigma_r^4})$, in which $\delta V_{i(1,1)}$ is the detection error in Eq. 12. In the same way, the error in Eq. 16 is $\delta V_{i(1,2)}/(2x_i y_i \sigma_r^2)$, and the error in Eq. 17 is $\delta V_{i(2,2)}/(2\sqrt{V_{i(2,2)}\sigma_r^2 - x_i^2 y_i^2 \sigma_r^4})$. If it is assumed that $\delta V_{i(1,1)}$, $\delta V_{i(1,2)}$, and $\delta V_{i(2,2)}$ are Gaussian random variables with the same variance, the following weights can be used in Eq. 18 to obtain the maximum-likelihood estimator of d_i:

$$w_\alpha = \frac{V_{i(1,1)} - x_i^2 y_i^2 \sigma_r^2}{V_{i(1,1)} + V_{i(2,2)} - x_i^2 y_i^2 \sigma_r^2}, \tag{20}$$

$$w_\beta = \frac{x_i^2 y_i^2 \sigma_r^2}{V_{i(1,1)} + V_{i(2,2)} - x_i^2 y_i^2 \sigma_r^2}, \tag{21}$$

$$w_\gamma = \frac{V_{i(2,2)} - x_i^2 y_i^2 \sigma_r^2}{V_{i(1,1)} + V_{i(2,2)} - x_i^2 y_i^2 \sigma_r^2}. \tag{22}$$

3.3 Direct Method

To optimize the computations, we should estimate the depth map directly without explicit determination of $g_x(\cdot; d)$, although this strategy generally requires a numerical search or an iterative update. We can construct two algorithms for the direct method, each of which employs a local optimization and a global optimization. In the following, we will briefly explain both algorithms. It should be noted that since the scheme examined in this study is based on spatial blur, we cannot expect high-resolution recovery. The proposed algorithms introduced below employ simple computations with no complicated techniques, such as those for recovering edges. If high resolution and a highly accurate recovery are needed, the results obtained here can be used as initial values for the methods based on differential schemes. When doing so, by applying image-warping processing with the initial depth values, the aliasing problem in the differential scheme can be effectively avoided [11,15,16].

Local Optimization Algorithm (LOA). For stable recovery, we assume a constant depth value in the local region $\mathcal{L}$ around each x. We can define the objective function with respect to the depth corresponding to each pixel based on the minimum least-square criterion and with a continuous form, as follows:

$$J_L(d(\boldsymbol{x})) \equiv \int_{\mathcal{L}} (f_m(\boldsymbol{x} - \boldsymbol{x}'') - f_{conv}(\boldsymbol{x} - \boldsymbol{x}''))^2 \, d\boldsymbol{x}'', \tag{23}$$

$$f_{conv}(\boldsymbol{x}) \equiv \int_{\mathcal{R}} g_{\boldsymbol{x}}(\boldsymbol{x}'; d) f_0(\boldsymbol{x} - \boldsymbol{x}') d\boldsymbol{x}'. \tag{24}$$

By minimizing this function at each x, we can recover separately the depth corresponding to each pixel. Therefore, a multivariate optimization is not needed, and we can adopt a one-dimensional numerical search.

Global Optimization Algorithm (GOA). By requiring a spatially smooth depth map, we can define the following functional to be minimized, based on the regularization theory of Poggio et al. [17]:

$$J_G(d(\boldsymbol{x})) = (1 - \lambda) \int (f_m(\boldsymbol{x}) - f_{conv}(\boldsymbol{x}))^2 \, d\boldsymbol{x} + \lambda \int \left\{ \left(\frac{\partial d(\boldsymbol{x})}{\partial x}\right)^2 + \left(\frac{\partial d(\boldsymbol{x})}{\partial y}\right)^2 \right\} d\boldsymbol{x}, \tag{25}$$

where λ is the weight value that adjusts the degree of the smoothness constraint requirement for the depth map, and the integration in Eq. 25 is carried out over the entire image. From the variational principle, the Euler-Lagrange equation for finding the solution of $d(\boldsymbol{x})$ is derived using $\nabla^2 \equiv \partial^2/\partial x^2 + \partial^2/\partial y^2$ as follows:

$$\nabla^2 d = -\frac{1 - \lambda}{\lambda} (f_m - f_{conv}) \frac{\partial f_{conv}}{\partial d}. \tag{26}$$

For the discrete computation and using (i, j), we can approximate the smoothness constraint in Eq. 25 as a description of an image position:

$$\left(\frac{\partial d(\boldsymbol{x})}{\partial x}\right)^2 + \left(\frac{\partial d(\boldsymbol{x})}{\partial y}\right)^2 \approx \frac{1}{5}\left\{(d_{i+1,j} - d_{i,j})^2 + (d_{i,j+1} - d_{i,j})^2\right\}$$
$$+ \frac{1}{20}\left\{(d_{i+1,j-1} - d_{i,j})^2 + (d_{i+1,j+1} - d_{i,j})^2\right\} \ (27)$$

Using Eq. 27 and the discrete representation of Eq. 26, we can minimize Eq. 25 by the following iterative formulation, where n is the iteration number:

$$d_{i,j}^{(n+1)} = \bar{d}_{i,j}^{(n)} + \frac{1-\lambda}{\lambda}\left(f_{m,i,j} - f_{conv}(d_{i,j}^{(n)})\right)\frac{\partial f_{conv}(d_{i,j}^{(n)})}{\partial d}, \qquad (28)$$

$$\bar{d}_{i,j}^{(n)} = \frac{1}{5}\left(d_{i+1,j}^{(n)} + d_{i,j+1}^{(n)} + d_{i-1,j}^{(n)} + d_{i,j-1}^{(n)}\right)$$
$$+ \frac{1}{20}\left(d_{i+1,j+1}^{(n)} + d_{i+1,j-1}^{(n)} + d_{i-1,j-1}^{(n)} + d_{i-1,j+1}^{(n)}\right).$$
$$(29)$$

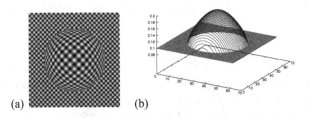

(a)   (b)

Fig. 3. Example of the artificial data used in the experiments: (a) original image; (b) true inverse depth map used for generating the blurred image.

4   Numerical Evaluation

In this paper, we use only the direct method to evaluate our scheme based on the motion blur; this is because the direct method can derive the optimal solution.

The proposed algorithms are based on the definition of the motion-blurred image in Eq. 3, and this depends strongly on the imaging system or how it is controlled. To observe the ideal motion blur, it is necessary to allow for sufficient exposure time, and during the exposure time, the camera has to be suitably controlled with small and random motions. Now, we are considering a real imaging system, and we will confirm immediately the validity of Eq. 3. We will use artificial data to examine the relationship of the size of the motion and the fineness of the texture on the performance of the proposed algorithms.

We artificially obtained motion-blurred images by using digital signal processing. First, we generated a huge number of images by using a computer graphics technique and a true depth map and then randomly sampling r according to the Gaussian distribution in Eq. 2. An artificial motion-blurred image was made by averaging these images. In this study, we imitated analog motion blur by averaging 10,000 images. Figure 3 shows an example of a reference image and a true inverse depth map. The image size used in the simulations is 256×256 pixels, which corresponds to $-0.5 \leq x, y \leq 0.5$, as measured using the focal length as one unit. In Fig. 3(b), the vertical axis indicates the inverse depth $d(x)$, where the focal length is one unit, and the horizontal axe indicate the position of the pixel in the image plane, which is marked every four pixels.

The LOA has a high computational cost at each pixel, and the GOA converges slowly. Hence, we evaluated a hybrid algorithm, in which the LOA is used sparsely in the image plane to obtain the initial values for the GOA. The plane indicating the background in Fig. 3(b) was used to supply the initial values for the LOA. Since the LOA was used for only a rough estimate, we used a block with 41×41 pixels as $\mathcal{L}$ in Eq. 23 without any special consideration, and applied the LOA once to each block. We adaptively determined the size of $\mathcal{R}$ in Eq. 24 according to the value of the depth updated in the optimization process. Therefore, $\mathcal{R}$ took a different size at each position in the image. We assumed a square region for $\mathcal{R}$, the side length of which was ten times as large as the larger value of the x-deviations and the y-deviation of $g_x(\cdot; d)$, which can be evaluated using Eq. 8.

We performed simulations with varying amounts of rotation σ_r of the camera. The recovered inverse depth maps are shown in Figs. 4, 5, and 6, with various values of λ used in the GOA. The relation between the root-mean-square error (RMSE) of the recovered depth map and the value of λ is also shown in Fig. 7. From Fig. 4, it can be easily seen that small camera rotations are inadequate for depth recovery, since the motion blur cannot be measured accurately. In Fig. 7(a), we see that since the measured information from small rotations is poor, the smoothness constraint indicated by λ is strongly needed to reduce the RMSE of the recovered depth map. On the other hand, large rotations make the point-spread function extensive compared to the spatial variation of the target shape, and hence the Gaussian function with the variance-covariance matrix in Eq. 8 is improper. Thus, the motion blur recognized by this model is smoother than the true blur in the image, and this causes an error in the recovered depth. This can be seen from the RMSE values in Fig. 7(c). We can see in Fig. 7(c) that since a smoother blur tends to recover a smoother depth, the smoothness constraint in Eq. 25 tends to increase the RMSE. Figure 8 shows the result with extremely large rotations of $\sigma_r = 0.016$. Such rotations are too large for the texture of the images used in this evaluation, and it was confirmed that the RMSE is almost independent of the value of λ. When σ_r is less than about 0.004, the proposed method does not obtain good results for the texture patterns used in this study. This is because the image motions are too small for the texture pattern, and hence there is little blurring. For this case, we can instead use our differential method [9].

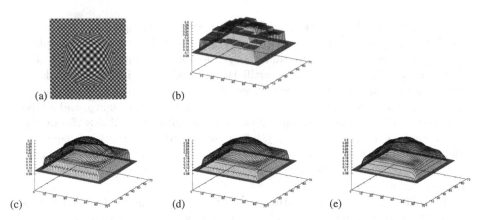

Fig. 4. Example of depth recovery with $\sigma_r = 0.006$: (a) motion-blurred image; (b) inverse depth recovered by LOA; (c) by GOA with $\lambda = 0.2$; (d) by GOA with $\lambda = 0.4$; (e) by GOA with $\lambda = 0.8$.

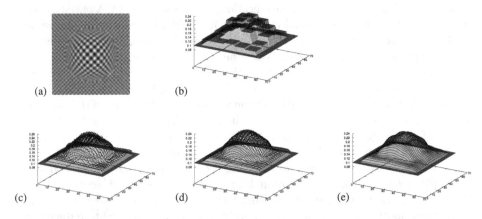

Fig. 5. Example of depth recovery with $\sigma_r = 0.008$: (a) motion-blurred image; (b) inverse depth recovered by LOA; (c) by GOA with $\lambda = 0.2$; (d) by GOA with $\lambda = 0.4$; (e) by GOA with $\lambda = 0.8$.

We also tried to recover the depth using striped images, which was insufficient for the method that used one-directional motion blur. Figure 9 shows the original image, the images blurred with $\sigma_r = 0.008$, and the recovered inverse depth map with $\lambda = 0.2$; this value of λ gives the minimum RMSE. From this result, we confirmed that our integral-based method is suitable for such an image.

The above simulations assumed a smooth shape that was suitable for the blur-based method. To determine how our method worked with discontinuous regions, we applied our method to the shape shown in Fig. 10(b) with the random dot pattern in Fig. 10(a). The simulation results of this data are shown in Fig. 11. The recovered inverse depth in Fig. 11(c) produces the minimum RMSE, and

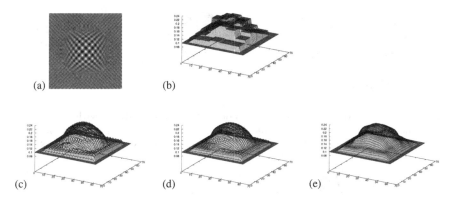

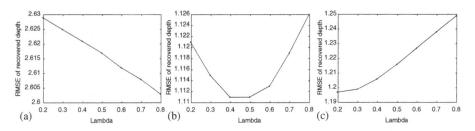

Fig. 6. Example of depth recovery with $\sigma_r = 0.01$: (a) motion-blurred image; (b) inverse depth recovered by LOA; (c) by GOA with $\lambda = 0.2$; (d) by GOA with $\lambda = 0.4$; (e) by GOA with $\lambda = 0.8$.

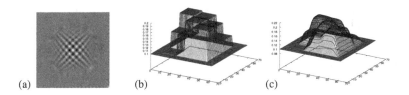

Fig. 7. Relation between the RMSE of the recovered depth and lambda: (a) $\sigma_r = 0.006$; (b) $\sigma_r = 0.008$; (c) $\sigma_r = 0.01$.

Fig. 8. Example of depth recovery with $\sigma_r = 0.16$: (a) motion-blurred image; (b) inverse depth recovered by LOA, with $\mathcal{L}$ set at 61×61 pixels; (c) by GOA with $\lambda = 0.4$, which is an example of the camera rotations being too large compared to the texture pattern.

from this we confirmed clearly that the motion-blur-based method is inadequate for the recovery of discontinuous regions.

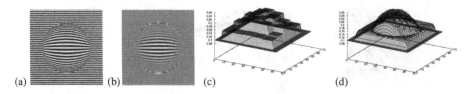

(a)   (b)   (c)   (d)

Fig. 9. Example of depth recovery for a horizontal striped pattern with $\sigma_r = 0.008$: (a) original image; (b) motion-blurred image; (c) inverse depth recovered by LOA; (d) by GOA with $\lambda = 0.2$, which is the minimum RMSE recovery (RMSE = 1.870).

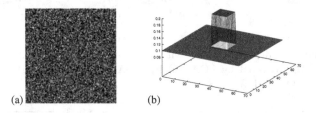

(a)   (b)

Fig. 10. Artificial data for evaluating a discontinuous shape: (a) original image; (b) true inverse depth map used for generating the blurred image.

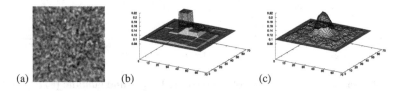

(a)   (b)   (c)

Fig. 11. Example of depth recovery for a discontinuous shape with $\sigma_r = 0.008$: (a) motion-blurred image; (b) inverse depth recovered by LOA; (c) by GOA with $\lambda = 0.5$, which is the minimum RMSE for a recovery (RMSE = 0.929).

5 Discussions

5.1 Parameter Determination

We understand that the region $\mathcal{L}$ in Eq. 23 should be determined according to the desirable resolution of the recovered depth map, while keeping the constraint that $\mathcal{L}$ must be larger than the deviation of $g_x(\cdot; d)$. This is in order to increase the accuracy and precision of the recovered depth. On the other hand, for $\mathcal{R}$ in Eq. 24, if there is no restriction on the cost of computations, it is best to use a very large value because of the infinite support of the Gaussian function.

In this study, since we used the LOA only to obtain the initial depth for GOA, we always used a square of 41×41 pixels as $\mathcal{L}$ shown in Sect. 4 without due deliberation. For $\mathcal{R}$, in order to reduce the numerical errors, we used a square large enough to cover the entire support of $g_x(\cdot; d)$, as explained in Sect. 4. For the true depth values, the size of $\mathcal{R}$ takes a value between 15×15 pixels and 19×19 pixels when $\sigma_r = 0.005$. As a result, when $\mathcal{L}$ is 41×41, it is large enough with respect to the size of $\mathcal{R}$. We confirmed that up to $\sigma_r = 0.012$, an $\mathcal{L}$ of 41×41 is sufficient for the size of $\mathcal{R}$, but for $\sigma_r = 0.016$, for the recovered result shown in Fig. 8, the size of $\mathcal{L}$ had to be expanded to 61×61 pixels for the LOA.

For setting the value of λ, in this study, we assumed that the value should be adjusted empirically while checking the validity of the recovered depth. In the future, we will adopt the expectation-maximization (EM) algorithm [18] used in [15,16] to solve this problem. In this algorithm, λ can be automatically determined using only the observed data set. In this framework, by modeling λ as a function of the image position using the Markov Random Field (MRF) model, a spatially adaptive λ can be determined.

5.2 Advantages Over Depth-from-Focus

At first, we considered that lack of focus would be detrimental to our proposed method. In this study, in order to simplify the explanation, we assumed an ideal camera with no defocusing, although actual cameras would be used in practice. If the camera rotations are not very large, however, which is assumed in this study from the beginning, the degree of the blur caused by defocusing is unchanged before and after the camera rotations. Our method uses a reference image and a blurred image for processing, and both have the same defocusing; hence, our method automatically cancels the defocusing.

We now explain the advantages of our method over the depth-from-focus method [19]. In the depth-from-focus method, the focus should be varied accurately in several different ways. However, in our method, a camera has only to be rotated randomly, i.e., accurate control of the camera is not required. Since, in our intended future method, the deviation of the random camera rotations will be estimated from the observed images, there will be no need to know the deviation before processing. Another advantage of our motion-blurred scheme is that, if necessary, many still images without motion blur can be averaged to generate a motion-blurred image. Depth recovery based on either motion blur or defocusing blur works for fine textures, but neither works for surfaces with blurred textures. However, if camera rotations are adopted, we can deal with a blurred texture by using the differential method [9]. Hence, we can adapt to the surface texture and recover the depth by switching between the integral method proposed in this study and the differential method.

6   Conclusions

We proposed a new scheme for recovering a depth map, using random camera rotations that imitate fixational eye movements, in particular, tremor-related movements. The proposed scheme can recover a depth map from the image blur. The two-step method and the direct method were introduced, and for the direct method two algorithms, i.e., the local optimization algorithm and the global optimization algorithm, were constructed based on this scheme. In this study, we approximated the motion-blurred image by averaging a huge number of images that were artificially generated by random motions of a camera. We have not yet examined the effectiveness of our method with real images from an actual imaging system; this is left for our future work. The simulations in this study did not consider lighting conditions or the reflection characteristics of the imaging target. Examination of the influence of specular reflection components will require thorough numerical evaluation and additional experiments.

By the simulations, we confirmed that the outline of the depth map can be recovered by using our method, although the accuracy may be insufficient. This method cannot be used for motions that are small relative to the texture pattern. For that case, the differential-based method [9] is effective. On the other hand, from the fundamental principle of our motion-blur-based scheme, the spatial resolution of the recovered depth is not very high, no matter how careful we are at selecting the size of the camera motion. This property was confirmed clearly by carrying out the performance evaluation for the object having discontinuous regions. For this case, we can use the results from this method as an initial value of the depth for the method in [15, 16]. We plan to unify these methods so that they can deal with a variety of situations. In particular, to combine the differential-based method [9] and the integral-based method, we will develop a suitable segmentation method, which will divide the observed images into regions of fine or rough texture (relative to the size of the camera rotations). Additionally, to combine the differential and the integral methods, the motion-blurred image must be generated by averaging many captured images without motion blur, instead of simply capturing an image with analog blur. In that case, it is desirable to average fewer images in order to reduce the computational cost and time, but this requirement cannot produce the ideal motion blur assumed in this study. Therefore, we have to improve the integral-based method in this study so that it performs well when the motion blur is insufficient.

References

1. Oliver, C., Quegan, S.: Understanding Synthetic Aperture Radar Images. Artech House, London (1998)
2. Jazwinski, A.: Stochastic Processes and Filtering Theory. Academic Press, New York (1970)
3. Prokopowicz, P.N., Cooper, P.R.: The dynamic retina: contrast and motion detection for active vision. Int. J. Comput. Vis. 16, 191–204 (1995)
4. Hongler, M.-O., de Meneses, Y.L., Beyeler, A., Jacot, J.: The resonant retina: exploiting vibration noise to optimally detect edges in an image. IEEE Trans. Pattern Anal. Mach. Intell. 25, 1051–1062 (2003)
5. Gammaitoni, L., Hänggi, P., Jung, P., Marchesoni, F.: Stochastic resonance. Rev. Mod. Phys. 70, 223–252 (1998)
6. Greenwood, P.E., Ward, L.M., Wefelmeyer, W.: Statistical analysis of stochastic resonance in a simple setting. Phys. Rev. E 60, 4687–4696 (1999)
7. Stemmler, M.: A single spike suffices: the simplest form of stochastic resonance in model neurons. Netw.: Comput. Neural Syst. 7, 687–716 (1996)
8. Martinez-Conde, S., Macknik, S.L., Hubel, D.H.: The role of fixational eye movements in visual perception. Nat. Rev. Neurosci. 5, 229–240 (2004)

9. Tagawa, N.: Depth perception model based on fixational eye movements using Bayesian statistical inference. In: International Conference on Pattern Recognition, pp. 1662–1665 (2010)
10. Horn, B.K.P., Schunk, B.G.: Determining optical flow. Artif. Intell. **17**, 185–203 (1981)
11. Simoncelli, E.P.: Bayesian multi-scale differential optical flow. In: Jähne, B., Haussecker, H., Geissler, P. (eds.) Handbook of Computer Vision and Applications, vol. 2, pp. 397–422. Academic Press, San Diego (1999)
12. Bruhn, A., Weickert, J.: Lucas/Kanade meets Horn/Schunk: combining local and global optic flow methods. Int. J. Comput. Vis. **61**, 211–231 (2005)
13. Sorel, M., Flusser, J.: Space-variant restoration of images degraded by camera motion blur. IEEE Trans. Image Process. **17**, 105–116 (2008)
14. Paramanand, C., Rajagopalan, A.N.: Depth from motion and optical blur with an unscented Kalman filter. IEEE Trans. Image Process. **21**, 2798–2811 (2012)
15. Tagawa, N., Kawaguchi, J., Naganuma, S., Okubo, K.: Direct 3-D shape recovery from image sequence based on multi-scale Bayesian network. In: International Conference on Pattern Recognition, pp. CD–ROM (2008)
16. Tagawa, N., Naganuma, S.: Structure and motion from image sequence based on multi-scale Bayesian network. In: Yin, P.-Y. (ed.) Pattern Recognition, pp. 73–98. In-Tech, Croatia (2009)
17. Poggio, T., Torre, V., Koch, C.: Computational vision and regularization theory. Nature **317**, 314–319 (1985)
18. Dempster, A.P., Laird, N.M., Rubin, D.B.: Maximum likelihood from incomplete data via the EM algorithm. J. Roy. Statist. Soc. B **39**, 1–38 (1977)
19. Nayar, S.K., Nakagawa, Y.: Shape from focus. IEEE Trans. Pattern Anal. Mach. Intell. **16**, 824–831 (1994)

Author Index